DISCOVER 6

EXPERIENCE 60

NEED TO KNOW 268

DISCOVER

The crystalline River Limmat bisecting Zürich

INSPIRE / PLAN / DISCOVER / EXPERIENCE

SWITZERLAND

SWITZERLAND

CONTENTS

WELCOME TO
SWITZERLAND

Forget yodelling, cheese, cuckoo clocks and chocolate, this country has so much more to offer. Magnificent natural beauty, charming medieval villages, cosmopolitan cities and a healthy dose of alpine air – Switzerland's small size belies its beguiling charms. The varied scene is coloured by a fascinating history and the unique mix of four official languages only add to the appeal. Whatever your dream trip to Switzerland includes, this DK Eyewitness travel guide is your perfect companion.

1 A warmly lit train passing the iconic Matterhorn.

2 Charlie Chaplin statue, overlooking Lake Geneva.

3 Evening in buzzy Zürich West.

4 Narcissus blooming across Les Pléiades, Vaud.

Once a group of independent cantons, the Swiss Confederation has come along way since its foundation in 1291. Today's federal state is an intriguing blend of different customs, languages and dialects, lending the country a rich heritage. The year's myriad traditional festivals, where alphorn players and Swiss wrestlers take centre stage, are woven into the country's cultural tapestry. And there are stunning historic landmarks to explore across the land, from the castles of Bellinzona in the south to St Gallen's abbey quarter in the north. As much as it is rooted in the past, Switzerland looks to the future, with cutting-edge nightlife in Zürich, world-class art galleries in Basel and superb fine dining across the country from Geneva to St Moritz.

Away from its buzzing cities, Switzerland is a land of the great outdoors, and the country's network of hiking, biking and skiing trails is as well organized as its public transport system. In a single day, you can encounter breathtaking glaciers, high altitude lakes and iconic mountains, and be back in time for fondue and schnapps.

With so many different things to experience, Switzerland can seem overwhelming. We've broken the country down into easily navigable chapters, with detailed itineraries, expert local knowledge and colourful, comprehensive maps to help you plan the perfect visit. Whether you're staying for a weekend, a week or longer, this DK Eyewitness travel guide will ensure that you see the very best Switzerland has to offer. Enjoy the book, and enjoy Switzerland.

REASONS TO LOVE
SWITZERLAND

Small in size but big on experiences, Switzerland is awash with fascinating sights, exhilarating activities and intriguing traditions, presented in one remarkably beautiful package. Here, we pick some of our favourites.

1 BERN'S OLD TOWN

A UNESCO World Heritage Site, the Swiss capital's medieval Old Town is a real beauty. Its charming *lauben* (covered walkways) shelter independent boutiques, little cafés and buzzing bars hidden beneath cellar doors *(p62)*.

SCENIC RAIL JOURNEYS *2*

Part of the fun of travelling around Switzerland is the journey itself. The country's rail routes are truly extraordinary, both as feats of engineering and for the incredible scenery they pass through.

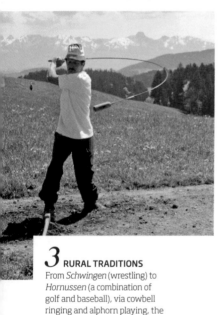

3 RURAL TRADITIONS

From *Schwingen* (wrestling) to *Hornussen* (a combination of golf and baseball), via cowbell ringing and alphorn playing, the past is still very much a part of modern Swiss life *(p32)*.

4 LAKE LIFE

Despite being a landlocked country, Switzerland's myriad lakes mean getting near the water is always easy. Lakeside beaches throng all summer with sunbathers and swimmers, while quiet hiking trails lead to remote alpine lagoons.

SLEDGING IN THE JUNGFRAU 5

Take an exhilarating toboggan ride in this stunning mountainous region. Top of the list is the longest run in Europe – the epic 15-km (9-mile) descent from the top of the Faulhorn to the village of Grindelwald.

FONDUE 6

Breathe in the irresistible aroma of molten cheese. The *moitié-moitié* – half Gruyère, half Vacherin Fribourgeois – is best washed down with a glass of local Chasselas wine.

HISTORIC TREASURES 7

Whether St Gallen Abbey, Bellinzona's castles or the fairytale Château de Chillon in Montreux, Switzerland's rugged terrain is littered with history-laden sights that rival its natural wonders for your attention *(p46)*.

ART IN BASEL 8

Art enthusiasts flock to Switzerland's cultural capital for its annual artistic showpiece Art Basel, but its world-class galleries and museums are a joy all year round *(p178)*.

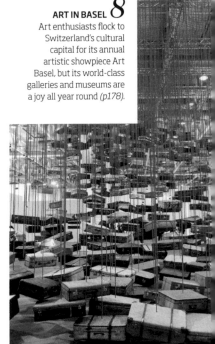

9 WORLD-CLASS SKIING

From the epic powder runs of Zermatt *(p90)* – the highest resort in Europe – to family-friendly slopes, Switzerland offers a remarkable choice for skiers, freeriders and snow-boarders on and off-piste.

10 HUT TO HUT HIKING

Join the Swiss in their national pastime – hiking to cosy cabins across the Alps. Whether run by the Swiss Alpine Club or privately owned, each offer the camaraderie of spending the night in the mountains.

ZÜRICH'S NIGHTLIFE 11

The largest city in Switzerland, Zürich is a go-to place for night owls. Head to dynamic Langstrasse *(p168)*, a reformed red-light district, for pubs, clubs and cocktail bars.

WINE TASTING IN THE LAVAUX 12

Blanketing the hillside above Lake Geneva *(p142)*, the terraced vineyards of the Lavaux are a fine place for a Swiss wine initiation. Take a stroll along the myriad wine trails, where *vignerons* (winegrowers) lure visitors with tastings.

EXPLORE
SWITZERLAND

This guide divides Switzerland into
eight colour-coded sightseeing
areas, as shown on the map below.
Find out more about each area on
the following pages.

Freiburg im
Bresigau

Mulhouse

Basel

Liestal

NORTHERN
SWITZERLAND
p174

Delémont

Olten

Lenzburg

Besançon

FRANCE

La Chaux-
de-Fonds

Solothurn

Langenthal

Sursee

Lucerne

Biel

Bielersee

Neuchâtel

Pontarlier

*Lake
Neuchâtel*

Murten

Langnau

Sarnen

Yverdon-
les-Bains

Fribourg

BERN
p62

Thun

Brienz

Thunersee

Brienzersee

WESTERN
SWITZERLAND
p130

Bulle

Spiez

Interlaken

Lausanne

*Lake
Geneva*

Vevey

Montreux

MITTELLAND,
BERNESE OBERLAND
AND VALAIS
p80

Nyon

Aigle

Sierre

Brig

GENEVA
p114

Monthey

Sion

Martigny

Zermatt

Annecy

Sallanches

Albertville

Bourg
St-Maurice

Aosta

ITALY

Chambery

Ivrea

0 kilometres   30

0 miles   30

N
↑

GETTING TO KNOW
SWITZERLAND

Cradled by Europe's highest peaks, Switzerland is the capital of alpine drama, and rich in world-class art, culinary adventures and fascinating folklore. Outside the cities, Switzerland is a land of mesmerising natural beauty with twisting valleys, dizzying mountains and shimmering lakes.

BERN

PAGE 62

The gateway to the Alps, Switzerland's oft-overlooked capital has a wealth of attractions – from its medieval Old Town (a UNESCO World Heritage Site) to urban swimming in the clean waters of the Aare River. The city is also the seat of Switzerland's government and the Houses of Parliament are often open to the public. Always at the heart of the country's intellectual culture, Bern is a laid-back place for serious thinkers. The former haunt of Albert Einstein has plenty of café-lined squares and pretty gardens to chew over the day's politics, ponder Modern Masters and debate matters of time and space.

Best for
A magnificent Old Town

Home to
Zytglogge, Kunstmuseum

Experience
The boutiques, cafés and restaurants hidden under the lauben, covered walkways that line the Old Town streets

PAGE 80

MITTELLAND, BERNESE OBERLAND AND VALAIS

One of the most beautiful areas in the country, this is the place to tick off half your bucket list. Mountain lovers should make a beeline to Interlaken to soak up the sky-high vistas and climb the Jungfraujoch or the Eiger. To the south, in the canton of Valais, looms the country's most famous peak: the Matterhorn. For the ultimate journey, catch the train to see hanging valleys and leviathan-sized glaciers from the comfort of a carriage.

Best for
Breathtaking panoramas from top-of-Europe summits

Home to
Zermatt and the Matterhorn, Aletsch Glacier

Experience
Hiking along the incomparable Aletsch Glacier

PAGE 114

GENEVA

The capital of the French-speaking part of the country is the jewel of the Swiss Lake District. Pocket-sized and impeccably clean, it offers timely distractions for clock-watchers and more casual travellers. The pedestrianized Old Town, a mini-maze of bijou squares and neo-classical cathedrals, is a delight to get lost in. Beyond the city limits, you'll find the famous CERN, the world's largest particle physics laboratory, the creased hills of Saint-Cergue, and enough lakeside vineyards and castles to keep you here longer than planned.

Best for
Museums, culture and lakeside excursions

Home to
Musee d'Art et d'Histoire

Experience
Taking a tram to the lovely Italianate district of Carouge, with its independent shops and Saturday market

$\rightarrow$

PAGE 130

WESTERN SWITZERLAND

Stretching from the Jura mountains and Vaud Alps to the shores of Lakes Geneva and Neuchâtel, this is one of the most densely inhabited parts of the country. City-breakers flock to buzzing university city Lausanne and the hip-shaking jazz bars of Montreux, while foodies relish the iconic cheese of Gruyères, fondue-friendly Fribourg and the Lavaux's winegrowing nirvana. In between all this let time slow down in the historical watchmaking hubs of Le Locle and La Chaux-de-Fonds.

Best for
Jazz, wine and watches

Home to
Lake Geneva, Château de Chillon

Experience
Taking the scenic Golden Pass train line from Montreux to Château d'Oex

PAGE 158

ZÜRICH

Often ranked as one of the world's most liveable cities, Zürich has more to offer than its reputation of wealth. Switzerland's largest city punches above its weight as a 21st-century design hub without losing its medieval mojo. Just take a stroll through the zigzagging lanes of the Old Town Niederdorf to the Limmat River, and you'll wend a path past weathered churches, candy-box clock towers, avant-garde galleries, traditional chocolatiers and high-end boutiques. Most visitors use it as a jumping off point, but the city's mix of culture and cuisine demands attention.

Best for
A city buzz

Home to
Schweizerisches Nationalmuseum

Experience
Swimming in a badi, an outdoor pool on the lake or river

NORTHERN SWITZERLAND

Encompassing the river lands of the Rhine, which winds from Basel's Old Town to Bodensee in the east, this region is full of contrasts. Basel is well known for its ambitious skyline – shaped by architects such as Mario Botta and Zaha Hadid – and few cities are so defined by their relationship with art. Elsewhere, hot springs have been attracting visitors to Baden since the Romans. To the east, the rolling vineyards of Regensberg yield some of the prettiest landscapes.

Best for
World-renowned art,
thermal springs

Home to
Basel Kunstmuseum, Baden

Experience
The huge annual expo Art Basel

$\rightarrow$

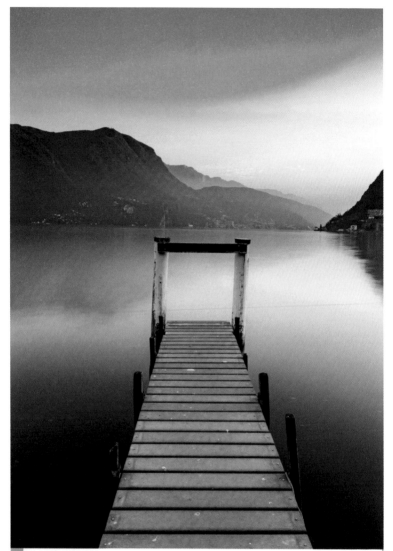

PAGE 200

CENTRAL SWITZERLAND AND TICINO

Most journeys through this alluring region begin in Lucerne, where a boat trip on Vierwaldstattersee drifts past jaw-dropping cliffs. To the south is the town of Andermatt, with five-star hotels and golf courses. On the other side of the Gotthard Tunnel spills Italian-speaking Switzerland, home to the lakeside towns of Locarno and Ascona, clifftop monasteries, crystal-clear swimming spots, and belly-hugging pizza and pasta.

Best for
Superlative scenery and tasty Italian food

Home to
Kloster Einsiedln, Bellinzona

Experience
Riding up – and up – the Burgenstock mountain's spine-tingling outdoor elevator

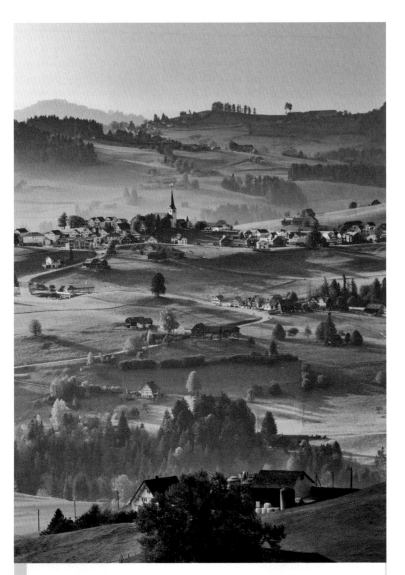

EASTERN SWITZERLAND AND GRAUBÜNDEN

The Switzerland of storybooks is alive in the east. Dairy farmers and cheese-makers get to work in postcard-ready mountain huts and picturesque farmsteads, while sawtooth peaks rise above turquoise lakes. The region is known for outdoor adventures and its famous "champagne powder" surrounding the ski towns of Arosa and Davos. Beyond the mountain resorts lie tranquil Lake Constance and historic St Gallen to the north.

Best for
Outdoor thrills, folk singing and traditional life

Home to
UNESCO-protected St Gallen Abbey, Swiss National Park

Experience
Participating in local celebrations

←

1 Bern's monumental
15th-century Münster.

2 Kleine Scheidegg ski
resort in Bernese Oberland.

3 Boats on Oeschinsee.

4 Interlaken's Old Town.

Switzerland's diverse regions are bursting with historic towns, breathtaking natural scenery and myriad activities. These itineraries will help you make the most of your visit to this beautiful country.

4 DAYS
in Bern and the Bernese Oberland

Day 1

Morning Start the day with a stroll round the arcades and boutiques of Bern's Old City (p62). Swing past the 15th-century Münster to marvel at its intricate tympanum before heading to the Zytglogge clock tower (p70).

Afternoon After lunch in the atmospheric Kornhauskeller (p73), take bus 12 to the wave-like Zentrum Paul Klee (p77) and immerse yourself in modern art.

Evening Head to the Altes Tramdepot (p75) for a great view of the Old City and enjoy traditional Bernese cuisine with a stein of house beer, brewed in copper vats right in the centre of the restaurant.

Day 2

Morning Take the train to the town of Interlaken (p84), which sits between the lakes Thun and Brienz. Explore Jungfrau Park (p103), then head to the pretty village of Lauterbrunnen (p102).

Afternoon Dine on a traditional Swiss lunch of *Flammenkuchen* (flambéed tarts) and fondue. The 141 bus will take you through lush countryside to the breath-taking Trümmelbach Falls, Europe's largest subterranean waterfall, and one of many that surround the village. From here you can hike into the "Black Monk" mountain to experience the full majesty of the ten glacier falls.

Evening Take the 141 onwards to the village of Stechelberg, where you can ascend the 2,970-m (9,744-ft) Schilthorn via a four-stage cable car. Its solar-powered revolving restaurant, Piz Gloria (p102), featured as Blofeld's lair in the 1969

Bond film, *On Her Majesty's Secret Service*. Dine on one of the legendary 007 burgers, then head down to the car-free village of Mürren (p104) for a night at the Alpenruh hotel (p101), near the cable terminus.

Day 3

Morning Hike or snowboard along some of Mürren's 51.5 km (32 miles) of trails, then take the train to have coffee at the historic Bellevue des Alpes hotel (p105).

Afternoon A short walk from the hotel yields fabulous views to the Männlichen, and deposits walkers at Eigergletscher train station. The train tunnels up through the mountains to Jungfraujoch (p103) for incredible glacial vistas. It's a 3-hour hike on the Eiger Ultra Trail (or a quick cable-car ride) back down to Grindelwald (p102).

Evening Ease those tired muscles in the sauna and spa rooms of Grindelwald's luxurious Grand Hotel Regina (p105).

Day 4

Morning Ride the cable car to Pfingstegg for a walk through Gletscherschlucht, a spectacular canyon of rock and ice with great views over the Bernese Oberland mountains. For a speedy return, head back to Pfingstegg and zoom down the summer toboggan run to Grindelwald.

Afternoon Enjoy a light lunch at C und M café (p102), then take the train back to Interlaken West for a leisurely steamer ride over Thunersee to the town that gave the lake its name. The pier is a few minutes' walk from the railway station for a train back to Bern.

←

1 People entering the sobering International Museum of the Red Cross and Red Crescent.

2 The audience mingling at the iconic Montreux Jazz Festival.

3 Rolling hills leading to Lutry.

4 Charlie Chaplin standing on the banks of Lake Geneva.

5 A visitor exploring a display at the Olympic Museum.

5 DAYS

in Western Switzerland

Day 1

Morning Starting at Geneva's Jet d'Eau *(p124)*, stroll north into the Old Town for coffee in the main square. Around the corner is Cathédrale Saint-Pierre *(p120)*, where far-reaching views reward those who climb the north tower.

Afternoon After a spot of lunch at Café Papon *(www.cafepapon.ch)*, catch the tram to visit the International Museum of the Red Cross and Red Crescent *(p126)*.

Evening Feast on contemporary Swiss cuisine at Chez Grégoire *(www.chez-gregoire.ch)* and test the mixologist's skills at Atelier Cocktail Club *(p125)*.

Day 2

Morning Take the train to Lausanne *(p134)* and explore the market (Wed and Sat, weekly). Climb the medieval market steps to visit the beautiful cathedral *(p132)*. Break for lunch at L'Eveché *(www.leveche.ch)*.

Afternoon Take the M2 metro down to Ouchy *(p139)* and the absorbing displays of the Olympic Museum *(p138)*. From here, it's an easy stroll to seasonal bar La Jetée de la Compagnie *(p139)* for an *apéro*.

Evening Book ahead for a table at live jazz club Chorus *(p136)* and enjoy dinner and drinks before the show starts.

Day 3

Morning Travel out to the medieval village of Lutry where the local market offers everything you need for a picnic in the terraced vineyards of Lavaux *(p145)*. If you're feeling energetic, you can hike the 11-km (7-mile) trail through the vines to the pretty town of St-Saphorin.

Afternoon From St-Saphorin, it's a three-minute train ride to Vevey *(p142)* and Chaplin's World, where re-created film sets and curated displays of personal items reveal the man behind the "Little Tramp". A ferry will get you there from Lutry in all of 30 minutes.

Evening Dine overlooking the water at Vevey's KJU *(p155)*, which turns into a club as the night wears on.

Day 4

Morning It's only five minutes by train from Vevey to Montreux *(p144)*, where you can follow the lakefront to Château de Chillon *(p146)*. Spend an hour or two exploring the medieval island and the 13th-century chapel of St-George.

Afternoon Catch a boat back to Montreux in time for lunch, then head to the summit of Rochers-de-Naye via a 55-minute cogwheel railway ride with stunning views over Lake Geneva *(p142)*.

Evening Enjoy dinner and drinks at the Montreux Jazz Café *(www.fairmont.com)*.

Day 5

Morning Take the train to the cheese-making town of Gruyères *(p152)*. Sample its famous cheese and learn how it's made at La Maison du Gruyère. Then head up the hill into the medieval centre.

Afternoon Tuck into a Le Gruyère fondue for lunch, and round things off with fresh meringues and cream, a local speciality. Explore the surreal world of H R Giger at the museum dedicated to his works.

Evening Journey back to Geneva, and enjoy a light dinner at buzzy open-plan restaurant L'Adresse *(www.ladress.ch)*.

8 DAYS
in Central Switzerland

Day 1

Hop on a train at Basel *(p178)* and speed past countryside to Schwyz *(p228)*, the birthplace of modern Switzerland, stopping in Zug for lunch. Once in Schwyz, check into Wysses Rössli *(wysses-roessli-schwyz.ch)*, a traditionally furnished 17th-century hotel overlooking the main square. Then find a café for a fortifying *Kirsch* (cherry schnapps); the area is famous for it. Later, enjoy seasonal, modern dishes at family-run restaurant Schwyzer-Stübli *(www.schwyzer-stubli.ch)*.

Day 2

Spend a couple of hours at the Museum of the Swiss Charters, where the earliest documents of the Swiss Confederation are kept. Round the corner is the Schweizeriches Nationalmuseum, which has interesting multimedia displays on life in Schwyz from 1300 to 1600. Take the Rolenflue-Mythenregion cable car up (and up) for pleasant mountain strolls. Return to town for a dinner of *Älpermagronen* (macaroni and cheese) made with Sbrinz, the quintessential cheese of the region.

Day 3

Catch the train to Lucerne *(p204)*, and get carried away in the Swiss Transport Museum *(p210)*. Take a picnic aboard a boat from the adjacent pier across to Alpnachstad for the world's steepest rack railway to wander Mount Pilatus *(p214)*. Then descend from Alpnachstad by the cable car to Fräkmüntegg, where there is a hair-raising toboggan run, and arrive in Lucerne's city centre in time for dinner.

Day 4

Start the day with a rendezvous with Modernist Masters at Lucerne's Rosengart Collection. Cross the Seebrücke to the Bourbaki Panorama to see the world's largest round mural, a visual history of the 19th century. Fill up on a hearty lunch at family-friendly Hofgarten, round the corner. Then catch a train to Stans *(p227)*, where you can board the funicular to Kälti, and transfer onto the double-decker open-top cable car up to the Stanserhorn summit. On your way back to Lucerne stop at Cubasia *(041 619 71 71)* in Stans for a spicy mix of Chinese and Cuban cuisine.

6

1 Pretty houses lining Basel streets.

2 Schwyz's church piercing the sky.

3 A bridge crossing the Reuss.

4 Amazing vistas at Pilatus.

5 Views from the Gotthard train.

6 A funicular climbing Monte Brè.

Day 5

Take a steam-powered paddle boat to Vitznau for a trip up to Mont Rigi *(p226)* on Europe's first rack railway. Pause for lunch at Rigi Kulm-Hotel *(www.rigikulm.ch)*, Switzerland's first mountain inn, and enjoy one of many walks in the area. Descend the mountain via Arth-Goldau for the train back to Lucerne.

Day 6

Take the Gotthard Panorama Express to Flüelen and then a train to Bellinzona *(p224)* to visit Castelgrande, Sasso Corbaro and Montebello. When hunger strikes at Montebello, sample some *salame* – a local specialty. Explore the pleasant historic town before taking the short trip to Locarno to watch the sunset over Lake Maggiore. Stay at the gorgeous Belvedere *(www.belvedere-locarno.com)*.

Day 7

Take the south train to Lugano *(p220)* for a meander through its pretty cobbled streets. At Cassarete, catch the funicular

up to Monte Brè for long views of Lake Lugano *(p218)* and the snow-capped mountains in the distance. Find a restaurant with a terrace for lunch, whatever time of year – cosy lap blankets are available when temperatures plummet. Return to the city centre and hail a cab to the small town of Montanola for a dinner of dry-rubbed pork and a bowl of wine at Grotto del Cavicc *(p231)* – a favourite haunt of Swiss author Hermann Hesse.

Day 8

Fuel up on Italian pastries and neat shots of espresso, at Café a Porter *(www.cafe-a-porter.ch)*, then enjoy a morning visiting the Piazza Castello museum in the former medieval palace of the Visconti family. Take one of Switzerland's most scenic railway journeys, the Centovalli. The narrow-gauge line to Domodóssola crosses numerous valleys over hair-raising bridges and viaducts, weaving through woods with views over the river hundreds of feet below. Change at Domodóssola, to return to Zürich or Basel.

A WEEK
in Valais

Day 1

From Geneva, take the train to the Rhône Valley beside Lake Geneva, which affords fabulous views of the French Alps and the Lavaux vineyard terraces. The train skirts the castle at Chillon *(p146)*, the backdrop of Lord Byron's poem, *The Prisoner of Chillon*. Disembark at Martigny *(p106)* to visit the impressive Fondation Pierre Gianadda, which hosts changing world-class art exhibitions. Come evening, watch the sun set over the ruins of the Roman amphitheatre, then dine on traditional wood-fired *raclettes*.

Day 2

After breakfast, take the branch railway from Martigny to Le Châble for the cable car to the famous ski resort of Verbier *(p106)*. For even more dramatic views, brave Europe's largest cable car to Mont Fort. In the winter test your mettle on bunny slopes and monster moguls, breaking for steaming mugs of hot chocolate. When it's warmer the region is famed for equally good hiking trails and bike paths. Return to Martigny and continue

east along the Rhône Valley to Leuk. From here the postbus will take you up the twisty mountain road to one of the spas of Leukerbad *(p113)*, such as Les Sources des Alpes *(www.sourcesdesalpes.ch)*.

Day 3

Spend a lazy morning recuperating in a thermal spa, followed by a wander round the historic village. Fuel up on some fine charcuterie in the brasserie, before testing your fitness on the former trading route to the Gemmipass, which zigzags up the mountain, offering ever-wider views. At the top is the historic Berghotel Schwarzenbach *(www.schwarenbach.ch)*, which inspired Guy Maupassant's short story *L'Auberge*. Head back to your hotel and go for a quick plunge in the pool back at the spa before dinner.

Day 4

Continue east to Visp and take the handy narrow-gauge railway up to the car-free resort of Zermatt *(p90)* and its iconic mountain, the Matterhorn. The fascinating

5

① Visitors admiring art at Fondation Pierre Gianadda.

② A panorama pointing out landmarks at the resort town of Verbier.

③ The iconic Matterhorn reflected in a clear mountain lake.

④ Walkers viewing the Aletsch Glacier.

⑤ Wooden chalets lining Zermatt.

Matterhorn Museum tells the story of the drama surrounding the first ascent in 1865 and describes how the mountain's distinctive silhouette has come to be so well known. One of the best walks from the town of Zermatt is the Matterhorn Trail to Schwarzee and its tiny chapel, passing through the hamlet of Zmutt where restaurants serve Valasian specialities. Have a drink (or stay) at the Monte Rosa hotel *(p105)* where famed mountaineer Edward Whymper stayed before his fateful ascent of the Matterhorn.

Day 5

Rise early to take the Gornergratbahn train to watch dawn break over one of the finest viewpoints of the Matterhorn, and grab a quick breakfast at the Kulmhotel Gornergrat *(www.gornergrat-kulm.ch)*. Take to the 360 Trail for great views of the Monte Rosa massif *(p112)* and a panorama of 29 peaks, or, if you're feeling energetic, try the longer Five Lakes Walk. Later, catch the train from Zermatt to Morel for the cable car up to Riederalp, gateway to the Aletsch Glacier *(p94)*.

Day 6

After breakfast, take the cable car to Moosfluh for the start of the spectacular Aletsch Panoramaweg, a 12-km (7-mile) walk beside the 23-km (14-mile) Aletsch Glacier, the centrepiece of the Aletsch Arena World Heritage Site. Stop for a reviving afternoon tea at Villa Cassel in Riederfurka, just above Riederalp; Sir Winston Churchill was a regular guest at Sir Ernest Cassel's holiday home here. Back in Riederalp, tuck into tasty locally sourced *chinoise* (hot pot) and *raclettes* at Derby restaurant and bar *(www.derby-riederalp.ch)*, then rock out to live music, performed here throughout the ski season. Stay overnight in one of the Swiss Alpine Club *(www.sac-cas.ch)* huts that can be found dotted around the area.

Day 7

Make your way to Morel for the train back to Geneva. Alternatively spend a leisurely day taking the scenic route to Zürich via Andermatt and the train through the scenic Schöllenen Gorge to Göschenen on the old Gotthard main line.

Monumental Peaks

A fundamental part of Swiss life, the Alps are a playground for hikers, bikers and rock climbers - and the ingenuity of Swiss engineering has made many peaks accessible to the less active visitor, too. Perhaps the most majestic of all is the iconic Matterhorn *(p90)*; this pyramid-shaped behemouth looms over the village of Zermatt *(p90)*. Still a challenge for even the most seasoned mountaineers, it's best admired from afar - take the train to the rocky ridge of Gornergrat for a stunning view of the majestic summit.

→

Two hikers walking over an icy path, with the Matterhorn in the distance

SWITZERLAND FOR
NATURAL
WONDERS

Switzerland brims with sublime natural beauty that has inspired painters, writers and photographers for centuries. But little can truly do justice to the immensity of its mountains, the sparkle of its alpine lakes and the sheer might of its glaciers. Prepare to bow down to Mother Nature.

Geological Marvels

Geological features carved out over millennia add their own unique beauty to this fascinating landscape, from Europe's largest waterfall to deep gorges. In western Switzerland, the one to see is the Creux du Van *(p156)*. A range of hiking trails, from a saunter to challenging treks, lead to breathtaking views across the amphitheatre of this grand canyon.

←

Sunlight curving along the towering walls of the Creux de Van

MAJESTIC MOUNTAINS

Pilatus
Paraglide on thermals around the mountain.

Rigi
Ride Europe's first mountain railway to the top.

Rochers-de-Naye
Spot marmots and alpine flowers on hiking paths.

Monte Generoso
Catch the rack railway to Ticino's most scenic spot.

Mont Fort
At the summit watch the sunrise over the valley.

Aletsch Glacier

Though many are shrinking at an alarming rate, Switzerland's enthralling glaciers remain an unforgettable experience. Among the most impressive is the 23-km (14-mile) Aletsch Glacier *(p94)*. It is particularly stunning when the glistening ice-river contrasts with the autumn forests around it.

←

A visitor getting up close to the thick wall of ice on the underside of the immense Aletsch Glacier

Enchanting Mountain Lakes

Landlocked Switzerland may be, but you're never far from water. Head into the mountains to seek out popular Oeschinensee *(p96)*, a swatch of turquoise surrounded by dramatic cliffs, or south to the sunny Mediterranean-esque Lake Lugano *(p218)*, a starting point for wonderful hikes.

→

Cows grazing in front of the placid expanse of Oeschinensee

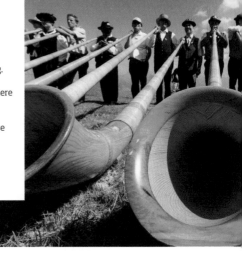

Blowing the Alphorn

A Swiss version of the didgeridoo, the alphorn was traditionally used by farmers to call their cows in for milking. In the 19th century alphorns became popular as musical instruments and there are now alphorn groups all over the country. Each year the Nendaz Alphorn Festival gathers many of these musicians together for a competitive three-day event where visitors can hear them play and join an alphorn-making workshop. The organizers also hold alphorn initiation courses.

→

Musicians in traditional dress at the Alphorn Festival

SWITZERLAND FOR
TRADITIONS

A forward-looking country in many ways, Switzerland is nonetheless rooted in tradition. While not everyone can yodel, there's a sense of pride around these customs and people flock to festivals that celebrate them. For visitors, they offer a fascinating glimpse into Switzerland's rural heart.

Wrestle With It

A sport dating back centuries, *Schwingen* (Swiss wrestling) pits two opponents against each other in a circle filled with sawdust. It has been a key feature of many rural festivals but the biggest event is Schwingfest, held every three years in front of thousands of people.

→

Two *Schwingen* competitors in the village of Boltigen

Yodel-Ay-Ee-Oooo

Originally a way for farmers in remote regions to call to each other, yodelling developed into song in the 19th century and is still going strong in Switzerland today; it also frequently features in contemporary folk music. The Älpli bar in Zürich is a good spot to watch live yodelling year-round, while each summer the national yodelling festival, Jodlerfest, attracts thousands of spectators. You can take yodelling lessons, and even take a degree at the University of Lucerne.

←

A yodelling group singing at a festival in traditional regalia

TOP 4 TRADITIONAL COSTUME

Schwingerhosen
Worn over trousers, these sackcloth shorts form a handle which a competitor may grab during a wrestling bout.

Edelweiss Shirt
This pale blue shirt is embroidered with a pattern of Switzerland's national flower.

Bredzon
Typical of the Fribourg region, this dark-blue short jacket with puffed sleeves is still worn by working dairy farmers.

Bredzo
This ornate overdress is worn by the women of the small Appenzell Innerrhoden canton.

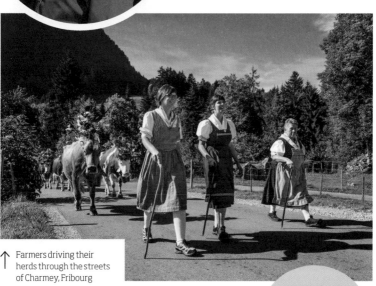

↑ Farmers driving their herds through the streets of Charmey, Fribourg

Till the Cows Come Home

Once the summer ends and the cheese is made, alpine farmers bring their cows back down to the valley for the winter. To celebrate, many villages stage a festival – Désalpage – with traditional music, food and drink stands, and cheese-making demonstrations. The cows sport large ceremonial bells and floral headdresses, while the farmers wear the traditional dress of their region.

210,000
The estimated number of cows grazing the hills and meadows of Switzerland.

Visitors perusing
exhibits at the Schweizer
Kindermuseum ↑

SWITZERLAND FOR
FAMILIES

With rope parks, toboggan runs, water parks and forests to high-tail it through, Switzerland is the perfect family getaway. In winter, the snow-dusted peaks become a fairy-tale landscape for children, while the summer thaw brings dozens of water-based attractions to life.

Into the Wild

Switzerland's great outdoors is a wonderland for children of all ages. In the winter, hit the bunny slopes in family-friendly resorts towns, such as Wengen *(p104)* and Kandersteg *(p105)*. When the weather warms, heed the call of mountain lakes and myriad hiking and cycling trails through Switzerland's natural wonders.

→

Walkers on the 5-Seenweg
(Five Lakes Walk), near Zermatt

Rainy Day Activities

Child-friendly museums are the perfect place to be when it's too rainy (or snowy) to be outside. Make for Zürich Schweizerisches Nationalmuseum *(p164)* and its "A Magic Carpet Ride Through History", an interactive journey that starts in an Arabian palace and ends on a vintage railway carriage. Over in Baden, "children's culture" is celebrated at the Schweizer Kindermuseum *(p193)*, where the whole family can play together.

The Schweizer Kindermuseum's elegant building, dating from 1890
↓

> 💬 INSIDER TIP
> ## Babies at High Altitude
>
> It's easier than you might think to travel with youngsters in Switzerland. Kids under six travel free on trains, and there is often space for prams. Resort town tourist offices have information on buggy-friendly walking trails, if baby-wearing is out of the question. Nappy-changing facilities are common, and some restaurants provide high chairs.

Theme Parks

With such large-scale landscapes on offer, Switzerland can appear daunting for little ones. They'll have no problem at Swissminiatur, an open-air park on the shores of Lake Lugano *(p218)* with pocket-sized models of monuments and national icons, plus tiny trains choo-chooing between the knee-high sights. In Graubünden, children can step back in time and re-create the adventures of Heidi, Switzerland's littlest explorer, at Heididorf *(www.heididorf.ch)*.

↑ Families enjoying the Swissminiatur park in Lake Lugano

Death by Chocolate

The Swiss won't let you forget that milk chocolate was invented in Switzerland in the 1880s, and it's possible to visit dozens of factories and artisan chocolatiers across the country to find out how they did it. Unearth the sweet history at Maison Cailler's historic Broc chocolate factory near Gruyères *(www.cailler.ch)*, or visit the Chocolarium of Maestrani in Flawil *(www.chocolarium.ch)*; it's the only chocolate factory in Switzerland that lets you onto the production floor.

$\longrightarrow$

Chocolate workshop at Maison Cailler's famous factory

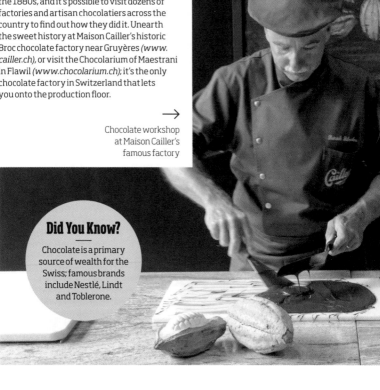

Did You Know?

Chocolate is a primary source of wealth for the Swiss; famous brands include Nestlé, Lindt and Toblerone.

SWITZERLAND FOR
FOODIES

Flanked by the powerhouses of France and Italy, Switzerland's culinary scene can get overlooked. Yet, its talented chefs and food fairs are quickly turning its cities into foodie destinations. Across the Alps you'll find age-old traditions and belly-hugging experiences that'll stay with you forever.

Regional Varieties

At the vanguard of the Swiss food revival is traditional go-to comfort food, and each region has its own classic dishes. In Graubünden, that's a tasty version of *Älplermagronen* (macaroni cheese elevated with speck), while in Zürich you'll find *Zürcher geschnetzeltes mit rösti* served in five-star restaurants and cosy taverns alike.

$\longleftarrow$

Hearty *Zürcher*, a dish with veal, onions, mushroom and a hash brown in a creamy sauce

Birchermuesli,
the wholesome
and classic Swiss
breakfast dish

←

A Hosanna to Healthy Living

Created by the famous Swiss physician Dr Bircher-Benner, Birchermuesli has rapidly changed the way the world eats breakfast. The simple meal is made from grated apple, cinnamon, rolled oats, seeds, nuts and dollops of yogurt – with the intention of combatting the ill effects of tuberculosis through better diet – and can be found at every hotel buffet. Strangely, it was actually never intended for breakfast, but as a starter to every meal.

TOP 4 FOOD FESTIVALS

St Moritz Gourmet Festival, January
Nine days of culinary highs in the mountains.

Food Zürich, May
Ten days with more than 150 dining events, from sizzling street food to five-star banquets.

Risotto Gran Prix, Locarno, September
Chefs go head-to-head in an open-air cook-off on the spectacular Piazza Grande.

Zibelemärit, Bern, November
This centuries-old festival celebrates the humble onion.

A World of Cheese

From Appenzeller to Sbinz, the Swiss love cheese and there is plenty of it to enjoy. Build an appetite on the Emmen Valley Cheese Trail, starting in Burgdorf, then tuck into some of the country's world-famous dishes, such as fondue (bubbling melted cheese for bread dipping) and *raclette* (grilled cheese for coating potatoes) – the subjects of lifelong obsessions for cheese-lovers everywhere. Cheesy festivals and artisanal markets can be relished across the country all year.

→
Dipping potatoes and
bread into a bubbling
cheese fondue

All Eyes on Basel

Basel is first and foremost a city of art and culture. There are more museums here than anywhere in Switzerland; it's the home of Art Basel (Europe's premier art show) and the term Art Brut (Raw Art) was coined here. Start at the Kunstmuseum *(p187)*, the world's oldest public fine art gallery, then pay homage to local hero and kinetic sculptor Jean Tinguely at Museum Tinguely *(p183)* on the banks of the Rhine. For 21st-century art, finish up at the Kunsthalle *(p181)*.

→

Visitors admiring works by Fernand Leger in the Kunstmuseum

SWITZERLAND FOR
ART LOVERS

Switzerland's artistic heritage is second-to-none, with a succession of world-class galleries, museums and renowned art fairs. National treasures include Alberto Giacometti, Ferdinand Hodler, Jean Tinguely and Paul Klee, but there are countless collections of Masters from around the world too.

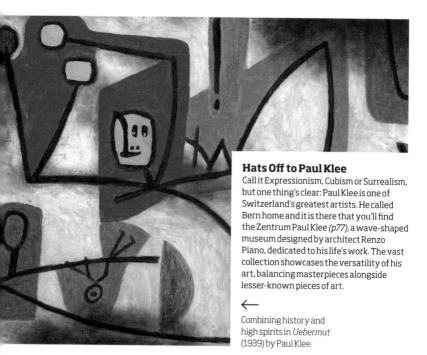

Hats Off to Paul Klee

Call it Expressionism, Cubism or Surrealism, but one thing's clear: Paul Klee is one of Switzerland's greatest artists. He called Bern home and it is there that you'll find the Zentrum Paul Klee *(p77)*, a wave-shaped museum designed by architect Renzo Piano, dedicated to his life's work. The vast collection showcases the versatility of his art, balancing masterpieces alongside lesser-known pieces of art.

←

Combining history and high spirits in *Uebermut* (1939) by Paul Klee

← A visitor perusing *Stone Line* (1977) by Richard Long, at Basel's Kunstmuseum

TOP 4 BEST ART MUSEUMS

Kunstmuseum Bern
Opened in 1879, this is one of Switzerland's oldest art museums.

Kunsthaus Zürich
A modern art home to international stars and homegrown heroes such as Giacometti and Hodler.

Lowenbrau Complex, Zürich
Once a brewery, now an unmissable cultural centre.

Musee d'Art et d'Histoire, Geneva
An impressive gallery in the west of the country.

Birthplace of Dadaism

Zürich's most famous art moment came during World War I when a counter-culture movement emerged focusing on anti-war politics and anti-bourgeois ethic. It was called Dadaism and its ground zero today is Cabaret Voltaire *(p171)*, one of Switzerland's most vibrant avant garde art spaces and jazz bars.

→ Performance art at Zürich's artistic nightclub, the Cabaret Voltaire

 INSIDER TIP
Comic Collection

Basel's Cartoon Museum *(www.cartoonmuseum. ch)* celebrates narrative drawing, with one of Europe's most kaleido-scopic collections of caricature, comics and graphic novels. In 2005, the quirky museum was extended and restyled by Swiss architects Herzog & de Meuron.

Bridging the Gap

Built in 2017 to connect two sections of the Europaweg, a summer hiking trail with views, the Charles Kuonen Suspension Bridge is the longest pedestrian bridge in the world. The daring walk across its 500-m (1,640-ft) length and sway 85 m (280 ft) above the valley floor. Once you've got a taste for it, try Glacier 3000's Peak Walk, which stretches between two mountain summits, or cross above the tongue of a glacier on the Trift bridge.

→

Charles Kuonen Suspension Bridge, with sweeping views of the peaks

Did You Know?

It takes the average hiker 10 minutes to cross the Charles Kuonen Suspension Bridge.

SWITZERLAND FOR
ENGINEERING

Switzerland's dramatic mountainscape has long been conquered by mountaineers but, since the 19th century, it has also been tamed by engineers. Whether you're an engineer or not, you can't fail to be impressed by these incredible pioneering feats, old and new.

Dam High

Switzerland's abundance of water means hydroelectricity is its primary power source. King of the dams is the 285-m- (930-ft-) high Grande Dixence *(p109)*, the world's tallest gravity dam. Take a guided tour inside the dam and walk across its scenic top. The daring can emulate James Bond by bungee jumping from the Contra Dam *(p45)*.

→

The Grande Dixence set deep within the mountains

On the Slopes

Switzerland's peaks have always presented a welcome challenge to engineers. Europe's first ever cogwheel mountain railway opened on Rigi mountain in 1871, while the Pilatusbahn, built in 1889, is still the steepest cogwheel in the world. Switzerland hasn't stopped leading the way ever since. The Matterhorn Glacier Ride cableway was named the world's highest when it opened in October 2018, and the Stoosbahn in Schwyz *(p228)* became the world's steepest classic funicular when it opened in 2017. Then, there's the Stanserhorn Cable Car in Stans *(p227)*, the world's first open-top cable-car ride.

←

The Stoosbahn funicular railway on the way up to the village of Stoos

TOP 3 — ALPINE ARCHITECTS

Herzog & de Meuron
The work of this renowned Swiss duo can be seen all over their home city of Basel, but they also designed the summit restaurant and cable car station at Chäserrugg.

Mario Botta
The Ticino-born architect has tackled Switzerland's challenging landscape several times, including designing the three-storey building at the top of Glacier 3000.

Bearth & Deplazes (1915–1959)
In an extraordinarily isolated location, the Monte Rosa hut was designed by this firm from Chur as a contemporary version of a medieval donjon.

On the Rails

In Switzerland, obstacles only make your train journey more interesting. The UNESCO World Heritage Rhaetian Railway takes passengers through 55 tunnels and over nearly 200 viaducts and bridges, while the Jungfraubahn burrows through the infamous north face of the Eiger *(p103)*. No less impressive is the 57-km- (34-mile-) long Gotthard tunnel *(p233)* under the Saint Gotthard massif, which is the world's longest and deepest rail tunnel.

↑ The Rhaetian Railway route passing the Bernina range

On the Water

In a country with around 7,000 lakes, much of local life takes place around - and across - the water. Paddle steamers cruise Lake Geneva (p142) and Lake Lucerne daily, in season. On Lake Maggiore (p234) speedboats ping-pong between Locarno and Ascona. Away from the lakes, river boats cruise the scenic Rhine between Schaffhausen (p242) and Stein am Rhein (p257).

←

A paddle steamer on the turquoise waters of Lake Geneva

SWITZERLAND FOR
SCENIC JOURNEYS

One of the best ways to appreciate the beauty of Switzerland's diverse landscape is to travel through it. Whether you're driving, walking or taking the train, you'll soon discover that there is truth in the saying "it's the journey not the destination".

Ride the Rails

The views outside train windows are just as impressive as the Swiss railways' obstacle-defying engineering (p41). Each time the Bernina Express (p274) emerges from one of the 55 tunnels between Chur and Tirano, the scene changes, from lakes to forest and back again. To really soak up the panoramas, ride the world's slowest "express" train, the Glacier Express (p274), which takes about seven hours to travel the mountainous 290 km (180 miles) between Zermatt and St Moritz.

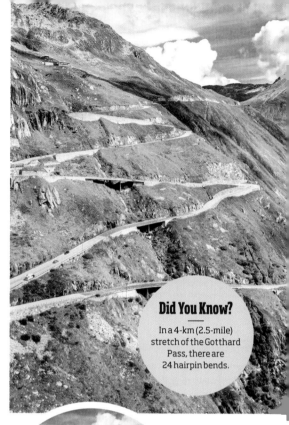

→

A series of hairpin bends on the Gotthard Pass

Hit the Road

Driving isn't always about speed and convenience; sometimes it pays to take the scenic route. The traffic-free Gotthard Pass *(p233)*, a route through the Swiss Alps, offers sweeping curves, hairpin bends and mountain views. The vistas from the Umbrail Pass – Switzerland's highest paved road – are similarly rewarding.

🔍 HIDDEN GEM
Flower Power

Zermatt's railway station marks the start of the Botanical Trail. This fairly easy 4-km (2.5-mile) hiking route offers sightings of ubiquitous edelweiss, rare orchids and wild ibex on its way to Trift.

Did You Know?

In a 4-km (2.5-mile) stretch of the Gotthard Pass, there are 24 hairpin bends.

←

Hiking along the rugged, ice-laden Aletsch Glacier Trail

Lace Up Your Boots

The Swiss swear that the best way to see their country is on foot and on summer weekends they love nothing more than donning hiking boots and heading up the nearest mountain. Join them on the Lauterbrunnental Glacial Valley route, which takes in 12 waterfalls, the 6-km (3.5-mile) Eiger Trail, the Aletsch Glacier Trail across Europe's largest ice flow or the Five Lakes Walk around the Matterhorn.

←

The iconic red Bernina Express trundling over a viaduct

Up, Up and Away

The glacially carved Swiss peaks are not only a playground for rock climbers, mountain bikers, skiers and snowboarders. Verbier contains some of the most well-reputed paragliding schools in Europe, while Appenzell's Ebenalp cable car affords access to consistent thermals for experienced flyers. For those who don't want to soar too high, airborne freedom can also be found on Grindelwald's First Flyer, a zipline with a one-two punch of Jungfraujoch's and Eiger's summit views.

→

A paraglider taking off in the breathtaking Bernese Highlands

Did You Know?

Paragliders use rising air created by solar radiation to get into the air, in a technque called thermalling.

SWITZERLAND FOR
THRILL-SEEKERS

With an enviable backdrop of sawtooth peaks, sheer canyon drops and hairline ridges, it's no surprise the Swiss have a love affair with white-knuckle adventures. Weekends see the cities empty out as locals embrace the elements, and there's ample opportunity to join them, too.

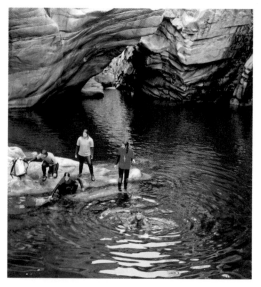

Adventure Awaits

Combining the best elements of hiking, climbing, swimming and abseiling, canyoning is a heart-racing activity. Sometimes, it's also the only way to access a hidden corner of the country. Switzerland's top canyoning spots include the Valle Verzasca *(p230)* and nearby Valle Maggia *(p231)*, where the Val Grande canyoning route takes in rock pools and waterfalls. Swiss River Adventures *(www.swiss riveradventures.ch)* shows beginners the ropes.

A group of visitors preparing for a dive in the serene waters of Valle Maggia

TOP 5 MORE GREAT ADVENTURES

Olympia Bob Run, St Moritz
The oldest bobsleigh track in the world.

Via Ferrata, Aletsch
Climb above the largest glacier in the Alps.

Whitewater Rafting, Lower Engadine
Thrills and spills on the river En.

Titlis Cliff Walk, Engelberg
Cross Europe's highest suspension bridge.

Mountain Biking, Lenzerheide
Home to a 6-km (3-mile) downhill run.

Follow 007

Opportunities abound for chasing adrenaline James Bond-style. Re-create the scene from *Goldfinger* (1964) by driving the Furka Pass *(p237)* as Sean Connery did, skiing down the slopes from Piz Gloria *(p102)* as shown in *On Her Majesty's Secret Service* (1969), or bungee jump off Contra Dam like Pierce Brosnan's 007 in *GoldenEye* (1995).

$\rightarrow$

The steep walls of the Contra Dam, and *(inset)* a bunjee jumper

Museums and More

The Schweizerisches Nationalmuseum *(p164)* in Zürich is the grand dame of Switzerland's cultural trove. Explore the galleries and you'll find some of the museum's best kept secrets, including sledges. The Swiss Open-Air Museum *(p89)* at Ballenberg has a hundred old buildings and actors to bring it to life.

A traditional building on display at the Swiss Open Air Museum

SWITZERLAND FOR
HISTORY BUFFS

With so many breathtaking natural attractions, it can be easy to overlook Switzerland's historical past. But the chance to observe Roman ruins, stout viscount castles and timeless UNESCO Heritage Sites shouldn't be passed up. Be sure to fit these unmissable national treasures into your schedule.

TOP 4 HISTORICAL SITES

Avenches Roman Amphitheatre
This amphitheatre hosts an opera festival and regular concerts.

Augusta Raurica, Basel
A Roman archaeological site on the south bank of the Rhine *(p196)*.

Rutli Meadow, Lucerne
The spot on the shores of Lake Lucerne where modern Switzerland was founded.

Sasso San Gottardo, Gotthard Pass
A former secret military bunker built in WW2, now a museum *(p232)*.

The Most Visited Castle

Discover a perfect marriage of history and locale at Château de Chillon *(p146)*, an island castle located south of Veytaux on Lake Geneva. The intriguing stories of the Counts of Savoy who controlled the fort, and its role as arsenal and prison, are rivalled only by the extraordinary natural drama that surrounds it.

The covered bridge leading to the popular, imposing Château de Chillon

UNESCO World Heritage Sites

In a country rich in UNESCO sights, it's hard to pick a favourite. Belinzona's magnificent castles *(p225)* and Bern's Zytglogge clock tower *(p70)* are among the best. The abbey at St Gallen *(p244)* is a perfect example of living history: its library has one of the world's most stunning book collections.

Celestial beings adorn the domed ceiling of St Gallen's abbey ↓

↑ The ornate façade and soaring twin towers of the abbey at St Gallen

→

Contestants in a bout of *Schwingen*, a Swiss form of wrestling

SWITZERLAND FOR
SPORTS FANS

Switzerland offers a wealth of variety for sports fans, from armchair pundits to anyone ready to play. The country is renowned for its world-class winter sports, down the slopes and on the ice, and as the summer heats up, so too do the tennis courts and biking trails.

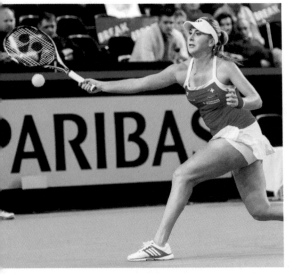

Anyone for Tennis?

Switzerland may have its medal-winning skiers and figure skaters, but tennis has become the de facto national sport thanks to a string of star players, such as Roger Federer and Belinda Bencic. The good news is there are plenty of places to practise, as well as a number of ATP World Tour championships at which to spectate. Consider the Geneva Open (May), Gstaad Open (Jul) or, the big one on Federer's home patch, the Swiss Indoors tournament in Basel (Oct–Nov).

←

Olympic gold medalist Belinda Bencic in action at the women's Fed Cup in Geneva

Keep up the Tradition

The Swiss have loved watching and playing sports for centuries. *Schwingen*, also known as Swiss wrestling, dates back to at least the 13th century. Bouts were originally fought between farmers and cattle herders and bulls are often still awarded as prizes. Other historic sports include *hornussen*, where players attempt to hit a heavy puck as far as possible, and *steinstossen*, where stones weighing up to 50 kg (110 lb) are thrown like a shot put.

TOP 4 **SPECTATOR SPORTS**

Ice Hockey, Davos
Catch the world's oldest ice hockey tournament.

Sailing, Geneva
Watch the Bol d'Or Mirabaud, the world's largest inland regatta.

Tour de Suisse Cycling, Various
Cheer on cyclists on this proving ground for the Tour de France.

Football, Various
Join fans at a local game between August and May.

→ Sculpture of cyclists in the Olympic Museum's expansive grounds

Active History

A meditative walk around the Olympic Museum in Ouchy *(p138)* is the perfect introduction to Switzerland's sport obsession. The International Olympic Committee is based in the city, but it's the museum where you can enjoy a comprehensive look into the history of the movement, including halls dedicated to Olympic torches, sports memorabilia and medals. Zürich, meanwhile, is home to the FIFA World Football Museum *(p171)*, which charts the highs and lows of the world's most popular sport *(p173)*. Understandably, the most famous attraction is a selfie with the original World Cup trophy.

→ A child at the FIFA World Football Museum

Heidi and Graubünden

Johanna Spyri's novel *Heidi* tells the story of an orphan girl who is taken to live with her grandfather high up in the Swiss Alps near Chur. The most popular work of Swiss fiction has been translated into 50 languages, and captured the imagination of children the world over. Kids can re-create her adventures at Heididorf *(p35)*, a village above Maienfeld *(p261)*.

Children reenacting characters Heidi and Clara walking across a meadow

SWITZERLAND IN
BOOKS AND FILM

Switzerland's jaw-dropping landscapes have inspired some of the most-read classics in English literature, and can often be seen as the backdrop to Hollywood blockbusters. There are museums, festivals and reenactments held across the country to honour Switzerland's affect on the imagination.

J R R Tolkien and Lauterbrunnen

For most *Lord of the Rings* fans, Middle Earth means New Zealand, yet it was the sheer cliffs, fairy tale grottoes and deep, dark forests of the rugged Bernese Oberland *(p80)* that inspired J R R Tolkien's elvish valleys, troll-filled woods and craggy fortresses.

→

The view of the Bernese mountains that surround turquoise Oscheninsee

INSIDER TIP
Licence to Chill

Sip martinis shaken to Bond's specifications at nearly 3,000 m (9850 ft) at the awe-inspiring revolving restaurant Piz Gloria *(p102)*, designed by Konrad Wolf.

Did You Know?

The Bond production team financed the completion of Piz Gloria in exchange for filming rights.

The Alps and 007

James Bond's high-altitude antics have brought viewers into the Alps three times. The first was *On Her Majesty's Secret Service* (1963), where its villain has a mountain lair on Schilthorn (now the Piz Gloria restaurant), and Bond embarks on a black run in an alpine blizzard. Next was the high-speed chase up to the Furka Pass in *Goldfinger* (1964). Then came the astonishing jump over the Contra Dam in *GoldenEye* (1995).

→

The terrace at Piz Gloria, with glorious mountain views across the Alps

←

The grizzly iron statue of Frankenstein's monster in Geneva

Mary Shelley and Geneva

The haunted (and hunted) scientist Victor Frankenstein was born when Gothic writer Mary Shelley was challenged to write a ghost story during a dark and stormy night while staying on Lake Geneva in 1816. The result was the instant horror classic *Frankenstein*, which has been commemorated all across the western tip of Switzerland. Visit the Plainpalais area of Geneva to see the statue of Frankenstein's monster; the grounds of private Villa Diodati, where Shelley was first struck with the idea; and the Martin Bodmer Foundation *(www. fondationbodmer.ch)*, which has an archive of material related to the book's creation.

Boarding Call

Skiing is the top choice of sport in Switzerland, however, there are also some resorts that favour snowboarders. With four snow parks, a freestyle slope and Europe's largest half-pipe, Flims Laax Falera is made for boarders. Take a lesson with LAAX School *(www.laaxschool. com)* before showing off your moves. Grindelwald *(p102),* in the Jungfrau region, is one of the best options for novice riders.

→

Snowboarding fun at Flims Laax Falera

SWITZERLAND FOR
SNOW SPORTS

Switzerland's mountains draw visitors all year round but for snow sports fans there's only one time to visit: winter, when the high altitude guarantees great powder. Whether you're after an adrenaline-fuelled ski session or a family-friendly toboggan-ride, Switzerland will not disappoint.

Cool Runnings

Adrenaline junkie? Visit St Moritz's Cresta Run, where the first competitive luge and bobsleigh races were held, and try your hand at skeleton bobsleighing *(www.cresta-run.com).* If you're after something a bit more gentle, hire a toboggan or *velogemel.* Invented in 1911 by a local businessman and wood-carver who faced mobility problems, the *velogemel* is a wooden snow-bike unique to the mountain village of Grindelwald *(p102).* It's easy to use: push off with your feet and steer with the two handlebars.

←

Snow sent flying through the air by the blades of a traditional toboggan

Take a Tube

The most family-friendly snow sport? Snow tubing, where parents and kids zoom down specially-designed slopes in inflatable tubes. And, with more snow tubing tracks than anywhere else in Europe, Switzerland offers plenty of opportunities to try it. Leysin *(p150)* has 11 tracks alone, including several for under-5s, and at Zermatt *(p90)* you can even snow tube on the glacier.

←

Icy tracks in Valais make for a fun snow tube ride

TOP 3 **FAMOUS SWISS SKIERS**

Madeleine Berthod (b 1931)
Won gold in the women's downhill at the 1956 Olympic Games.

Vreni Schneider (b 1964)
Voted "Swiss Sportswoman of the Century".

Simon Ammann (b 1981)
Recipient of four individual Winter Olympic gold medals.

Hit the Slopes

With scores of ski resorts and thousands of kilometres of pistes, it's little wonder the Swiss Alps are a popular training ground for the best winter sports athletes. If you're after classic alpine skiing, choose a mega resort, such as Verbier *(p102)* or Davos *(p261)*. For glitz and glamour, it's hard to beat Zermatt *(p86)* and Gstaad *(p102)*. St Moritz *(p264)*, meanwhile, is a top choice for cross-country skiers.

HIDDEN GEM
Empty Slopes

Swiss ski slopes are world famous, but there are still some under-the-radar pistes if you know where to look. Car-free Bettmeralp, for instance, rewards intrepid skiers with empty runs.

→

A skier zooming across the powdery slopes of the Zermatt ski resort

A YEAR IN
SWITZERLAND

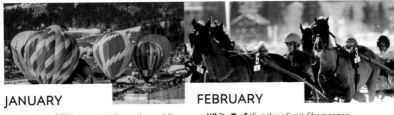

JANUARY

Inferno Downhill (*late Jan*). In Mürren, the world's oldest and longest downhill ski race is open to all.

World Economic Forum (*late Jan*). Davos plays host to heads of state and public events.

△ **International Hot Air Balloon Festival** (*late Jan–early Feb*). Competition and passenger flights high above Château d'Oex in the Alps.

FEBRUARY

△ **White Turf** (*first three Suns*). Champagne flows as thoroughbred horses make snow fly on St Moritz's frozen lake.

Carnival (*late Feb–early Mar*). It's party time in every village during *Carnaval* (in French), or *Fastnacht* (in German), with world-famous parades in Basel and Lucerne.

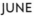

MAY

Combats de Reines, Aproz (*early May*). In Aproz, the unique Herens breed of feisty cow lock (blunted) horns in bovine battle to determine next year's "Queen of queens".

△ **International Cheese Festival** (*1st Sun*). Visitors - and judges - snaffle samples made by cheesemakers from around the world, vying to be crowned Supreme Champion in Gruyères.

JUNE

△ **Art Basel** (*mid-Jun*). World-renowned art fair, with sister events in Miami and Hong Kong.

Montreux Jazz Festival (*end Jun*). Music fans flock to venues across the city for this legendary festival. Acclaimed artists perform everywhere from intimate cafés to Montreux's huge Stravinski auditorium.

OCTOBER

Chestnut Festival (*mid-Oct*). During a celebration of chestnuts across Ticino, more than 2,000 kg (4,400 lbs) are consumed in a day in Ascona.

△ **Swiss Toy, Bern** (*mid-Oct*). The country's largest toy fair is held every year in Bern, showcasing everything from stuffed toys shaped as alpine marmots to cutting-edge digital devices.

SEPTEMBER

△ **Désalpage** (*mid-Sep–early Oct*). Bringing the cows down from high alpine pastures is celebrated in every rural Swiss village, with children leading highly decorated cows through the streets.

MARCH

△ **Engadine Marathon** *(second Sun)*. Well over a thousand cross-country skiers trudge across frozen lakes and woods to rustic S-chanf; open to all.

International Motor Show *(mid-Mar)*. Geneva's 10-day extravaganza launches futuristic designs, as well as the next year's family cars.

Verbier Xtreme *(end Mar–early Apr)*. Skiers and snowboarders compete with pros on Verbier's challenging terrain.

APRIL

Festichoc *(early Apr)*. Visitors tour artisan workshops, ride on the chocolate train and sample all the chocolate they can stomach in Versoix for free.

△ **Landsgemeinde** *(late Apr)*. Switzerland's unique open-air assembly takes place in Appenzell, where some 3,000 citizens stand and vote on all public matters.

JULY

Paléo *(late Jul)*. An eclectic range of rock, blues and funk is performed in circus tents around Nyon.

△ **Swiss Open** *(end Jul)*. The world's best tennis players battle it out on impeccable clay courts for the title of champion, in Gstaad's ultra-chic surroundings.

AUGUST

△ **Swiss National Day** *(1 Aug)*. During the day, a parade snakes through Zurich, while bonfires and fireworks illuminate every mountaintop across the country by night to celebrate the founding of the Swiss Confederacy.

International Film Festival *(mid-Aug)*. Thousands of spectators grab a seat in Locarno for outdoor viewings on a huge screen, of premieres, as well as old favourites.

Lucerne Festival *(mid-Aug–mid-Sep)*. Internationally renowned summer programme of galas and concerts showcase the best of classical music.

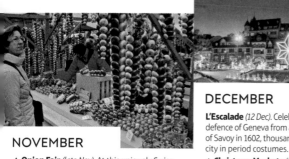

NOVEMBER

△ **Onion Fair** *(late Nov)*. At this uniquely Swiss event, people flock to Bern from across the country to ring in the onion harvest. A wild confetti-throwing battle signals the official end of the festival.

DECEMBER

L'Escalade *(12 Dec)*. Celebrating the successful defence of Geneva from an attack by the Duke of Savoy in 1602, thousands march through the city in period costumes.

△ **Christmas Markets** *(throughout)*. Open-air markets appear across the country. While the ones in Basel, Bern, Zürich and Montreux are among the biggest, Stein am Rhein and Fribourg's are particularly charming.

A BRIEF
HISTORY

Thanks to its strategic location, Switzerland has been highly sought for centuries. In 1291, the Swiss Confederation was created to stave off foreign rule. The alliance expanded until modern Switzerland was born in 1848. Although its international neutrality has kept it out of many major events, this small country remains one of the continent's powerhouses.

The Crossroads of Europe

As early as 500 BC, the lands that now comprise Switzerland were settled by two tribes, the Celtic Helvetii and the Etruscan Rhaetians. By 58 BC, the region was incorporated into the Roman Empire and peace and prosperity reigned: agriculture flourished, towns grew and new roads encouraged trade. From the 5th to the 13th centuries, different factions fought over the territory until it was swallowed into the Holy Roman Empire in the 800s; it continued to be a battleground for powerful feudal families, notably the Habsburgs, Savoys and Zähringens.

1 A 17th-century map showing Basel.

2 The 1315 Battle of Morgarten against the Habsburgs.

3 A statue depicting folk hero William Tell.

4 Destruction of icons during the Reformation in 1524, Zürich.

Timeline of events

390 BC
Gallic armies heading for Rome cross the Grand St Bernard Pass.

217 BC
Hannibal comes over the Alps with his elephants.

200 BC onwards
The Roman rulers introduce their religion, language and underfloor heating.

500s BC
The Helvetii and Rhaetian tribes begin to settle in the Alps.

742
A feudal system develops as Charlemagne draws the region into the Holy Roman Empire.

3

2   4

Birth of the Swiss Nation

In 1291, men from Unterwalden, Schwyz and Uri, the "Three Forest Cantons", gathered to form an alliance against foreign power. The Swiss Confederation was born, eventually giving rise to the legend of William Tell, the heroic countryman who defied Habsburg rule. Over the next 200 years, other cantons joined the fight for independence, which they finally gained in 1499. Renowned for their valour, Swiss troops became sought after as mercenaries. However, a shock defeat at the 1515 Battle of Marignano led the nation to declare an "eternal peace" with France; this led to laws preventing the Swiss from fighting in foreign wars, and gradually brought about complete neutrality.

The Reformation

The Protestant Reformation of the early 16th century created bitter conflict between Catholic cantons and those embracing the new creed of reformers such as Huldrych Zwingli (1484–1531) and Jean Calvin (1509–64). Despite this religious rift, all the cantons remained loyal to the Confederation throughout the wars of religion that swept Europe in the 17th century.

MÈRE ROYAUME'S FOOD FIGHT

On 11 December 1602, the Duke of Savoy's troops attempted to scale Geneva's walls in a surprise attack. Catherine Cheynel ("Mère Royaume"), a mother of 14 children, grabbed a cauldron of hot vegetable soup and poured it over the attackers, killing one of them. This caused such a commotion it roused the townspeople to defend their city.

1291

The Swiss Confederation stands against the Habsburgs.

1506

The Swiss Guard is engaged to protect the Vatican.

1315

The Swiss defeat the Habsburgs at the Battle of Morgarten, consolidating the Confederation; the 1499 Swabian War brings independence.

1516

Huguenot refugees introduce the craft of clock making.

1680s–90s

Swiss mathematicians Jacob and Johann Bernoulli work on probability and calculus.

The Foundation of Modern Switzerland

Napoleon invaded Switzerland in 1798 and replaced the cantons of the Confederation with the short-lived, unpopular Helvetic Republic. The Swiss Confederation was restored in 1803, but French jurisdiction lasted until Napoleon's defeat by a British-led coalition of European armies at Waterloo in 1815. In the wake of civil war, a new constitution, drawn up in 1848 and revised in 1874, established today's system of direct democracy, with the cantons collectively ruled by a federal assembly in Bern. With political stability, the country flourished. New commercial banks were established, and the construction of the railway network and new roads opened up alpine areas to burgeoning tourism; industries from watchmaking to chocolate manufacture thrived.

Neutrality through Two World Wars

During both the World Wars, Switzerland maintained a state of armed neutrality. As a result, it was sought after by both the Allied and Axis countries as a location for commerce (thus boosting the growth of the Swiss banking industry), espionage

WOMEN'S SUFFRAGE

Swiss women were only granted the right to vote in federal elections in 1971; in 1991 Appenzell Innerrhoden became the last canton to give women a vote on local issues. Since then, women have made great strides in the political arena. In 2010, the country was one of just five worldwide to have more women than men in the cabinet that year.

Timeline of events

1863
Henri Dunant establishes the Red Cross; he receives the first Nobel Peace Prize in 1901.

1874
A revision of the Swiss constitution allows direct democracy by referendum.

1912
Carl Jung publishes his ground-breaking book, *Psychology of the Unconscious*.

1914–18
Switzerland organizes Red Cross units but remains neutral during World War I; the 1919 Treaty of Versailles reaffirms Swiss neutrality.

and secret diplomacy. It also became a safe haven for refugees fleeing violence from all across Europe, even as it provided anonymity for Nazi officials seeking to exchange pillaged gold and other looted assets for hard currency. The postwar years coincided with a period of unprecedented financial and industrial growth as the country, unscathed by the ravages of war, basked in its insular neutrality and political isolationism.

Switzerland Today

Although this small, wealthy alpine nation still enjoys its political neutrality and its role as a tax haven, it has now finally become more involved in European matters. The country joined the United Nations in 2002 and the Schengen Agreement in 2005 as a result of public voting, and signed the Paris climate agreement in 2016, although it remains firmly outside the EU to date. As it looks to redefine itself in a changing world, Switzerland's asylum and immigration laws have become highly contentious. Nonetheless, as host to the headquarters of several important international organizations, it continues to play a key role in world affairs.

1 Artwork depicting Napoleon at Zürich.

2 Swiss General Guisan during World War II, 1939.

3 Women campaigning for the vote in 1971.

4 People strolling down Rennweg in Zürich.

Did You Know?

The date of Henri Dunant's birthday – 8 May - is celebrated as World Red Cross Day.

1996
The "Nazi Gold" scandal reveals Swiss banks had bolstered the German economy.

2018
The government initiates "national empowerment", sponsoring tourism in Tunisia to try to curb illegal immigration.

1928
The inaugural Winter Olympics are held in St Moritz.

2008
The nation scraps routine passport controls at all its borders.

EXPERIENCE

Cross-country skiers on the Zermatt skipass

BERN

Lying on a narrow, elevated spit of land set in a sharp, steep-banked bend of the River Aare, the city of Bern was founded by Berthold V, Duke of Zähringen, in 1191. According to legend, the duke decided to name the new settlement after the first animal that he killed on his next hunt: this was a bear *(Bär)*, and the duke duly named the town Bärn. After the demise of the Zähringen dynasty, Bern became a free town. Growing in power and prosperity, it joined the Swiss Confederation in 1353.

In 1528, the Bernese declared themselves in favour of the Reformation, and supported the Protestant cause. By the 16th century, Bern, led by a prosperous nobility, was a powerful city-state that in the 17th and 18th centuries further expanded its territory through the annexation of surrounding lands. It lost some of its territories following an invasion of Napoleonic forces in 1798, but it remained important enough to be chosen as the Swiss capital in 1848. In the early 20th century Albert Einstein published his theory of relativity in Bern, and the city became home to prominent anarchists, thus securing Bern's reputation as a place of progress.

BERN

Must Sees
1. Münster St Vinzenz
2. Kunstmuseum
3. Zytglogge

Experience More
4. Bärenplatz
5. Bundeshaus
6. Marktgasse
7. Kramgasse
8. Erlacherhof
9. Münstergasse
10. Gerechtigkeitsgasse
11. Rathaus
12. Bear Park
13. Kunsthalle

14. Schweizerisches Alpines Museum
15. Museum für Kommunikation
16. Bernisches Historisches Museum
17. Naturhistorisches Museum
18. Zentrum Paul Klee

Eat
1. Lötschberg
2. Confiserie la Praline

Drink
3. Café Einstein au Jardin
4. Turnhalle
5. Kornhauskeller

1 Ⓜ3

MÜNSTER ST VINZENZ

🅐C3 🅐Münsterplatz 🚌12, 30 🕐Winter: noon–4pm Mon–Fri, 10am–5pm Sat, 11:15am–4pm Sun; summer: 10am–5pm Mon–Sat (from 11:15am Sun) 🌐bernermuenster.ch

A splendid example of the German-influenced late Gothic style, Bern's Münster is the most recent of Switzerland's great Gothic cathedrals. Work on the cathedral began in 1421, however it was not until 1893, when the spire was added, that the building was finally completed.

Replacing a smaller church the Münster is the country's tallest cathedral and largest ecclesiastical building, at just over 100 m (328 ft) high. It was originally located outside the city walls, near what is now Kreuzgasse; today the cathedral dominates Münsterplatz in the city's Old Town. The architect Matthäus Ensinger of Ulm designed it as a three-aisle basilica with fan vaulting, side chapels and a tower. The main construction took place during the city's conversion from Catholicism to Protestantism. As a result, the choir's religious symbols are Catholic, while the arms on the ceiling's keystones are Protestant.

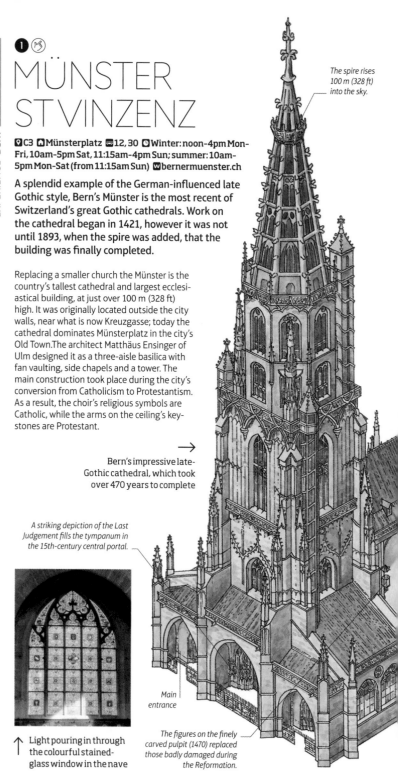

The spire rises 100 m (328 ft) into the sky.

→
Bern's impressive late-Gothic cathedral, which took over 470 years to complete

A striking depiction of the Last Judgement fills the tympanum in the 15th-century central portal.

↑ Light pouring in through the colourful stained-glass window in the nave

Main entrance

The figures on the finely carved pulpit (1470) replaced those badly damaged during the Reformation.

↑ The Münster's tower and spire, piercing the sky above Bern's quaint Old Town

The central stained-glass panel in the choir depicts Christ's Passion and Crucifixion.

The nave culminates in the stained-glass windows of the choir.

GREAT VIEW
The Tower

Fortune favours the brave. For a small fee, you can climb up the 344 steps that scale the cathedral's tower to the lookout point, which perches high above the entrance. The reward is fantastic views, spilling over the rooftops of the city across to the snow-covered mountains of the distant Bernese Oberland.

Flying buttressess transmit the weight of the roof outwards and downwards to the outer walls.

The rib vaulting, by Daniel Heintz, dates from the 1570s.

↑ The figures of the Foolish Virgins standing on the left side of the main doors

2 🎨 🖼 🖥 🏛

KUNSTMUSEUM

📍B3 🏠Hodlerstrasse 8-12 🚊11, 18, 20, 21 🕙10am-9pm Tue, 10am-5pm Wed-Sun 🌐kunstmuseumbern.ch

Housing over 3,000 paintings, and 48,000 other items including drawings, prints and photographs, Bern's Museum of Fine Arts is Switzerland's oldest art museum with a permanent collection and the perfect place to explore centuries of world-class art.

Spanning the 14th to the 20th centuries, the Kunstmuseum's constantly evolving collection includes Early Renaissance paintings, 16th- and 17th-century Old Master paintings, and 19th- and 20th-century French paintings, including works by Delacroix, Manet, Monet, Cézanne, Braque, Gris, Picasso, Klee and Kandinsky. Look out, in particular, for Picasso's *Drunken Doze*, a work from his early Blue Period, and Klee's *Ad Parnassum*, a piece produced at a time when he was fascinated with Pointillism. Swiss artists, among them Ferdinand Hodler and Albert Anker, are well represented.

The museum runs public tours on Tuesdays and Sundays – though only occasionally in English – and a children's workshop on Saturdays and Sundays (once a month in English).

GALLERY GUIDE

The layout of the Kunstmuseum is quite simple: its collection of Old Master paintings is displayed in the basement, while the 19th-century paintings are exhibited on the ground floor, alongside temporary exhibitions. The 20th-century collection, comprising work by Picasso and Klee, occupies the first floor.

1 This winter landscape of broken ice carried downstream by a wide river *(Ice on the River)* was painted in 1882 by the Impressionist Claude Monet.

2 Visitors survey some of the well-curated works on display at the Kunstmuseum.

3 Busts line the walls of the Kunstmuseum's grand 19th-century staircase.

↑ Working alongside paintings by Ferdinand Hodler, inside the Neo-Renaissance Kunstmuseum *(inset)*

ZYTGLOGGE

◆B3 ♠Bim Zytglogge 1 ▣6,7,8,9 ▣10,12,19,30 ◷Apr-Oct & 26-31 Dec: 2:30-3:20pm daily ⊞zeitglockenturm.ch

The eclectic Zytglogge, also widely known as the Zeitglockenturm, is Bern's most striking central landmark. Located at the heart of the medieval Old Town – a UNESCO World Heritage Site – this clock tower is one of the most visited sights in the city.

The clock tower was the town's west gate from 1191 to 1250, when it was superseded by the Käfigturm. Rebuilt after the fire of 1405, the Zytglogge was then used as a prison. Its astronomical clock was made by Caspar Brunner in 1527–30 and contains mechanical figures, including bears and a crowing cock that begin their procession on the clock's east face four minutes before it strikes the hour. A guided tour allows visitors to observe the clock's original mechanism, as well as see the rooms in the tower and admire the view. English-language tours take place on Wednesdays, Saturdays and Sundays.

Internal mechanics of the ↑ astronomical clock on display in the tower

 GREAT VIEW
Nighttime Sight

Although the views from the tower are impressive, you don't need to buy a ticket to appreciate the Zytglogge. From Easter to October and in the run-up to Christmas, the clock tower is illuminated after dusk each day, making it a magical sight.

↑ Detail of the astronomical clock, with its brightly coloured face and dials

THE TOWER'S BELL

With a diameter of 127 cm (50 in) and a weight of 1,400 kg (3,100 lb) the tower's hour bell has remained unchanged since the tower's construction. An inscription carved on the bell reads, in Latin: "In the October month of the year 1405 I was cast by Master John called Reber of Aarau. I am vessel and wax, and to all I tell the hours of the day." Below it hangs the smaller quarter hour bell, cast in 1887 to replace the cracked 1486 original.

↑ The tall spire and clockface of the Zytglogge rising above the red-roofed buildings of the Old Town

↑ The softly lit arcade
under Bern's iconic
Zytglogge, at twilight

EXPERIENCE MORE

❹ Bärenplatz

◊B3 🚊**6, 7, 8** 🚌**12, 30**

This elongated esplanade looks more like a wide street than a square. Seamlessly continued by another square, Waisenhausplatz, on its north side, only a fountain marks the division between the two.

Bärenplatz (Bear Square) is named after the bear pits that were once located here; since 2009, the bears have been housed in a Bear Park on the other side of the River Aare (p75). The Waisenhausplatz (Orphanage Square), now a police headquarters, owes its name to the former orphanage that was once housed in this fine Baroque building.

On the east side of both squares stand the Dutch Tower and the **Käfigturm** (Prison Tower). The Käfigturm has a slender lantern tower topped by a spire. It was incorporated into a wall that was built to the west as Bern expanded, and was the town gate from 1250 until 1350. From 1643 to 1897 the tower was used as a prison, and since 1999 it has been a venue for political seminars, forums and exhibitions.

On its southern side the square adjoins Bundesplatz, which is lined with cafés; a fruit and flower market is held here on Tuesday and Saturday.

Käfigturm

◊Marktgasse 67 📞**031 322 75 00** 🕐**2–6pm Mon (from 10am Tue–Fri), 10am–4pm Sat** 🚫**Mid-Jul–mid-Aug**

❺ Bundeshaus

◊B4 ◊Bundesplatz 3 🚌**10, 19** 🌐**parlament.ch**

The imposing seat of the Federal Assembly, the Bundeshaus (parliament building) stands on a cliff overlooking the Aare

> **Did You Know?**
>
> Bern hosted the 1954 World Cup Final, in which West Germany defeated Hungary.

> **INSIDER TIP**
> **Lights On Bern**
>
> Every autumn, the Bundeshaus exterior stars in the highly inventive Rendez-vous Bundesplatz, a brightly coloured sound and light show. Performances are free of charge and take place several times a day.

valley. Although it faces north onto Bundesplatz, its most attractive aspect is from the south – from Monbijoubrücke, a bridge on the Aare.

The building was designed by W H Auer in a bold Neo-Renaissance style, and completed in 1902. Its central part contains a spacious domed hall, with paintings illustrating important events in Swiss history. Access is by guided tour only. Free English-language tours take place on Saturdays at 2pm (book online in advance).

The Bundesterrasse, a wide promenade behind the Bundeshaus, offers a panoramic view of the Alps. A funicular near the western side of the Bundeshaus takes visitors down to the bottom of the Aare valley.

The medieval Käfigturm, the old town gate, on picturesque Marktgasse ↑

6

Marktgasse

📍B3 🚋6, 7, 8, 9 🚌10, 12, 19, 30

Laid out in the 13th century, Marktgasse runs east to west from the Zytglogge, the original town gate, to the Käfigturm, the later gate. Now the centre of Bern's shopping district, Marktgasse has two Renaissance fountains: the Anna-Seiler-Brunnen, which commemorates the woman who founded Bern's first hospital in 1354, and the Schützenbrunnen (Musketeer Fountain). On the adjoining Kornhausplatz is the macabre Kindlifresserbrunnen (Ogre Fountain).

Off the northwestern side of Kornhausgasse stands the Französische Kirche (French Church). Built in the 12th century, it is the oldest church in Bern. It was taken over by French Protestants, most of them Huguenot refugees, in the 17th century.

←

The Neo-Renaissance façade of the stately Bundeshaus

7

Kramgasse

📍C3 🚋6, 7, 8 🚌10, 12, 19, 30

With Gerechtigkeitsgasse, its eastern extension, Kramgasse marks the main axis of Bern's early medieval town plan. It is lined with handsome historic buildings fronted by long arcades and has three fountains: the Zähringerbrunnen (1542), with a bear in armour holding the standard of Berthold von Zähringer, Bern's founder; the Simsonbrunnen (1545), with a figure of Samson subduing a lion; and the unadorned Kreuzgassbrunnen (1778). Located at Kramgasse 49 is the **Einsteinhaus**, where the great German physicist and mathematician Albert Einstein lived from 1903 to 1905 and where he began to develop the theory of relativity while working at the patent office. Einstein's apartment is now a museum, displaying his writing desk and other objects from his time in Bern.

Einsteinhaus

🏠Kramgasse 49
🕐11am–4pm daily
🌐einstein-bern.ch

DRINK

Café Einstein au Jardin

Perch on the garden terrace, with a famous Einstein brew in hand, and admire the view.

📍C4
🏠Münsterplattform
🌐einstein-jardin.ch

Turnhalle

This cool bar is located in a former school. Chill out with a local brew in front of the open fire or in the busy courtyard.

📍B3
🏠Speichergasse 4
🌐turnhalle.ch

Kornhauskeller

Enjoy brews under vaulted ceilings at Bern's most sumptuous beer cellar.

📍B3
🏠Kornhausplatz 18
🌐kornhaus-bern.ch

Erlacherhof

♀ C3 ⌂ Junkerngasse 47
🚌 12, 30 🕐 Closed to visitors

Junkerngasse was once home to Bern's wealthiest citizens. At No 47 is the Erlacherhof, a Baroque mansion built by Hieronymus von Erlach, mayor of Bern, and completed in 1752. Designed in the French style, its wings are set at a right angle to the main building, enclosing a grand courtyard. To the rear is a formal French garden.

The Erlacherhof is now the official residence of the mayor of Bern and the seat of the city's government.

Münstergasse

♀ C3

Running parallel to nearby Kramgasse, Münstergasse links Theaterplatz with

One of the weekly markets held on the medieval cobbled street of Münstergasse

EAT

Lötschberg
This place has large communal tables, no reservations and a cheesy menu.
♀ B3
⌂ Zeughausgasse 16
🌐 lotschbergbern.com
Ⓢ Ⓢ Ⓢ

Confiserie la Praline
A little restaurant and bakery with old-world charm and tasty treats.
♀ D1
⌂ Rütlistrasse 2
🌐 lapraline.ch
Ⓢ Ⓢ Ⓢ

Münsterplatz, which is lined with arcaded buildings. On Tuesday and Saturday mornings (and Thursday from April to October), this square is filled with a busy meat and cheese market. During Advent, it is replaced by a large Christmas market.

Where Münstergasse and Theaterplatz meet stands the **Stadt- und Universitäts-bibliothek**, the City and University Library. This 18th-century building stages exhibitions on the history of Bern and on literary subjects.

A fountain with the figure of Moses holding the Ten Commandments stands at the corner of Münstergasse and Münsterplatz, opposite the Münster. He points to the second of them, which forbids idolatry, one of the main tenets of the Reformation.

On the Münster's south side is the Münsterplattform, a terrace with trees and Baroque pavilions from which there are views over the River Aare.

Stadt- und Universitätsbibliothek
⌂ Münstergasse 61 📞 031 631 92 11 🕐 8am-7pm Mon-Fri, 8am-5pm Sat & Sun

Gerechtigkeitsgasse

♀ C3

Some of the oldest and most beautiful arcaded buildings in Bern line this street. Many of them were built as guild houses, and their façades are heavily decorated with motifs reflecting the relevant trade. Gerechtigkeitsgasse, or Street of Justice, also has a fountain, the Gerechtigkeitsbrunnen, which features a figure personifying Justice.

Where Gerechtigkeitsgasse leads to Nydegggasse a castle once stood, probably about 100 years before Berthold V chose the location as a secure spot on which to establish a new town. In the late

15th century the castle was replaced by a small church, the Nydeggkirche, and in the 19th century a stone bridge, the Nydeggbrücke, was built over the deep gorge of the Aare, connecting the Old Town with Bern's eastern end.

Rathaus

C3 **Rathausplatz 2**
12, 30 **sta.be.ch/en**

The seat of the canton and the city of Bern's legislative assembly since it was built in 1406–16, the Rathaus is an attractive building with an elegant Gothic façade and double staircase.

Since the 15th century, the Rathaus has undergone several major restorations, and the ground floor was completely rebuilt in 1939–42. However, it still retains its Gothic character. The Visitors' Gallery is open to the public when the assembly is in session, and free guided tours are held once a month (book ahead online).

Near the Rathaus stands the Neo-Gothic Catholic church, Kirche St Peter und Paul, completed in 1858.

Bear Park

D3 **Grosser Muristalden 6** **12** **24 hrs by appointment** **tierpark-bern.ch**

Located near the town's old bear pits, this forested 6,000-sq-m (64,590-sq-ft) modern park is home to three brown bears. Sloping down to the river, the park has numerous caves and pools that provide the bears with a truly natural environment. There is no feeding time, rather food is hidden for the bears to forage.

Next to the old bear pits, in a former tram depot, is one of the town's two helpful tourist offices, as well as a restaurant serving local cuisine and beer brewed on the premises.

A steep path from the old bear pits leads up to the Rosengarten, containing over 200 varieties of roses.

Kunsthalle

C4 **Helvetiaplatz 1**
6, 7, 8 **19** **11am–6pm Tue–Fri, 10am–6pm Sat & Sun** **kunsthalle-bern.ch**

The Kunsthalle, a building in the Modernist style, was founded in 1918 and has retained its prominence as a showcase for modern art. It has no permanent collection, but stages a continuous programme of exhibitions by prominent artists.

BERN'S BEARS

Brown bears have been indelibly associated with Bern since the town was founded in 1191. They were kept in pits (Bärengraben) on the far side of the Nydeggbrücke, just across the river from the Old Town's eastern extremity, from the early 16th century. The old pits are still there, linked by a tunnel to the Bear Park.

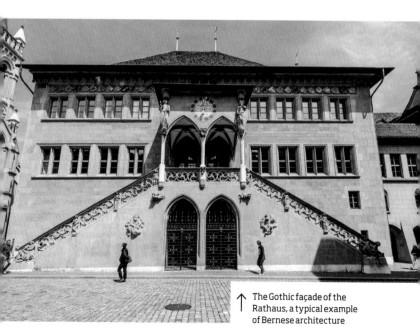

↑ The Gothic façade of the Rathaus, a typical example of Bernese architecture

14

Schweizerisches Alpines Museum

📍B4 🏛Helvetiaplatz 4
🚃6, 7, 8 🚌19 🕐10am-
5pm Tue-Sun 🌐alpines
museum.ch

Through various multimedia, including videos, dioramas and paintings inspired by the Alps' scenery, this museum describes the geology, topography, climate and natural history of the Swiss Alps, and documents all aspects of human activity in the mountains.

The displays include a graphic explanation of how glaciers are formed, how they are melting and a model of the Bernese Oberland. Separate sections are devoted to various aspects of Alpine life, including transport, industry, tourism and winter sports. The daily life and culture of alpine people are also described, as are current concerns for the environment. One exhibit in the section devoted

to the history of mountaineering is *The Climb and the Fall*, part of two dioramas by Ferdinand Hodler, illustrating the history of the conquest of the Matterhorn.

15

Museum für Kommunikation

📍C4 🏛Helvetiastrasse 16
🚃6, 7, 8 🚌19 🕐10am-5pm
Tue-Sun 🌐mfk.ch

The history of the human endeavour to make contact across long distances is compellingly laid out at the

Museum of Communication. The displays span the gamut from bonfires to satellites. Multimedia presentations dive into radio, described as "the window to the world", and how cyborgs are the progeny of simple punch cards. The new permanent collection gets visitors singing along with karaoke and trying their hand at hacking.

Also new are the "communicators", a group of expert hosts who move through the museum to get conversations flowing. The ever-changing temporary exhibitions might include digital detoxing or political cartoons.

> 💬 INSIDER TIP
> **Swim in the River Aare**
>
> On a particularly hot day nothing beats being carried along in the bracing current of Bern's River Aare. Jump in the river for a swim or bathe in the refreshing Marzili swimming pool.

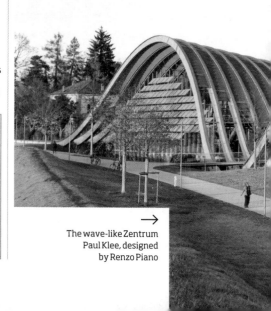

→
The wave-like Zentrum Paul Klee, designed by Renzo Piano

An exhibit in the interactive Museum für Kommunikation

 ⑯

Bernisches Historisches Museum

📍C4 🏛Helvetiaplatz 5
🚋6, 7, 8 🚌19 🕙10am–5pm
Tue–Sun 🌐bhm.ch

Laid out over seven floors of a Neo-Gothic building reminiscent of a medieval fortified castle, Bern's Museum of History holds some 500,000 artifacts and is also home to the Einstein Museum.

Among the most interesting exhibits here is a spine-chilling depiction of the Dance of Death, a copy of a 16th-century monastic wall painting, but the pride of the museum is its collection of 12 Burgundian tapestries, the oldest of which date from the 15th-century. Among the most notable is the Millefleurs-tapisserie (Thousand Flowers Tapestry).

Other sections are devoted to archaeology, with displays of Stone Age, Ancient Egyptian, Celtic, Roman and Islamic artifacts. The Einstein Museum provides an engaging account of Albert Einstein's ground-breaking discoveries, as well as the life and loves behind the genius.

---

⑰

Naturhistorisches Museum

📍C4 🏛Bernastrasse 15
🚋6, 7, 8 🚌19 🕙2–5pm
Mon, 9am–5pm Tue, Thu &
Fri, 9am–6pm Wed, 10am–
5pm Sat–Sun 🌐nmbe.ch

With roots dating to the early 19th century, Bern's Museum of Natural History is one of the oldest museums in Switzerland. It is best known for its numerous dioramas of stuffed animals shown in re-creations of their natural habitats. There are sections devoted to Africa, Asia and the Arctic, but the most impressive displays focus on the wildlife of the Alps. On view is the stuffed body of Barry, a St Bernard dog famous for his feats of mountain rescue in the 19th century. The museum also has a large collection of alpine minerals and fossils.

Did You Know?

A skilled musician, Paul Klee chose the visual arts because modern music was "creatively unattractive".

⑱

Zentrum Paul Klee

📍F3 🏛Monument im
Fruchtland 3 🚌12 🕙10am–
5pm Tue–Sun 🌐zpk.org

This arts centre houses the world's largest collection of works by Swiss artist Paul Klee (1879–1940). Of the 4,000 paintings and drawings in its collection, about 200 are on display at any one time. There are temporary exhibitions, guided tours and events such as concerts, theatre, readings and workshops, as well as a separate children's museum, Creaviva. The undulating building by Italian architect Renzo Piano, and the surrounding sculpture park, are designed to blend in with the landscape.

A SHORT WALK
OLD TOWN

Distance 2 km (1 mile) **Nearest tram** 6, 7, 8
Time 30 minutes

With long cobbled streets lined with red-roofed houses and picturesque arcades, Bern's Old Town (Altstadt) is the best-preserved historic town centre in Switzerland. The layout of its streets, which are punctuated by colourfully painted fountains, has remained largely unchanged since the early 15th century. This was also the period when the Münster and the Rathaus, two of its great landmarks, were built. While the western district of the Old Town is filled with shops and busy street markets, its older eastern district has a more restful atmosphere.

↑ Zytglogge's ornate golden clock face

Now a cultural centre, the 18th-century **Kornhaus** *granary was built over vaulted wine cellars that currently house a restaurant.*

Französische Kirche

FINISH

0 metres 100
0 yards 100

SPEICHERGASSE

START

ZEUGHAUSGASSE

The **Bärenplatz** *(p72) overlies the spot where a moat once ran, along Bern's west side.*

NEUENGASSE

MARKTGASSE

BÄREN–PLATZ

Heiliggeistkirche *is one of the finest Protestant churches in Switzerland.*

SPITALGASSE

BUNDES–PLATZ

SCHAUPLATZGASSE

The main axis through the Old Town begins at the Käfigturm (Prison Tower) on **Marktgasse** *(p73). It was the city's western gate in the 13th and 14th centuries.*

The Bundeshaus, with its paintings of historical events, overlooks the **Bundesplatz** *(p72).*

Did You Know?

The Französische Kirche is the oldest church in Bern.

Gerechtigkeitsgasse (p74) marks the eastern section of the main axis through the Old Town. The house at No 68 is the Weavers' Guild, the façade featuring a gilt griffin. Another striking landmark is a fountain with a statue of Justice.

Locator Map
For more detail see p64

BERN

Old Town

From 1191 to 1250 the **Zytglogge** (p70) clock tower was the city's western gate, and it was later used as a prison. Its chimes begin at four minutes before the hour.

Rathaus (p75), the town hall, is fronted by a double staircase and a Gothic loggia that leads to the main entrance.

POSTGASSE

GERECHTIGKEITSGASSE

RATHAUSGASSE

KRAMGASSE

SNHAUSPLATZ

THEATER-PLATZ

MÜNSTERGASSE

MÜNSTERPLATZ

The most striking feature of Bern's Gothic cathedral **Münster St Vinzenz** (p66) is the magnificent central portal, surrounded by painted figures.

HAUSGASSE

On Tuesday and Saturday mornings the arcades along **Münstergasse** (p74) host a bustling street market.

The main axis through the Old Town is continued by **Kramgasse** (p73). This street begins at the Zytglogge, the clock tower marking the western limit of the oldest part of the Old Town.

→
Relief on the main portal of Bern's Münster St Vinzenz

79

MITTELLAND, BERNESE OBERLAND AND VALAIS

Peppered with the cultural centres of Basel and Bern, these three regions in the western central section of Switzerland are beloved for their combination of magnificent, diverse landscapes and artistic heritage. The rolling farmland and numerous lakes attracted Celtic tribes to the Mittelland in around 500 BC. Following the Roman conquest in 15 BC, the region became crisscrossed with roads that linked the towns that sprung up across the plateau. By the Middle Ages, these roads brought skilled craftsmen and trade to cities across the Mittelland and Bernese Oberland, such as Bern and Solothurn. At the same time, the people of Valais, in the south, had developed engineering methods to build a new trade route across the St Gotthard Pass. This new route allowed formidable alliances to be forged between centres of power in the north and south, so strengthening the ever-expanding Swiss Confederate.

While much of the region remained agricultural, by the 19th century the more mountainous areas began to develop a thriving tourist industry. Artists and writers, from Felix Mendelssohn to Mark Twain, flocked to hike in the fresh mountain air. Today the large international resorts of Verbier, Crans-Montana, Zermatt and Saas-Fee draw tourists year-round.

MITTELLAND, BERNESE OBERLAND AND VALAIS

Must Sees

1. Interlaken
2. Thun and Thunersee
3. Brienz and Brienzersee
4. Zermatt and the Matterhorn
5. Aletsch Glacier
6. Oeschinensee

Experience More

7. Olten
8. Solothurn
9. Weissenstein
10. Biel/Bienne
11. Meiringen
12. The Emmental
13. Giessbachfälle
14. Grindelwald
15. Jungfraujoch
16. Lauterbrunnen
17. Wengen
18. Mürren
19. Adelboden
20. Kandersteg
21. Gstaad
22. Martigny
23. Verbier
24. Grand St Bernard Pass
25. The Simmental
26. St-Pierre-de-Clages
27. Sion
28. Sierre
29. Barrage de la Grande Dixence
30. Trient Valley
31. Val d'Hérens
32. Val d'Anniviers
33. Monte Rosa
34. Crans-Montana
35. Saas-Fee
36. Simplon Pass
37. Brig
38. Leukerbad

A charming street in Interlaken, backed by blue-tinged mountains ↑

 1

INTERLAKEN

🅰 C4-D4 🅱 Bern 🚉 Interlaken Ost, Interlaken West
ℹ Interlaken: Marktgasse 1; www.interlaken.ch

Sitting on a narrow strip of land between Thunersee *(p86)* and Brienzersee *(p88)*, Interlaken owes its name to the 12th-century monastery founded here, named Inter Lacus, meaning "between lakes" in Latin. Today a popular resort, the town makes an excellent base for skiers in winter and for mountaineers and hikers in summer, as well as for visitors looking to make the most of the surrounding lakes.

  ①

Heimwehfluh

🏠 Därligenstrasse 32
🕐 Apr-Oct: 8:30am-4:30pm daily 🚫 Nov-Mar
🌐 heimwehfluh.ch

The Heimwehfluhbahn, one of Switzerland's oldest funiculars, has been transporting viewpoint chasers to the top of Heimwehfluh hill since 1906. The funicular takes just a couple of minutes to reach an altitude of 680 m (2,230 ft), and rewards passengers with splendid views along the way.

At the top of the hill, there is a huge adventure playground, a model railway and a restaurant appropriately named Panorama, which overlooks Interlaken and the surrounding villages.

Between April and October, visitors can take the Rodelbahn, a summer

> **GREAT VIEW**
> **On High**
>
> The Eiger, Mönch and Jungfrau peaks can be seen from the summit of mountain Harder Kulm, which overlooks Interlaken. The Two Lakes Bridge offers stunning views from a glass-floored platform.

sledging run through the Rugen forest, to get back to town from the hill. It's a thrilling ride.

  ②

Kunsthaus Interlaken

🏠 Jungfraustrasse 55
🕐 2-5pm Mon-Sat, 11am-5pm Sun 🌐 kunsthaus interlaken.ch

Interlaken's most important art museum opened in 2009 and is housed in a striking, modernist gallery. Inside, the Kunsthaus hosts a variety of temporary exhibitions focused primarily on the Swiss Alps. The programme explores how local and international artists interpret the Alps' landscape, way of life and history. Aside from art, the gallery hosts regular film screenings, workshops and concerts.

  ③

Bödelibahn

🏠 Kanalpromenade 1
🕐 May-Oct 🚫 Nov-Apr
🌐 boedelibahn.business.site

Bödeli is the local name for the strip of land between

commentary to learn all about the history of Bödeli, or simply take in the picturesque alpine views.

---

 ④

Unterseen

Separated from Interlaken by the Aare, Unterseen (literally meaning Lower Lake) was an important fortified town in the Middle Ages, controlling trade in the Lütschin valleys and over the passes towards Central Switzerland and Italy. Today, Unterseen has a far more laidback feel than Interlaken, and its pretty Old Town makes for a glorious stroll at any time of day.

At the centre of the Old Town lies Stadthausplatz, where the imposing Stadthaus houses a café and restaurant. Just off the square is the **Reformierte Kirche** with its 15th-century clock tower. Nearby, a 17th-century rectory is now home to the quirky

Tourismuseum, which traces the history of tourism in the Jungfrau region. Exhibitions explore the history of the Alpine railways and the development of winter sports from their beginnings (look out for the early examples of ski lifts and bobsleighs) to the challenges posed by climate change today. The highlight of the museum is the exhibition on the history of mountaineering, which includes feats by the earliest mountaineers, who climbed the Eiger in little more than a suit and tie.

Reformierte Kirche
🏠 Kirchgasse 3
🕐 Summer: 9am–6pm daily; winter: 9am–5pm daily

Tourismuseum
♿ 🏠 Obere Gasse 26
🕐 Apr–Oct: 2–5pm Wed–Sun; Nov–Mar: 2–5pm Wed & Sun
🌐 tourismuseum.ch

Thunersee and Brienzersee where Interlaken sits. In 1872, a train line was constructed along the strip, linking Därligen on Thunersee with Bönigen on Brienzersee's shore. The track beyond Interlaken was removed when passenger services ended in the 1960s.

Today, a road train known as the Bödelibahn follows the original tracks between Bönigen and Interlaken. During the 60-minute journey, passengers can listen to recorded

> **Today, Unterseen has a far more laidback feel than Interlaken, and its pretty Old Town makes for a glorious stroll at any time of day.**

THUN AND THUNERSEE

 C4–D4 🏠 Bern 🚌🚋🚐 ℹ️ Bahnhof; www.thun tourismus.ch

Famed for its turquoise waters, Thunersee is the larger of the two lakes that surround Interlaken, and offers many watersports, including sailing and diving. At its northern end, on the River Aare, lies the market town of Thun, whose origins go back to 1191, when Berthold V, Duke of Zähringen, built a hilltop castle here.

①

Thun Altstadt

Thun's Old Town spreads out beneath Schloss Thun, along the right riverbank. Obere Hauptgasse, its main street, runs parallel to the river, and is split into two levels. The upper walkway is built on the roofs of the arcaded buildings lining the lower street, so pedestrians must step down to enter the shops below. Alleys off Obere Hauptgasse lead up to the castle.

②

Schloss Thun

🏠 Schlossberg 1 🕐 Feb & Mar: 1–4pm daily; Apr–Oct: 10am–5pm daily; Nov–Jan: 1–4pm Sun 🌐 schlossthun.ch

Perched on a hill above Thun, this castle has impressive views of the town and the Bernese Oberland. Inside the castle's massive turreted keep is a museum that traces the town's history. Other rooms in the castle contain collections of household objects, weapons and uniforms. Also on the hill is Stadtkirche, the town's church.

Did You Know?

In 1969, the Swiss government dumped more than 6,500 munitions in Thunersee.

③

Schadau Park

Set on the river's left bank, Schadau Park is a beautiful English garden, where you can admire seasonal plants and dine in Schloss Schadau, a mid-19th-century palace that has been transformed into a restaurant. There's also a Neo-Gothic folly and a pavilion, which houses the **Wocher Panorama**, an 1814 painting by Marquard Wocher that records daily life in 19th-century Thun. It's the oldest such panorama in the world.

↑ The charming chalets of Thun, clustered on the banks of Thunersee

Thun Altstadt
 Schloss Thun

Wocher Panorama

⊗ 🏠Seestrasse 45, Schadaupark ⏰Mar–Oct: 11am–5pm Tue–Sun; Jul & Aug: 10am–6pm daily
🌐thun-panorama.ch

Schloss Oberhofen

🏠Oberhofen 🚌21 ⏰May–Oct: 11am–5pm Tue–Sun
🌐schlossoberhofen.ch

On Thunersee's northern shore is Schloss Oberhofen, once the castle-home of the von Oberhofen family. Originally built in the early 13th century, it has been remodelled many times over the years. The most extensive renovations were made in the mid-19th century when it was given its present Romanesque appearance.

The castle has served as a museum dedicated to its previous residents since the 1950s. Highlights include the 15th-century chapel, which has some beautiful murals, the smoking room at the top of the keep and the exhibition dedicated to the legions of staff who kept the castle running over the years. Don't miss the gardens.

St Beatus Höhlen

🏠Seestrasse 30, Sundlauenen 🚌21 ⏰Mar–Oct: 9am–5pm daily 🚫Nov–Feb 🌐beatushoehlen.swiss

Legend has it that a terrifying dragon once lurked inside the St Beatus caves. Look out for the creature yourself as you explore the 1 km (0.5 miles) of the cave system that is open to the public. Along the way, you'll discover many grottos, stalagmites and stalactites, and impressive limestone formations. The temperature in the caves is around 8°C, so dress appropriately.

Above ground, there is an on-site restaurant with lake views and a museum tracing the cave's natural history.

Kunstmuseum

🏠Hofstettenstrasse 14 ⏰10am–5pm Tue–Sun (to 7pm Wed) 🌐kunstmuseumthun.ch

Built in the French Renaissance style that was popular in the 1870s, the former Grand Hotel Thunerhof sits on the River Aare. Since the 1970s, it has housed the Kunstmuseum's collection of Swiss artworks, ranging from 18th-century Bernese landscapes to 20th-century Dada and Pop Art pieces. The museum does not display a permanent collection; three or four themed exhibits are usually on at any one time.

③

BRIENZ AND BRIENZERSEE

🅰C4-D4 🅱Bern 🚉 ℹHauptstrasse 143, Brienz; 033 952 80 80

East of Interlaken (p84), the clear waters of Brienzersee stretch out beneath forested slopes and waterfalls. Some 14 km (9 miles) long and almost 3 km (2 miles) wide, Brienzersee is smaller and less developed than Thunersee (p86), making it much more appealing to some visitors. At the lake's eastern end is Brienz, the main town on the lake's shore, which makes a good base for hiking, fishing and watersports.

①

Rothorn Bahn

🅰Hauptrasse 149, Brienz
🕐May-Oct: 8am-6pm daily
🚫Nov-Apr �🆆brienz-rothorn-bahn.ch

Since 1892, steam locomotives have been pushing the little red carriages of the Brienz-Rothorn rack railway up to the 2,350-m (7,710-ft) summit of the Rothorn, the highest peak in the Emmental Alps. While onboard, passengers are treated to panoramic views of Brienzersee; there are also several intermediate stops on the route, allowing visitors to hike part of the way. At the top of the Rothorn is Gipfel, a good restaurant, with a large terrace where you can dine alfresco and enjoy breathtaking views of no fewer than 693 other mountain peaks.

Reservations for seats aboard the Rothorn Bahn should be made in advance, as numbers are limited.

②

Schule fur Holzbildhauerei

🅰Schleegasse 1
🕐Exhibition: 10:30am-5pm Wed-Sun �ll🆆museum holzbildhauerei-ch

Being the centre of Swiss woodcarving, Brienz is full of shops selling all kinds of wooden objects such as toys and furniture. The workshops of the renowned Schule für Holzbildhauerei are open to visitors during term-time. Here, students can be seen at work, and there's also an exhibition of their finished pieces.

③

Geigenbauschule

🅰Oberdorfstrasse 94
📞033 951 18 61
🕐By appointment

Another speciality of Brienz is violin-making. Aspiring violin-makers learn their craft at the Geigenbauschule, a training school. Sign up for a guided tour or visit the on-site exhibition, which showcases some of the violins that have been made here over the years.

↑ The enchanting town of Brienz, nestled along the lake

Bernatone Alphornbau

🅐 Habkern 🕒 8am–noon & 1–5pm daily (workshop visits by appointment only) 🌐 bernatone.ch

One of the most recognizable cultural symbols of the Swiss Alps, a traditional alphorn, or alpenhorn, is carved from a single piece of softwood (usually spruce but sometimes pine). Discover how alphorns are made at the Bernatone Alphornbau, a workshop and educational centre located in the village of Habkern. Here, members of the Tschiemer family will take you through the age-old process of crafting alphorns and tell you about the history of this instrument, which dates back to at least

> **HIDDEN GEM**
> **Spring in your Step**
>
> Behind Haupstrasse, Brienz's main street, is Brungasse, a narrow cobbled street lined with pretty 18th-century wooden chalets. Come spring, their balconies overflow with flowers.

the 15th century, as well as of Swiss cattle herding, a practice that is entwined with the alphorn's past. You can even try your hand at playing the instrument yourself here and, if you discover that you have a natural talent, you can purchase one from the family's shop on site.

Swiss Open-air Museum Ballenberg

🅐 3 km (2 miles) E of Brienz 🕒 Mid-Apr–Oct: 10am–5pm daily (grounds from 9am) 🌐 ballenberg.ch

From simple alpine chalets to entire farmsteads, about 100 historic rural buildings and 250 farmyard animals fill this 66-hectare (160-acre) open-air museum. The buildings here are mainly constructed from wood, although some brick and stone examples can also be found, and come from several regions of the country. Some of the houses at the museum have workshops, where craftsmen using authentic tools and original machinery demonstrate various crafts and trades, including weaving, spinning and cheese-making.

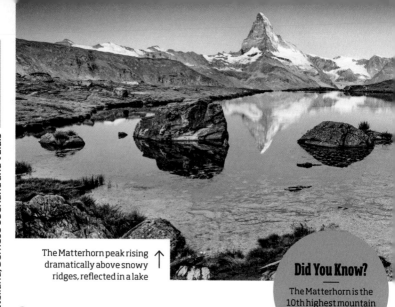

The Matterhorn peak rising dramatically above snowy ridges, reflected in a lake ↑

4

ZERMATT AND THE MATTERHORN

◫C5 ◫Valais ◫ ⓘBahnhofplatz, Zermatt; www.zermatt.ch

At 4,478 m (14,692 ft), the Matterhorn is Switzerland's most famous mountain. The small pastoral village of Zermatt, located at its base, grew quickly at the end of the 19th century to serve climbers tackling the peak. Today, it is a major ski resort and is home to Europe's largest network of pistes. Opportunities for climbing, hiking, glacier skiing and snowboarding abound, too.

①

Gornergratbahn

◫Bahnhofplatz ◷7am–9:50pm ⓦgornergrat.ch

Climbing to an altitude of 3,089 m (10,135 ft), the Gornergratbahn was the country's first electrified, and Europe's highest, rack railway when it opened in 1898. It operates year-round, transporting skiers to the pistes in winter and hikers to the trails in summer. Along the 9-km (6-mile) route, passengers are rewarded with magnificent views of the Matterhorn, many glacial lakes, and dense forests from its specially designed carriages. At the top, there are both short trails and fauna and flora trails (wild ibex are a common sight), as well as longer hikes. The summit is also home to the Kulmhotel Gornergrat, Europe's highest hotel, which serves sunset suppers in its restaurant.

Did You Know?

The Matterhorn is the 10th highest mountain in Switzerland.

②

Matterhorn Museum Zermatlantis

◫Kirchplatz ◷3–6pm daily ⓦzermatt.ch/museum

Underneath Zermatt's central Kitchplatz, and accessed via a glass hut, Zermatlantis chronicles the heroic yet often tragic story of the early attempts to conquer the Matterhorn. Alongside a reconstruction of the first successful ascent in 1865 are personal effects of some of the climbers who did not make it. The collection also shows you how 19th-century mountaineering expeditions transformed the town.

> **INSIDER TIP**
> **Take a Hike**
>
> Hikers of all abilities are spoilt for choice by the scores of trails around Zermatt. The pick of the lot is a four-hour walk to the top of Gornergrat (3,089 m/10,135 ft). A cog railway carries you back down to Zermatt.

91 tunnels, and granting unrivalled views of the Swiss Alps. If you don't have time for the full route, the section from Zermatt to Brig is the most dramatic.

---

③

Glacier Express

🏠 Zermatt station
🕐 Summer: 8:50am & 9:50am; winter: around 8:50am ⓦ glacierexpress.ch

It's been dubbed the world's slowest express, but the train service from Zermatt to St Mortiz is not to be hurried. The full trip takes 7.5 hours, carrying passengers across 291 bridges and through

---

④

Pfarrkirche St Mauritius

🏠 Englischer Viertel 8
ⓦ pfarrei.zermatt.net

The oldest church in Zermatt, St Mauritius dates back to the 13th century, although the current church building, with its soaring spire, was built in 1913. The stunning painting on the ceiling of the central nave, *Noah's Ark*, was added in 1980.

In the church's courtyard is the Mountaineers' Cemetery. A poignant reminder of just how many lives have been lost on the Matterhorn and nearby peaks, it contains the graves of more than 50 climbers. Most of the simple yet moving tombstones carry an explanation of how the respective climber died – avalanche, rockfall, crevasse – but one memorial to a young American climber carries the striking message: "I chose to climb".

CLIMBING THE MATTERHORN

The extreme difficulty involved in reaching the Matterhorn's summit made it the last of the great Swiss mountains to be conquered. In 1865, a team led by the British explorer Edward Whymper made it to the top, but four of the climbers died during the descent. Even so, the Matterhorn remains a huge draw for experienced climbers across the world to this day.

---

⑤

Sunnegga

A modern funicular takes less than five minutes to climb up to Sunnegga's summit, where you can enjoy a definitive view of the Matterhorn.

In winter, Sunnegga is a ski area with gentle slopes. In summer, it serves as the starting point of the Five Lakes Walk, which culminates in a dip in Leisee's glacial waters.

THE SWISS ALPS

About two-thirds of Swiss territory consists of Alpine and sub-Alpine areas, giving the country diverse landscapes. At lower elevations up to 1,500 m (5,000 ft), agricultural land and deciduous trees predominate. These give way to coniferous forests, which above 2,200 m (7,200 ft) in turn give way to scrub and Alpine pastures. At altitudes above 3,000 m (9,800 ft), mosses and lichens cover a desolate rocky landscape, above which are snowfields, glaciers and permanently snow-covered peaks.

FORMATION OF THE ALPS

About 70 million years ago, the Adriatic Microplate began to drift northward, colliding with the rigid European Plate. While the oceanic floor that lay between them was forced downwards, the Adriatic Microplate was thrust upwards, creating the Alps. This upheaval, which continued until 2 million years ago, caused the upper strata of rock to fold over on themselves. The older metamorphic rocks, thrust up from the substratum, thus form the highest part of the Alps, while the more recent sedimentary and igneous rocks make up the lower levels. The action of glaciers during successive ice ages then scoured and sculpted the Alps, giving them their present appearance.

Jura mountains

Western Alps

European Plate

Mantle

Mittelland plateau

↑ Drawing of a cross-section of the Alps, showing the actions of tectonic forces

ALPINE GLACIERS

Vestiges of the Ice Age, Alpine glaciers continue their erosive action. As they advance, they scour valley floors and sides, carrying away rocks, which are ground and then deposited as lateral and terminal moraines. Glacial lakes fill basins scooped out by glaciers. Hanging valleys were created when glaciers deepened the main valley.

Alpine plants and animals

Edelweiss

▷ With many ballads sung in its praise, star-shaped Edelweiss is the country's most famous flower. It grows among rocks at altitudes up to 3,500 m (11,500 ft). A symbol of purity and love, the woolly-leafed plant has become increasingly rare and is now a protected species.

The Alpine ibex

A species of wild goat with backward-curving horns, the Alpine ibex lives above the treeline for most of the year. It is extremely agile over mountainous terrain.

Gentian

◁ Intensely blue in colour and trumpet-like in shape, this flower grows in rock crevices and in woodlands. Its roots are used in the pharmaceutical industry.

The chamois

This goat-like antelope lives between wooded mountainsides and the snowline. Agile and shy, it is seldom seen at close range. It was once hunted for its hide, which makes a very soft leather, but hunting quotas are now imposed.

Alpenrose

◁ An evergreen species of rhododendron, alpenrose - also known as snow-rose - grows mostly at altitudes of 2,500 m (8,200 ft). Its pink-red blossoms create large clusters of dense colour. The plant and its seeds can be poisonous if ingested.

The marmot

▷ Difficult to spot but easy to hear, this rodent lives in burrows high on the valley slopes. Found throughout the Alps, marmots are particularly abundant in Graubünden and Ticino. When disturbed, they emit a piercing, high-pitched whistle.

Southern Alps

Direction of tectonic thrust

Adriatic Plate

Mantle

5 (M3)

ALETSCH GLACIER

D5 **Valais** **Jungfraujoch** **Bahnhofstrasse 7, Riederalp; www.aletsch.ch**

A vast river of ice that stretches for more than 23 km (14 miles) from the Jungfrau region down to the Massa Gorge, the Aletsch Glacier is the longest in the Alps and the most spectacular of all Switzerland's eternal ice fields.

The result of a vast accumulation of snow around 18,000 years ago, the glacier is part of the Jungfrau-Aletsch Protected Area, which was declared a UNESCO World Heritage Site in 2001. The best way to experience the Aletsch Glacier is to take one of the guided walks that traverse its expanse. These tours can vary in length from a couple of hours to long hikes that run over two days. Setting off from the cable car station above the ski resort of Riederalp, these walks allow visitors to explore the glacier, and its caves and tunnels, some of which are stunningly lit when the light of the sun penetrates the walls of ice. Special night excursions into these caves and tunnels can be arranged with experienced guides. The glacier is encircled by 32 dramatic peaks, accessible by cable car; the summits of Eggishorn and Bettmerhorn – both well over 2,500-m- (8,200-ft-) high – offer awe-inspiring panoramic views of the glacier from above.

A mountaineer making a night-time descent into one of the glacier's caves ↑

↑ The spectacularly located Jungfraujoch Station, high above the Aletsch Glacier

↑ A group of walkers standing back to admire a section of the glacier

CLIMATE CHANGE

Although the sheer size of the Aletsch Glacier means that it is reacting more slowly to climate change than smaller glaciers, since around 1870 this ice mass has lost over 3 km (2 miles) in length; since 1980 alone, it has lost an incredible 1.3 km (1 mile) and more than 300 m (980 ft) of its thickness. By 2100, it is estimated that around 90 per cent of the ice will have disappeared. In 2007, the American photographer Spencer Tunick had hundreds of people pose naked for a photoshoot on the glacier in order to draw attention to the negative effects of global warming.

Did You Know?

The glacier's icy mass holds a whopping 27 billion tons of ice.

Panoramic view over the ↑ icy path formed by the Aletsch Glacier

6

OESCHINENSEE

D4 **Bern** **Kandersteg** **From Kandersteg**
oeschinensee.ch/en

Cradled between glaciers and ancient pine woods and surrounded by fiercely steep mountains, Oeschinensee is one of Switzerland's most stunning glacial lakes. It is also the western gateway to the Jungfrau Aletsch UNESCO World Heritage Site.

Few places in the country are as picture perfect as Oeschinensee, nestled between the sheer drop of the Blüemlisalp and a prettily wooded shore. Set at a height of 1,578 m (5,177 ft), the lake is usually frozen in winter. Ice skating is possible some years, while ice fishing is a popular activity from January to March: the lake is home to delicious rainbow trout and Arctic char. Some gentle skiing is also available on the slopes surrounding the lake. The lake is at its best during the summer, when its crystal-clear, turquoise waters beckon brave swimmers: fed by a series of mountain creeks, the water remains ice-cold all year. Kayaking and hiking lure outdoorsy types, while thrill-seekers make a beeline for an exhilarating *via ferrata* (protected climbing route) and the epic summer toboggan run. Most visitors just come to relax and enjoy the peaceful surroundings with a picnic hamper full of tasty local produce. The easiest way to access the lake is via the cable car from the village of Kandersteg (*p105*), followed by a short shuttle ride or a pleasant 25-minute walk.

VIA FERRATA

The mountain village of Kandersteg is the starting point of the Kandersteg-Allmenalp *via ferrata*. Starting at the railway station, this tough climb soon becomes vertical, and requires the use of iron cam hooks drilled into the rock. The Allmibach river itself is crossed using two rope bridges.

↑ Boating on the sparkling waters of Oeschinensee against an awe-inspiring backdrop of snowy peaks

1 In winter, visitors and locals come out to ice skate and walk on frozen Oeschinensee.

2 Wooden chalets are dotted around the shores of the lake.

3 The Kandersteg-Allmenalp *via ferrata* goes through stunning mountain landscapes, passing a 350-m- (1,150-ft-) high vertical wall and crossing four lovely waterfalls created by the Allmibach river.

EXPERIENCE MORE

7

Olten

🅐D3-D4 🚋Solothurn 🚌🚊
🛈Frohburgstrasse 1;
www.oltentourismus.ch

The small town of Olten is set in a picturesque location on the banks of the River Aare. Pedestrian access to the old part of the town is provided by the Alte Brücke, a covered bridge dating from 1802.

The Old Town is dominated by the tall Gothic belfry of a church that was demolished in the 19th century. There are many fine historic houses, particularly on Hauptgasse and along the Old Town's riverbank. Also of interest are the 17th-century monastery church and the Neo-Classical Stadtkirche, which dates from 1806–12 and is decorated with detailed paintings by draughtsman and caricaturist Martin Disteli. Many works by this local artist, along with 19th- and 20th-century paintings, installations and sculpture, are exhibited in the **Kunstmuseum**.

Kunstmuseum
⌖ 🏛Kirchgasse 8
🕐2–5pm Tue–Fri, 10am–5pm Sat & Sun 🖥kunstmuseumolten.ch

8

Solothurn

🅐C3 🚋Solothurn 🚌🚊
🛈Hauptgasse 69; www.solothurn-city.ch

Acclaimed as Switzerland's most beautiful Baroque city, Solothurn was founded by Celts but later became the second-largest Roman town north of the Alps. From here, boats depart for Biel/Bienne, and explore a particularly scenic stretch of the Aare.

Solothurn's monumental Neo-Classical **St Ursen Kathedrale**, was built from 1763 to 1773, and is flanked by friezes depicting the city's patron saints, Ursus and Victor, martyred by the Romans. The treasury in the crypt is open for guided tours only. The climb up to the bell tower is worth it for the sweeping views over the rooftops to the surrounding countryside.

Nearby is the former arsenal, the **Altes Zeughaus**, now a museum of militaria, including arms and uniforms used by Swiss mercenaries who served as bodyguards to popes and French kings. The town's small art gallery, the **Kunstmuseum**, contains some fine Old Masters, including the Madonna of

Solothurn (1522) by Hans Holbein the Younger. Ferdinand Hodler's dramatic depiction of William Tell emerging from the clouds, painted in 1897, is iconic.

St Ursen Kathedrale
⌖ 🏛Hauptgasse 📞032 626 46 46 🕐Church: 8am–6:30pm daily; tower: Apr–Oct: 9:30am–5:30pm Mon–Sat, noon–5:30pm Sun

Altes Zeughaus
⌖ 🏛Zeughausplatz 1
🕐1–5pm Tue–Sat, 10am–5pm Sun 🖥museum-alteszeughaus.so.ch

Kunstmuseum
⌖ 🏛Werkhofstrasse 30
🕐11am–5pm Tue–Sun, 10am–5pm Sat & Sun
🖥kunstmuseum-so.ch

9

Weissenstein

🅐C3 🚋Solothurn 🚠From Oberdorf 🛈Hauptgasse 69 Solothurn; www.solothurn-city.ch

Some of the most spectacular views of the Mittelland can be enjoyed from the summit of the Weissenstein, a ridge of the Jura that rises like a

← The Old Town of Olten, located on the banks of the River Aare

The stunning Jura mountains dotted with high alpine meadows ↑

rampart 1,284 m (4,213 ft) high. It is situated 10 km (6 miles) north of Solothurn. It is accessible by road or rail to Oberdorf, from where you can either hike to the summit or take a telecabine (closed on Monday and Tuesday).

On the ridge is the newly renovated hotel Kurhaus Weissenstein, with a restaurant. This is a good base for hiking, rock climbing and paragliding in summer, and for sledging in winter. Among the area's other attractions are a botanical garden and the Nidleloch, a limestone cave.

Biel/Bienne

🅰C3 **🏠Bern** 🚗🚌🚆
ℹ️Bözingenfeld/Champ;
www.biel-seeland.ch

Biel, known as Bienne in French, is the second-largest town in the canton of Bern. Founded in the 13th century,

it was ruled by the prince-bishops of Basel until the 19th century. Biel/Bienne's principal industry is watch-making and its factories produce some of the world's leading brands, such as Omega and Rolex. It is Switzerland's largest bilingual town: three-fifths of its inhabitants speak French, and the rest German.

The town is set on the shores of the Bielersee (or Lac de Bienne) at the point where the River Schüss (or Suze) flows into it. Set on a hill, the Old Town has narrow cobbled streets and fountains. Its nucleus is a square known as the Ring, which is surrounded by fine arcaded houses. One of them is the house of the guild of foresters. It has a 16th-century circular turret topped by an onion dome. Also on the square is the 15th-century church of St Benedict, with impressive late-Gothic stained-glass windows.

At the intersection of Burggasse and Rathausgasse,

west of the Ring, stands the Rathaus, the Gothic town hall, which dates from the 1530s. It is fronted by a Fountain of Justice. The late 16th-century Zeughaus, or arsenal, nearby is now used as a theatre.

In two adjacent buildings, Schwab and Neuhaus, the **Neues Museum Biel** imagines 19th-century bourgeois life with displays of domestic interiors. Other sections are devoted to industry, archaeology, and 19th- and early 20th-century paintings by local artists. Further down Seervorstadt the dynamic **Centre Pasquart** stages a programme of changing exhibitions of contemporary art and photography.

There are boat trips on the lake, including services to Solothurn, medieval Twann and pretty La Neuveville.

Neues Museum Biel
🔷 🏠Seervorstadt 52
🕐11am–5pm Tue–Sun
Ⓦnmbiel.ch

Centre Pasquart
🔷 🏠Seervorstadt/
Faubourg du Lac 71–73
🕐Noon–6pm Wed & Fri,
noon–8pm Thu, 11am–6pm
Sat & Sun Ⓦpasquart.ch

> Some of the most spectacular views of the Mittelland can be enjoyed from the summit of the Weissenstein, a ridge of the Jura that rises like a rampart.

The valley of Emmental, with its unspoiled meadows and mountain backdrop ↑

 11

Meiringen

🅰D4 🏛Bern 🚆🚌
🛈Bahnhofplatz 12;
www.haslital.ch

This small town lies in the heart of the Hasli valley, the Upper Aare valley to the east of Brienzersee. It is a historic settlement, dating back to c 1234, and has always been the political capital of the surrounding valley due to its strategic location at the foot of several alpine passes. Today, Meiringen is a snow sports resort in winter, and a base for hiking and mountain biking in summer.

Meiringen lies near the **Reichenbachfälle**, the waters

← A statue of Sherlock Holmes in Conan Doyle Place, Meiringen

chosen by the writer Arthur Conan Doyle as the scene of Sherlock Holmes's "death" after a struggle with Professor Moriarty. The town's quirky **Sherlock Holmes Museum**, which is found beneath the deconsecrated English Church, features a representation of the famous detective's drawing room at 221B Baker Street, London. From Meiringen a funicular takes visitors to the top of the Reichenbachfälle. From here there is a stunning view of the cascading waters.

Also of interest in Meiringen is the little church of St Michael at the top of the town, built in 1684 over a Romanesque crypt. It replaced the original village church, which was built in the 9th or 10th century and destroyed by a flood. Close by, to the east of the town, is the ruined castle of Restiturm, which was originally built in the 13th century to protect and control trade through the mountainous passes. Information boards around the site tell the castle's history.

Between Meiringen and Innertkirchen is the impressive **Aareschlucht**, a deep gorge cut by the River Aare.

Did You Know?

Switzerland produces more than 450 varieties of cheese, with Emmental the most exported.

Reichenbachfälle

📞033 972 9010 (funicular)
🕐May–Oct: 9am–5:30pm daily (last ascent 5:15pm)
🚫Nov–Apr

Sherlock Holmes Museum

🔗 🏛Bahnhofstrasse 26
🕐May–Oct: 1:30–6:30pm daily (Jul & Aug: to 9pm Thu); Nov–Apr: 4:30–6pm Wed & Sun 🌐sherlockholmes.ch

Aareschlucht

🕐Apr–mid-Jun & mid-Sep–Nov: 8:30am–5:30pm; mid-Jun–mid-Sep: 8:30am–6:30pm 🚫Dec–Mar
🌐aareschlucht.ch

 12

The Emmental

🅰C3 🏛Bern 🚆🚌
🛈Langnau, Schlossstrasse 3; www.emmental.ch

The Emmental, the long, wide valley of the River Emme,

has a beautiful landscape of green meadowland, grazed by cows. The valley, criss-crossed with excellent cycling and hiking routes, is dotted with traditional wooden chalets with high roofseaves that brush the ground.

Farming and traditional customs are central to the valley's local culture. This is also where the famous Emmental cheese is made, most of it by hand. At the **Schaukäserei** (show dairy) in Affoltern, visitors can see every stage in the process of producing this holey, nutty-tasting cheese. It is on sale in the dairy's shop and on the menu in its restaurant, and is also available in inns up and down the valley.

Burgdorf is a small town located in the north of the Emmental. The old part of the town is perched on top of a hill. It features arcaded houses, a Gothic church, and a 7th-century castle founded by the Zähringers. Further up the valley, the quiet village of Trubschachen has pottery workshops where colourful local wares are made and offered for sale.

The Emmental also has the longest arched wooden bridge in Europe. Built in 1839, the Holzbrücke spans the Emme just downstream of the village of Hasle-Rüegsau.

Schaukäserei
 Schaukäsereistrasse 6, Affoltern ◷ 9am–5pm daily 🖥 emmentaler-schaukaeserei.ch

---

⑬
Giessbachfälle
🏔 C3 🚉 Bern 🚌🚆

At 400-m- (1,312-ft-) high, this waterfall thunders down a verdant hillside into the valley below. It's at its most impressive during late spring and early summer, when the sheer volume of meltwater means that it can be heard from some distance away.

The best way to reach Giessbachfälle is via a ferry ride across Brienzersee from Brienz (p88). From the jetty, take Switzerland's oldest **funicular**, dating from 1879, up to the Grandhotel Giessbach. Once a stately home, it's now a hotel that marks the starting point of a circular hiking route to the falls. The highlight of the two-hour route is when the path passes behind the water.

The falls are illuminated at night, proving a lovely sight for those dining or staying at the hotel.

Funicular
◈ ◷ Jun–Oct: 10am–5:30pm daily 🚫 Nov–May

STAY

Hotel Bären
An 18th-century village coaching inn near Wilderswil station. Ask for a room over-looking the Eiger.

🏔 C4
🏠 Oberdorfstrasse 1, Wilderswil 🖥 baeren.ch

Chalet zum Steg
A gorgeous chalet in the hills above Meiringen. Large apartments are available for families.

🏔 D4 🏠 Balmstrass 69, Meiringen 🖥 chalet zumsteg.ch

Grandhotel Giessbach
Ideal for romantic getaways, this opulent hotel offers lovely views of both Brienzersee and Giessbachfälle.

🏔 C3 🏠 Brienz
🖥 giessbach.ch

↑ The waters of the dramatic Giessbachfälle, gushing down a hillside

14 Grindelwald

 D4 Bern
 Dorfstrasse 110;
www.grindelwald.ch

The road and railway lines into the mountains diverge just south of Interlaken. One branch carries into the Lauterbrunnen valley towards Mürren; the other heads east along the Lütschen valley to Grindelwald. From here, many visitors immediately jump onto the Wengernalp cog railway up to Kleine Scheidegg, from where the Jungfraubahn train climbs up to Jungfraujoch, the highest railway station in Europe, granting breathtaking views at the summit and along the way. But Grindelwald rewards those who stop here.

EAT

Bergrestaurant Bussalp
Climb through cow-dotted fields for hearty mountain fare.

 D4 Bussalp, Grindelwald
 bussalp.ch

(SF) (SF) (SF)

Piz Gloria
A revolving restaurant offering good food and down-to-earth prices.

 C5 Schilthorn, Mürren schilthorn.ch

(SF) (SF) (SF)

C UND M
Great pastries in a former ski school chalet with views to the Eiger.

 D4 Almisgaessli 1, Grindelwald cundm-grindelwald.ch

(SF) (SF) (SF)

Grindelwald, a popular destination in the Swiss Alps ↑

Nestled beneath the Eiger, Wetterhorn and Mettenberg this lively resort village has long been one of the most popular destinations in the Alps. In winter it offers plenty of snow sports, with excellent pistes and the opportunity to try the ubiquitous *velogemel*, and in summer great hiking. A one-hour walk east of the village leads to a wooded trail up to the Oberer Gletscher, a glacier inching its way down the Wetterhorn. Another popular hike takes walkers from the cable car station at First (a minor summit on the slopes of the Schwarzhorn) to Bachsee, a gorgeous lake set amid pretty alpine meadows.

The First summit is also home to the spectacular **First Cliff Walk** – a raised metallic structure bolted onto the rock face that snakes above the summit. This narrow walkway leads to a viewing platform that affords unrivalled pano-ramic views of the Eiger. When it's time to descend from First, you can either ride a mountain cart or take the **First Flyer Zipline**, which speeds downhill at 80 km/h (50 mph) to the Schreckfeld intermediate cable car station.

First Cliff Walk
  Bergstation First
 Dec-Oct: 8:30am-5:30pm daily Nov

First Flyer Zipline
  Bergstation First
 May & Jun: 11am-3:15pm daily; Jul-mid-Aug: 10am-4:30pm daily; mid-Aug-Oct: 11am-4pm daily Nov-Apr

15 Jungfraujoch

 D5 Bern and Valais
 Höheweg 37, Interlaken; www.jungfrau.ch

South of Interlaken lies the Bernese Oberland's most impressive mountain scenery, centred on a triple-peaked ridge: the Eiger (3,970 m/ 13,025 ft), the Mönch (4,099 m/ 13,448 ft) and the Jungfrau (4,158 m/ 13,642 ft). An effi-cient network of rail and cable car routes from Interlaken (*p84*) makes it easy to travel around this ridge.

One of the best-known rail excursions travels up to the Jungfraujoch. This icy saddle, lying just below the summit of the Jungfrau, has been dubbed the "Top of Europe", and at 3,454 m (11,332 ft) above sea level, the train station here is the highest on the continent.

As there are two different routes up to the Jungfraujoch,

this excursion can easily be done as a circular journey. Trains head from Interlaken to Lauterbrunnen. Here, you can change to the rack railway that climbs up through the village of Wengen *(p104)* and on further up to the dramatic station at Kleine-Scheidegg, directly beneath the famous north face of the Eiger.

Different trains head from Interlaken up to Grindelwald, where you again change, this time to the rack railway, which climbs up to Kleine-Scheidegg from the other direction. From Kleine-Scheidegg, a separate line heads up through tunnels and along the mountain face to the Jungfraujoch itself. From April to September seat reservations are recommended. The cogwheel railway stops twice, at the Eismeer and at the Eiger Wall, from where visitors can enjoy magnificent views.

Lauterbrunnen

🅰 C4/D4 🄰 Bern 🚉🚌
🆆 lauterbrunnen.swiss

Unspoiled Lauterbrunnen is the world's deepest U-shaped valley, a rough-hewn glacial gorge hemmed in by steep walls cut by 72 waterfalls. A local legend claims that, in 1911, the 19-year-old J R R Tolkien found inspiration for the fictional landscape of Middle Earth, the setting for *The Lord of the Rings* (1954), here. Similarly, the German poet Johann Wolfgang von Goethe is said to have broken into verse, namely the *Song of the Spirits over the Waters* (1779), on seeing the 297-m-(974-ft-) Staubbach Falls, Switzerland's highest free-falling waterfall.

During summer, Staubbach Falls are accessible via a narrow yet easy path from Lauterbrunnen village to a natural rock balcony. Information panels along the route explain the various natural phenomena that led to the fall's formation. The round trip takes about three hours to complete.

In winter, skiers descend on Lauterbrunnen to tackle the 2,000-m (6562-ft) ski run from the summit of Schilthorn to Lauterbrunnen. The village is also one of Switzerland's most popular destinations for cross-country skiers. One 16-km (10-mile) route passes several frozen waterfalls along the way.

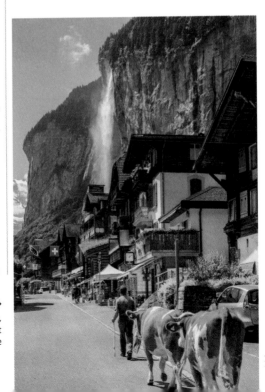

→
Lauterbrunnen village, set in a magnificent wild valley gorge

Wengen

🏔️ D4 🚆 Bern 🚉
ℹ️ Dorfstrasse; www.
wengen.ch

At an altitude of 1,274 m
(4,180 ft), the car-free resort of
Wengen overlooks the pretty
Lauterbrunnen valley. This is
classic Swiss alpine scenery,
with snowy peaks, sheer cliffs,
cascading waterfalls and
verdant, rolling meadows
where the cows graze.

Mountain trains heading
from Lauterbrunnen climb
towards the Jungfraujoch
(p103), stopping midway at
Wengen. A village of chalets
and large hotels tucked on
a shelf of southwest-facing
pasture, Wengen is blessed
with long hours of sunshine
even in winter and has a long
history of being a popular
mountain holiday destination,
just like its neighbours Mürren
and Grindelwald (p102).

Skiing terrain is extensive
and especially suited to
families, and in summer the
countryside around Wengen
offers superb hiking. Trails
lead down to the flower-filled

Did You Know?

There are over 500
kilometres of sign-
posted hiking trails
around Wengen.

meadows around Wengwald,
and up to Männlichen (which
can also be reached by cable
car). From here visitors can
enjoy spectacular views down
over Grindelwald on one side
and the Lauterbrunnen valley
on the other.

Mürren

🏔️ D4 🚆 Bern 🚉
ℹ️ Höhemaate 1074B,
Mürren; www.muerren.ch

From Lauterbrunnen (p103)
there are two ways of reaching
the small car-free village of
Mürren, on the opposite side
of the valley from Wengen.
Both routes are spectacular. A
cable car rises to Grütschalp,

from where a tram takes a
scenic route along the cliff
edge to reach Mürren. Alternatively, buses travel along
the valley-floor road (past a
striking series of waterfalls at
Trümmelbach) to Stechelberg,
from where a cable car climbs
to Mürren, perched 1, 638 m
(5,374 ft) above sea level. The
views, down the valley and
up to a dazzling panorama of
snowy crags, are astounding.
Another cable car heads
further up, to the ice-bound
summit of the Schilthorn
(2,970 m/9,744 ft), where there
is a revolving restaurant, Piz
Gloria (p102), famously featured as the villain's lair in
the James Bond film, On Her
Majesty's Secret Service (1969).

Adelboden

🏔️ C5 🚆 Bern 🚉
ℹ️ Dorfstrasse 23; www.
adelboden.ch

Located at the head of the
Engstligental, a wide valley,
Adelboden is an attractive
village with chalets, pleasant
streets and well-kept gardens.

↑ The charming mountain
village of Mürren set amid
spectacular alpine scenery

↑ The mountain village of Kandersteg, an ideal base for skiing or hiking

The small 15th-century parish church here is of interest for its frescoes and stained-glass windows created by Augusto Giacometti. The village also has an interesting museum documenting local history and daily life in the Engstligental.

Adelboden is primarily a resort, with 72 ski lifts and some 210 km (130 miles) of pistes in the Adelboden-Lenk ski-pass region. The town also offers facilities for extreme sports, as well as ice rinks for skating and curling. In summer it's a base for mountain biking and hiking.

The Engstligenfälle, spectacular waterfalls tumbling from Engstligenalp, 4 km (2.5 miles) above Adelboden, are accessible by cable car. There are several hiking trails, which lead to higher altitudes, including Ammertenspitz (2,613 m/8,573 ft), and also down past the falls.

20

Kandersteg

 C4 🚉 Bern 🚉
🛈 Äussere Dorfstraae 26; www.kandersteg.ch

The village of Kandersteg stretches out along the valley of the River Kander, west of the Jungfrau massif. The village is located near the north entrance to the old Lötschberg Tunnel, through which trains run for 15 km (9 miles) under the Lötschberg to emerge at Goppenstein, in eastern Valais. In 2008, a 35-km- (22-mile-) tunnel opened beneath the old line, massively cutting travel times.

Apart from its attractive 16th-century parish church, Kandersteg's main interest to visitors is as a resort. In winter, the gentle slopes around the village make ideal skiing pistes for beginners. In summer the village turns into a popular base for hiking, biking and paragliding or simply for exploring the stunning lakes and soaring mountains.

Oeschinensee, a small lake surrounded by towering cliffs, can be reached by a chair-lift from the eastern edge of the village. Fit hikers can take the trail back down to Kandersteg. Blausee, an enchanting small boating lake surrounded by a pine forest, is a ten-minute drive north of Kandersteg.

Nearby, the lofty peak of the Blüemlisalphorn (3,671 m/12,044 ft) and its impressive neighbour the Hockenhorn (3,297 m/10,820 ft) offer mountaineers a somewhat more demanding challenge. The Lötschenpass hut is a handy spot to overnight during multi-day treks.

STAY

Berghaus Bort
A small chalet hotel with simple, sparsely furnished rooms drenched with sunshine.

 D4 🚉 Bortweg 44, Grindelwald
📞 033 853 17 62

ⓢⓕ ⓢⓕ ⓢⓕ

Ruedihaus Kandersteg
A large rustic house dedicated to tradition: no metal, no plastic and no Wi-Fi.

 D4 🚉 Hinder de Büele, Kandersteg
🌐 doldenhorn-ruedihus.ch

ⓢⓕ ⓢⓕ ⓢⓕ

Alpenruh
A cosy hotel, near Mürren cable terminus, with stunning views and large family rooms.

 D5 🚉 Eggli 954B, Mürren 🌐 alpenruh-muerren.ch

ⓢⓕ ⓢⓕ ⓢⓕ

Grand Hotel Regina
Palatial luxury with a pool and spas, just steps from the train station.

 D4 🚉 Dorfstrasse 80, Grindelwald 🌐 hotel regina.ch

ⓢⓕ ⓢⓕ ⓢⓕ

Bellevue des Alpes
Unrivalled views and true comfort provided for seasoned climbers and casual walkers.

 D4 🚉 Kleine Scheidegg 🌐 scheidegg-hotels.ch

ⓢⓕ ⓢⓕ ⓢⓕ

↑ The village of Gstaad, with its traditional Swiss architecture

21

Gstaad

 C5 🏛 Bern 🚌🚂 ℹ Haus des Gastes; www.gstaad.ch

Given it is one of Switzerland's most famous resorts, Gstaad is a surprisingly small village, its size out of proportion to its international prestige. At the junction of four valleys, it connects into a larger regional ski-pass network, including the Diablerets Glacier.

In summer Gstaad attracts numerous visitors who come to enjoy rock climbing, hiking, cycling and rafting on the turbulent waters of the Saane. By remaining faithful to traditional architecture, the town has maintained its romantic character. Its main street, the Promenade, is lined with shops, cafés and galleries.

22

Martigny

🅐 B5 🏛 Valais 🚂🚌 ℹ 6 Ave de la Gare; www. martigny.com

Located where the Dranse and Rhône rivers meet, at the point where the latter curves

to the north, Martigny was established by the Romans as Octodorus in about 15 BC. Excavations have unearthed a complex of Roman buildings, among them baths, an amphitheatre and a temple dedicated to Minerva.

The town is dominated by the Tour de la Bâtiaz, a 13th-century fortress set on a promontory. In Martigny's old district are the 15th-century Maison Supersaxo and the Chapelle Notre-Dame-de-Compassion, built in the 1620s, both worth a visit.

Martigny's main attraction is the **Fondation Pierre Gianadda**, a museum built on the ruins of a Gallo-Roman temple. Among its several collections, the Musée Archéologique Gallo-Romain contains statues and artifacts uncovered during excavations. The Musée de l'Auto, in the basement, showcases vintage cars, including Swiss-made models. A small number of paintings, by Cézanne, Van Gogh and Toulouse-Lautrec and other artists, are shown in the Salle Franck, while important temporary exhibitions are staged in the main gallery.

Nearby is **Barryland**, a "living museum" dedicated

to the famous St Bernard dogs that were once kept at the Grand St Bernard Pass monastery and who were trained by monks to sniff out travellers lost in snow or avalanches. The museum also keeps a number of dogs on site, which you are allowed to pet at certain times of day.

Fondation Pierre Gianadda

⬦ 🏛 59 Rue du Forum 🕐 Jun–Nov: 9am–7pm daily; Dec–May: 10am–6pm daily 🌐 gianadda.ch

Barryland

⬦ 🏛 Route du Levant 34 🕐 10am–6pm daily 🌐 barryland.ch

23

Verbier

🅐 C5 🏛 Valais 🚌 ℹ Place Centrale; www.verbier.ch

Verbier is Switzerland's most extensive ski area, with terrain to suit every skier, from gentle slopes to some of the most challenging pistes. That, plus its beautiful location, climate, cosmopolitan atmosphere and vibrant nightlife, have made it a celebrity favourite. At an altitude of 1,500 m (4,921 ft), the resort lies on a wide plateau with fine views of peaks in Switzerland, Italy and France. Just below Verbier lies the Val de Bagnes, a picturesque valley and one of the country's best kept secrets.

Verbier's ski-pass area covers more than 400 km (248 miles) of on- and off-piste runs. The highest point is Mont Fort, at 3,330 m (10,925 ft). From there are far-reaching views as far as Mont Blanc. In summer, there are two golf courses and good hiking trails.

Xtreme Verbier is a winter event in which skiers and snowboarders swoop down steep mountain faces studded with cliffs. In summer the town hosts the Verbier Festival, an international festival of classical music with free workshops. August sees the world's best horse riders compete in a prestigious dressage event.

㉔
Grand St Bernard Pass

 B6 Valais

 Grand-St-Bernard;
www.saint-bernard.ch/en

Situated on the border with Italy at an altitude of 2,469 m

$\rightarrow$

The 17th-century church within the Grand St Bernard Pass hospice

(8,100 ft), the St Bernard Pass is the oldest of all Alpine pass routes, in use since 800 BC.

The pass is named after Bernard of Menthon, Bishop of Aosta, who built a hospice for travellers here in 1049. It has been inhabited by monks ever since. It welcomes travellers all year round – access in winter is by skis or snowshoes. There is also an interesting museum that documents the history of the pass.

The St Bernard Pass is closed to vehicles all winter, with snow common in June. However, the St Bernard Tunnel provides a year-round route between Switzerland and Italy.

㉕
The Simmental

 C4 Bern

 Rawilstrasse 3, Lenk;
www.lenk-simmental.ch

The Simmental, the beautiful long valley of the River Simme, is divided into two sections. Nieder Simmental, the lower section, runs from the town of Spiez – where the River Simme enters Thunersee (Lake Thun) – westwards to Boltigen. Here the valley veers to the south, becoming Obere Simmental, the upper section. This part stretches up a little above the valley to the holiday resort and spa town of Lenk, near the source of the Simme.

Several charming villages lie along the Simmental, among them Erlenbach, the starting point for whitewater rafting down the Simme.

> INSIDER TIP
> **The Simmental Cycle Route**
>
> Head out on this enjoyable flat-terrain bike route, which winds its way over tarmacked and natural paths from Lenk to Erlenback (lenk-simmental.ch).

26
St-Pierre-de-Clages

 B5 □ Valais ▣▣

The tiny medieval village of St-Pierre-de-Clages is set on the southern, vineyard-covered slopes of the Rhône valley. Apart from an annual book festival and some well-stocked antiquarian bookshops in the village, its main attraction is a beautiful Romanesque church with an octagonal bell tower. Dating from the late 11th to the early 12th century, it was originally part of a Benedictine priory. The rib-vaulted interior is almost entirely devoid of decoration, and this pleasing austerity is accentuated by the unadorned stonework of the walls and columns. The stained glass dates from 1948.

27
Sion

□ C5 □ Valais ▣▣
🛈 Place de la Planta;
www.siontourisme.ch

The capital of the canton of Valais sits along the Rhône, at the foot of two hills. Four castles stand guard over the town of Sion: Valère, Tourbillon, Majorie and Montorge, each dating back to the 13th century or earlier. The

> **Four castles stand guard over the town of Sion: Valère, Tourbillon, Majorie and Montorge, each dating back to the 13th century or earlier.**

surrounding Rhône valley is renowned for its apricots and indiginous Fendant vineyards.

The **Château de Tourbillon** itself is now in ruins, but many of the ramparts remain. The chapel, with ribbed vaulting and carved capitals, contains medieval wall paintings. The nearby **Château de Valère** is a 12th-century fortified church with 15th-century murals and the world's oldest working organ, dating from 1430.

Château de Tourbillon

🕒 Mid-Mar-Apr & Oct-mid-Nov: 11am-5pm daily; May-Sep: 10am-6pm daily 🔒 Mid-Nov-mid-Mar 🌐 tourbillon.ch

Château de Valère

📞 027 606 47 15 🕒 Jun-Sep: 10am-6pm daily; Oct-May: 10am-5pm Tue-Sun

28
Sierre

□ C5 □ Valais ▣▣ 🛈 10 Place de la Gare; www.sierretourisme.ch

 Located in the Rhône valley, Sierre

(Siders in German) lies on an invisible linguistic border separating French speakers from their German compatriots. The town enjoys a wonderfully sunny climate and is surrounded by vineyards. It contains several historic buildings, including a 16th-century castle, the Château des Vidomnes. The Baroque town hall contains a small museum of pewter objects.

The local winemaking tradition is documented by the **Wine Museum Sierre**, which has fascinating collections displayed in two places. One part occupies a wing of the 16th-century Château de Villa in Sierre, the other the 16th-century Zumofenhaus in Salgesch (Salquenen in French), a village east of Sierre. The scenic 6-km (4-mile) Sentier Viticole, or wine route, wends through villages and

> 🔍 HIDDEN GEM
> ### Lac St Léonard
>
> Between Sion and Sierre lies Europe's largest underground lake, Lac St Léonard (www.lac-souterrain.com). You can visit it mid-March to November – in summer, concerts are staged on the water.

The Lac des Dix framed by alpine peaks and the Grande Dixence dam

vineyards, with a number of wine-tasting stops along the way. The route connects the museum's two parts.

Wine Museum Sierre

⊛⊛ 🏛 Château de Villa, 6 Rue Ste-Catherine 🕐 Mar-Nov: 2-6pm Wed-Fri, 11am-6pm Sat & Sun 🕐 Dec-Feb 🌐 museeduvin-valais.ch

---

 29

Barrage de la Grande Dixence

🅰 C6 🏛 Valais 🚌 Late Jun-mid-Oct 🌐 grande-dixence.ch

The world's highest gravity dam and the greatest feat of modern engineering in Switzerland, this extraordinary hydroelectric dam towers 285 m (935 ft) high, across the River Dixence, at the head of the Val d'Hérémence.

The Lac des Dix, the stretch of water that fills the valley above the dam, is surrounded

 ←

Sion, capital of the French-speaking Valais, dramatically set amid rocky outcrops

by mountains. Rising to the west is Rosablanche (3,336 m/ 10,945 ft); to the east soars Les Aiguilles Rouges (3,646 m/ 11,962 ft); and to the south climbs Mont Blanc de Cheilon (3,870m/12,697 ft) and Pigne d'Arolla (3,796m/12,454 ft). A cable car runs from the foot of the dam, where there is a restaurant, up to the lake. From here you can hike to the Cabane des Dix, a mountain refuge, walk around the lake or take the six-hour hike to the small resort of Arolla.

Val d'Hérémence joins the Val d'Hérens (p110) at the small town of Hérémence. The town is a good base for skiing on the eastern slopes of Mont Rouge, and also for hiking in the mountains.

 30

Trient Valley

🅰 B6 🏛 Valais 🚆🚌🚠 ℹ Rue de la Poste 3, Martigny; www.vallee dutrient.ch/en

Connecting Martigny to Chamonix in France over the narrow Forclaz Pass, Trient is an almost forgotten valley of tranquillity and pastoral life. A rack-railway train, the "Mont Blanc Express",

carries passengers along the edge of the valley, offering views car drivers will never see on the road. Especially spectacular is the journey up to the lake and dam at **VerticAlp Emosson** on the Swiss border, involving three types of funicular.

Hikers can walk all the way up to the permanent ice of Trient Glacier. Along the way are the village of Le Trétien, famed for its centuries-old wooden buildings, and the natural rock swimming pool at Les Marécottes. Hikers can spend the night in one of the Swiss Alpine Club's mountain huts dotted across the terrain.

VerticAlp Emosson

🏛 Route du Châtelard 6, Le Châtelard 🚌 🕐 Jun-mid-Oct: 9am-5pm daily 🕐 Mid-Oct-May 🌐 verticalp-emosson.ch

---

Did You Know?

One of the funiculars up the Trient Valley to Emosson climbs at an incline of 87 per cent.

The unspoilt Val d'Anniviers, a side valley in the Valais, popular with hikers

31
Val d'Hérens

C5 **Valais** **13 Rue Principale, Euseigne; www.valdherens.ch**

Stretching southeast from Sion, the tranquil Val d'Hérens (Eringertal in German) reaches into the Pennine Alps. This pretty valley has enchanting scenery and is home to pretty villages with wooden chalets. Traditions are kept alive here, making it seem a world away from modern life.

A striking geological feature of the Val d'Hérens is a cluster

 The dramatic jagged rocks that form the Pyramides d'Euseigne

of rock formations known as the Pyramides d'Euseigne. Visible from the valley road, these sawtoothed outcrops of rock jut out of the hillside like fangs. They were sanded into shape during the Ice Age by the erosive action of wind, rain and ice. Each point is capped by a rock, which protected the softer rock beneath from erosion, so producing these jagged formations.

The village of Evolène, 15 km (9 miles) south of the village of Euseigne, is a good base for hiking. At the head of the valley, amid lush Arolla pine forests and flowery meadows, is the hamlet of Les Haudères, where there is a Geology and Glacier Centre with an interesting museum. Beyond this small outpost, the Val d'Hérens extends into tree-lined Val d'Arolla. At the end of the road sits the small resort of Arolla.

32
Val d'Anniviers

C5 **Valais** **valdanniviers.ch**

A popular destination in the summer for hikers, the rugged Val d'Anniviers begins across from Sierre and runs up to the

 INSIDER TIP
Hike the Valais Bisses

The *bisses* are irrigation channels that run throughout the Valais. Some of them have been there for centuries, and many are now restored and make excellent hiking paths. Some are vertigo-inducing, set along a cliff edge; others are more gentle.

glaciers of Zinal to the south. Surrounded by the high peaks of the Pennine Alps and cut by the River La Navisence, the valley is dotted with villages which offer visitors skiing in the winter, and hiking and cycling in the summer.

Near the entrance to the valley perches the unspoilt mountain village of Vercorin. From Soussillon you can journey to medieval Chandolin, a village of quaint wooden chalets and fantastic views. From Vissoie it is worth going to sun-drenched Saint-Luc at 1,650 m (5,413 ft) for a breathtaking view of the Val d'Anniviers. From there you can proceed up to the top of Bella Tola (3,025 m/9,925 ft).

Grimentz is a fascinating village, full of traditional tall wooden chalets built on the underlying bedrock. From here, hiking trails lead up to the Moiry dam and the Glacier de Moiry. The highest village in the valley is Zinal at 1,670 m (5,479 ft). This resort is a ski centre in winter and a good base for summer hiking. From Zinal guides can be hired for the climb to the summit of the Zinal-Rothorn (4,221 m/ 13,848 ft), the Pyramide des Besso, Oberes Gabelhorn and Pointe de Zinal. There are also many easier peaks and highly scenic rambling routes.

 33

Monte Rosa

 C6 ◻ Valais
◻ Gornergrat

The Monte Rosa massif spans Swiss and Italian territory, and possesses the highest peak in Switzerland and the second highest in the Alps after Mont Blanc: the Dufourspitze, which peaks at 4,634 m (15,203 ft). Because of its shape, Monte Rosa is easier to climb than the Matterhorn.

Situated on its Italian side, near the summit at 4,556 m (14,947 ft), is the Capanna Regina Margherita, the highest mountain shelter in Europe, built in 1893. The Monte Rosa massif is encircled by the Gornergletscher, a vast glacier and the second-largest glacial system in the Alps; stretching lower down are the usually deserted slopes of Stockhorn and Gornergrat.

34

Crans-Montana

◻ B5/C5 ◻ Valais ◻
◻ cransmontana.ch

The fashionable ski and golf resort of Crans-Montana lies on a plateau north of the Rhône valley, with a clear view of the Valais Alps to the south. In the late 19th century, as the fashion for mountain holidays grew, Crans and Montana expanded and merged into one legal entity.

Crans-Montana can be reached by road from Sion, and from Sierre either by a road that winds up through vineyards and pasture, or by funicular. This very sunny resort has a network of cable cars and ski lifts, accessing over 140 km (87 miles) of pistes and the glacier of Plaine Morte, a popular destination for cross-country skiing. The resort is best known, however, for high-altitude golf. Two nine-hole courses, plus the legendary Swiss Masters links, with views over the Rhône Valley, make Crans-Montana Switzerland's premier golf centre. And at this altitude, balls fly an incredible 20 per cent further than at sea level.

↑ The winding road up to the popular ski resort of Crans-Montana

A roadside rest stop amid the hills around Saas-Fee in springtime

35 Saas-Fee

A D5 **A** Valais **i** Obere Dorfstrasse 2; www. saas-fee.ch

A village dating back to the 13th century, Saas-Fee, in the Pennine Alps, has been a resort since the early 19th century. It is the main town in the Saas Valley, through which flows the River Saaser Vispa. It has a magnificent setting at the foot of the Dom (4,545 m/ 14,911 ft) and is surrounded by other tall peaks.

The car-free resort has many traditional wooden chalets, which are built on high walls. Saas-Fee, more than many resorts in the area, cherishes its traditional rural culture, and several local traditions are enacted for visitors. These include processions marking Corpus Christi, cow fights and yodelling contests, folk festivals celebrating Swiss National Day, and the late-spring festival Alpaufzug, which marks the time when cows are taken up to their summer pastures. The Saaser Museum, with a reconstruction of a typical local house, and beautifully preserved crafts and costumes, is devoted to the region's folk traditions and culture.

All around the village, in winter or in summer, are vistas of mammoth glaciers and steep crevasses. Year-round skiing is possible on the Feegletscher (Fairy Glacier) in the Mischabel massif; it is the highest massif to lie entirely in Switzerland.

In summer, there is a range of hiking trails, from easy strolls to demanding treks, that lead into the surrounding peaks or to other sites, such as Mattmarksee, an artificial lake. A cable car also runs up to the rocky outcrop of Felskinn (3,000 m/9,800 ft). From here, the Alpine Metro makes the journey up to Mittelallalin, where you can savour the panorama from Allalin *(041 27 957 17 71)*, the highest revolving restaurant in the world at a height of 3,500 m (11,480 ft).

36 Simplon Pass

A D5 **A** Valais **=** 631 **i** Simplon Dorf; www. simplon.ch

The Simplon Pass is one of the most important routes between western and southern Europe. Connecting Switzerland and Italy, it also marks the border between the Pennine and Lepontine Alps. The route has been in use since the Stone Age, and so has played an essential role in trade since the Middle Ages.

The strategic importance of the pass was recognized by Napoleon, on whose orders a new road was built here in 1800–06. This road is about 64 km (40 miles) long and runs from Brig, over the pass and through the village of Simplon, down to the Italian town of Domodossola. Napoleon's road is passable virtually all year round. A railway tunnel under the pass was built in 1906, as an alternative crossing.

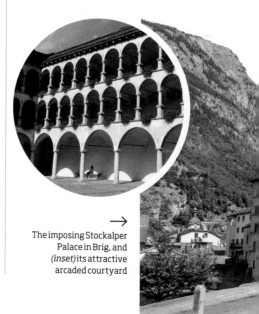

→ The imposing Stockalper Palace in Brig, and *(inset)* its attractive arcaded courtyard

Brig

D5 ⊕ Valais ⊕
🛈 Bahnhofplatz 1; www.
brig-simplon.ch

Built over a Roman settlement, Brig is the major town in the Upper Valais. It lies at the crossroads of the main alpine routes leading over the Simplon, Furka, Grimsel and Nufenen passes and through the Lötschberg Tunnel. Set on the Rhône, the bridges that span the river at this spot give the town its name. During the 17th century, the trade route to Italy, leading over the Simplon Pass, was controlled by the Stockalper family of merchants. Kaspar Jodok Stockalper von Thurm gave Brig its finest monument, a Renaissance-Baroque palace built between 1658 and 1678. The building is set with three

> Leukerbad
> (Loèche-les-Bains
> in French) is one
> of the highest spa
> resorts in Europe.

tall square towers crowned by cupolas Caspar, Melchior and Balthazar. The palace has an arcaded courtyard and a chapel dedicated to the Three Kings, with an ornate silver altarpiece made by Samuel Hornung of Augsburg.

38
Leukerbad

C5 ⊕ Valais ⊕
🛈 Rathausstrasse 8;
www.leukerbad.ch

At the head of the Dala valley, at an altitude of

CUSTOMS OF THE LÖTSCHENTAL

The Lötschental is a remote valley just east of Leukerbad. For centuries the valley's inhabitants were isolated from the outside world during winter, and they have retained many ancient rituals, customs and traditions. One such custom is Tschäggättä, a festival that lasts from Candlemas until Shrovetide. Young bachelors don sheepskin coats, with the fleece on the outside and cowbells strapped to their waists, and wear grotesque masks *(left)*. Masked processions are held during the last week of the carnival.

1,400 m (4,595 ft), Leukerbad (Loèche-les-Bains in French) is one of the highest spa resorts in Europe. The therapeutic properties of its hot springs, which are rich in calcium, sulphur and gypsum, have been famed since Roman times.

Leukerbad has many public spa complexes, with pools and many other facilities, including treatments and rehabilitation programmes.

Above the resort, and accessible by cable car, lies the breathtaking Gemmi Pass, found on the hiking trail to Kandersteg *(p105)* and the Bernese Oberland.

GENEVA

The capital of Switzerland's westernmost canton, with which it shares its name, Geneva nestles against the shores of Lake Geneva (Lac Léman), where the Rhône and the Arve divide. It was settled by the Celtic Helvetii around 450 BC, who were attracted by the fertile land and defensive position. The same appealed to the Romans, who swooped in to secure the city in 121 BC. Fought over for centuries by different factions, the city gained its independence in 1536. By that point, the city of Geneva was established as a prosperous centre of trade, and on its way to becoming a stronghold of the Reformation. Known as the Protestant Rome, the city attracted Protestant refugees from across Europe. These newcomers both increased the city's wealth and boosted its cosmopolitan character. Artists and philosophers soon followed, adding to the city's culture. The city's reputation as a place of mediation and civility was cemented in 1864, when the International Red Cross was founded by a group of Genevois. In the century that followed, the League of Nations and later the United Nations made their home here. Now home to more than 200 international organizations, including CERN, one of the world's most advanced laboratories, it remains a centre of international cooperation.

GENEVA

←

1 Mont Salève cable car.

2 A paddle steamer docking on Lake Geneva.

3 The Jet d'Eau, seen from Geneva's cathedral.

4 Touring Maison Tavel.

2 DAYS
in Geneva

Day 1

Morning Start the day discovering early Geneva at the city's oldest house, 12th-century Maison Tavel *(p125)*. Spend a couple of hours diving into Geneva's fascinating history, then, once you've worked up an appetite, swing by one of the lively local markets to choose picnic treats from stalls crammed with fresh produce.

Afternoon Visit the home of the Large Hadron Collider at CERN *(p127)* for a fascinating 3-hour (pre-booked) tour. If you'd rather be out in the fresh air, hop on bus 8 for an easy outing up "Geneva's mountain", Mont Salève instead. Get off at Veyrier-Douane, where it's a mere 10-minute walk across the Swiss–French border (remember your passport) to the foot of the cable car that ascends the mountain. Travel to the top and pop into the summit restaurant for coffee with a stupendous view over the city and Lake Geneva. Follow the paths that cling to the rockface. There are glorious views to be found round every corner.

Evening Return to the city for an atmospheric dinner aboard the *Savoie* paddle steamer, built in 1914. As you dine, the boat passes numerous landmarks, including the impressive Jet d'Eau *(p124)*, a powerful water fountain that has become symbolic of the city.

Day 2

Morning Enjoy a leisurely morning croissant by the river, then take a walk through the university campus to the International Red Cross and Red Crescent Museum *(p126)*, where the well-curated three-part permanent exhibition takes visitors on an emotional journey to highlight humanitarian efforts around the world. From there, head over the Arve river via the cross-hatched Hans-Wilsdorf bridge and make your way to Carouge, Geneva's very own "Little Italy". Towards the neighbourhood's southern end is La Clemence *(www.laclemence.ch)*. Serving up an excellent coffee, it's the perfect spot for a *petit pause*.

Afternoon Allow some time to take in the sights, sounds and delicious smells of this dynamic neighbourhood. Once a hamlet built in the Sardinian style, it is now a bohemian enclave, filled with artisan boutiques, craftsmen's workshops and quaint streets lined with independent bistros and cosy cafés.

Evening Stroll back along the river towards the Old Town and dine at the iconic Café-Restaurant de l'Hôtel de Ville *(p127)*. Dating from 1764, it is steeped in the old-fashioned charm of a neighbourhood bistro, serving up classic Genevois dishes such as traditional Fricasée de porc (spiced pork stew).

❶

CATHÉDRALE ST-PIERRE

📍C4 📍6-8 Cour St-Pierre 🚌36 🕐Archaeological site: 10am-5pm daily; church: Jun-Sep: 9:30am-6:30pm Mon-Fri, 9:30am-5pm Sat, noon-6:30pm Sun; Oct-May: 10am-5:30pm Mon-Sat, noon-5:30pm Sun 🌐cathedrale-geneve.ch

Built over a span of some 70 years from 1160 to 1230, with later additions, Geneva's vast cathedral is a mish-mash of styles, from the Gothic to the Neo-Classical and a mix of Catholic and Protestant symbolism.

Archaeological evidence, unearthed in the 1970s, show that there has been a Christian church on this site since at least AD 360. A complex of 4th-century ecclesiastical build-ings were erected here – and subsequently built over repeatedly until the 1100s, when the complex was razed and work began on the present Gothic-Romanesque cathedral. While the cathedral faced a programme of reinvention, as religious aesthetic principles changed, the original structure remained largely untouched until 1976, when exca-vations under and around the cathedral were started. Today, beneath the cathedral, an archaeological museum displays remains from some of the 4th-century buildings, as well as the findings of excavations from the surrounding area.

John Calvin's chair is in the nave.

A triforium surmounts the arches in the groin-vaulted nave.

→

The cathedral, a mix of architectural styles and religious symbolism

🔺 GREAT VIEW
City Panorama

Climb the narrow steps (all 157 of them) that wind up the north tower to enjoy the spectacular panoramic views over the city.

Main entrance

The flamboyant 15th-century Chapelle des Macchabées

The tall spire was added in the 19th-century.

Tomb of Henri de Rohan

Romanesque and Gothic stonework capitals survived the Reformist purge.

With intricately carved back panels and canopy, the stalls originally stood near the choir.

① A riot of colour fills the presbytery, from the stained-glass windows to the brilliantly painted ceiling.

② An exquisitely carved animal in the stalls is a survivor of the purge of the Reformation.

③ A bas relief of St Pierre stands outside Geneva's austere cathedral.

Timeline

360s
▽ A Christian church consecrated on this site.

1160-1230
▽ Construction of original cathedral.

1500s
▽ Flamboyant interiors removed by Reformers in favour of austerity.

1970s
▽ Remains of the 4th-century church uncovered during renovations.

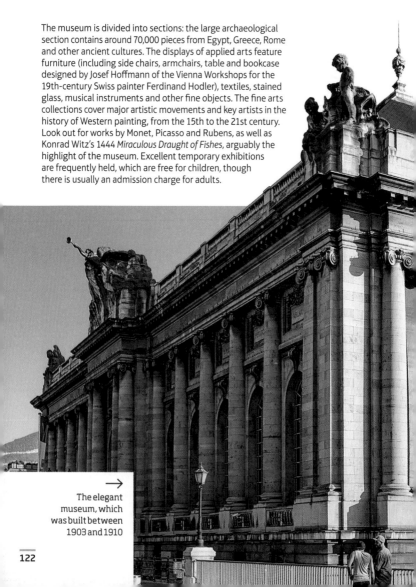

2 🎨 🍴 🛍

MUSÉE D'ART ET D'HISTOIRE

📍D4-D5 🏛2 Rue Charles-Galland 🚌7 🕐11am-6pm Tue-Sun
🌐mah-geneve.ch

Geneva's impressive Museum of Art and History, presenting paintings, sculpture and artifacts covering prehistory to the present day, is the city's largest art museum. Visitors can easily spend several hours here perusing the vast collection, which consists of over half a million items.

The museum is divided into sections: the large archaeological section contains around 70,000 pieces from Egypt, Greece, Rome and other ancient cultures. The displays of applied arts feature furniture (including side chairs, armchairs, table and bookcase designed by Josef Hoffmann of the Vienna Workshops for the 19th-century Swiss painter Ferdinand Hodler), textiles, stained glass, musical instruments and other fine objects. The fine arts collections cover major artistic movements and key artists in the history of Western painting, from the 15th to the 21st century. Look out for works by Monet, Picasso and Rubens, as well as Konrad Witz's 1444 *Miraculous Draught of Fishes*, arguably the highlight of the museum. Excellent temporary exhibitions are frequently held, which are free for children, though there is usually an admission charge for adults.

→
The elegant museum, which was built between 1903 and 1910

GALLERY GUIDE

In the basement are displays of archaeological discoveries made in the Geneva region, while archaeological exhibits from ancient civilizations occupy the lower ground floor. Also on the ground floor are rooms devoted to the applied arts; temporary exhibitions are hosted here too. The first floor is closed to the public, but paintings and sculptures are displayed on the second floor, representing artists from across Europe who lived and worked from medieval times to the modern age.

1. In his 1907 *Le Bain Turc* Swiss artist Félix Vallotton (1865–1925) pays homage to Neo-Classical painter Jean-Auguste-Dominique Ingres's masterpiece *The Turkish Bath*.

2. Venus bids farewell to Adonis before setting off on a fatal hunt in this marble statue carved by Antonio Canova (1757–1822); Venus is based on one of Canova's most famous models.

3. The *Miraculous Draught of Fishes* is part of the altarpiece that Konrad Witz made for the Cathédrale St-Pierre *(p120)* in 1444. In the background is a view of Geneva.

Did You Know?

A huge renovation for the museum was postponed after Genevans rejected the idea in 2016.

EXPERIENCE MORE

↑ Geneva's spectacular Jet d'Eau shooting water into the sky

❸
Jet d'Eau

⊙ E2 **⌂** Off Quai Gustave-Ador 🚌 2, 6, E, G

Located on a jetty on the south bank of Lake Geneva, the Jet d'Eau is one of the world's highest fountains, shooting a plume of water 140 m (460 ft) into the air, at a rate of 500 litres (110 gallons) per second and a speed of 200 km per hour (125 mph). It came into existence almost by accident.

In the late 19th century a purely functional fountain was set up to relieve excess water pressure while a reservoir system was being installed. The fountain was so popular that the authorities decided

to construct a permanent fountain, which became more spectacular as more powerful pumps were installed. Visible from afar and floodlit after dark, the Jet d'Eau is the pride of Geneva and has been adopted as the city's emblem.

❹
Île Rousseau

⊙ C3 **⌂** Pont des Bergues 🚌 6, 8, 9, 25

A walkway jutting out from the centre of the Pont des Bergues leads to a medieval bastion in the Rhône. Now known as the Île Rousseau, it is named after Jean-Jacques Rousseau (1712–78), the writer and philosopher of the Enlightenment who was one of Geneva's most distinguished citizens.

❺
Jardin Anglais

⊙ D3 **⌂** Quai du Général-Guisan 🚌 2, 6, 7, 8, 9, 10, 12

Laid out on the lakeside at the foot of the Old Town, the Jardin Anglais (English Garden) offers an open view of the harbour and quayside buildings. At its entrance is the Horloge Fleurie, a large floral clock. This tribute to Switzerland's clock-making

tradition, created in 1955, has eight intersecting wheels and features 6,500 flowering plants.

Protruding from the lake at a point just north of the Jardin Anglais are two stones brought down by glaciers during the Ice Age. They are known as the Pierres du Niton (Neptune's Stones); the larger of the two was once used as the reference point from which altitude was measured in Switzerland.

❻
Musée Barbier-Mueller

⊙ C4 **⌂** 10 Rue Jean-Calvin 🚌 36 **⊙** 11am–5pm daily **🌐** barbier-mueller.ch

Almost hidden away in a back street near the Cathédrale St-Pierre (p120), this art museum with stunning works from tribal and classical antiquity. It was founded in 1977 to preserve a collection begun in 1907 by the Muellers, a family of art collectors. On display are sculptures, masks and other artifacts from Africa, Asia and Oceania, as well as items from the ancient world.

❼
Place du Bourg-de-Four

⊙ C4 🚌 36

Probably overlying Geneva's Roman forum, the Place du Bourg-de-Four was the city's marketplace in the Middle Ages. Today, lined with 16th-century houses, art galleries and antiques shops, and with busy cafés and restaurants, the square is still the hub of Geneva's Old Town.

The imposing Palais de Justice on the southeastern side of the square was built in 1707–12 and has been used as the city's law courts since 1860.

← The Île Rousseau and Quai des Bergues on the River Rhône

↑ Place du Bourg-de-Four, the bustling heart of Geneva's Old Town

Nearby, on Rue de l'Hôtel-de-Ville on the southwestern side of the square, stands the Hôtel de Ville. Built in the 15th century, it was originally the city hall and now serves as the seat of the cantonal authorities. The Tour Baudet, a tower dating from 1455 and the oldest part of the city hall, once housed the cantonal archives. On the ground floor of the Hôtel de Ville is the Alabama Room, where the Geneva Convention was signed in 1864 and where the International Red Cross was recognized as a humanitarian organization. It was also here that the League of Nations assembled for the first time, in 1920.

 8

Maison Tavel

🔲 C4 🏠 6 Rue du Puits-St-Pierre 🚌 36 🕐 11am–6pm Tue–Sun 🌐 mah-geneve.ch

Built by the Tavel family, this fine limestone building is the oldest house in Geneva. The Gothic façade, with three tiers of windows and a turret at one corner, is decorated with the Tavel coat of arms, as well as with curious stone sculptures of animal and human heads. Although it was rebuilt after the fire of 1334, which destroyed much of Geneva, the earliest record of the house goes back to 1303.

Maison Tavel now houses the Musée du Vieux Genève, a museum devoted to daily life in Geneva from the 14th to the 19th centuries. While the basement is reserved for temporary exhibitions, the rest of the house is filled with exhibits, including coins, ironwork, tiles, wooden doors and other elements of ancient houses. Twelve rooms on the second floor illustrate urban life in the 17th century. In the attic is a huge model of Geneva, made in 1850, before the city's medieval fortifications were demolished. A *son-et-lumière* presentation highlights points of interest on the model.

A separate section is devoted to Général Dufour (1787–1875), the son of a Genevan clockmaker who created a 1:100,000-scale topographic map of the country. As commander of the Federal forces during the civil war of 1847, he managed to defeat the separatists. He was also a founder of the International Red Cross – the neutral organization that assists victims of war and violence – which has its headquarters nearby *(p126)*.

DRINK

Atelier
Perfectly balanced wines and hand-mixed cocktails in an industrial-chic setting.

🔲 E3 🏠 Rue Boissonnas 16 🕐 Sun 🌐 atelierlounge.ch

Qafe Guidoline
A large bar, with a terrace, which serves a wide range of craft beer and cocktails. DJs spin discs here on the weekends.

🔲 C1 🏠 Rue des Pâquis 24 🌐 qafe guidoline.ch

International Red Cross and Red Crescent Museum

F5 **17 Avenue de la Paix** **8, 20, 22, F** **Apr-Oct: 10am-6pm Tue-Sun; Nov-Mar: 10am-5pm Tue-Sun** **redcrossmuseum.ch**

Moving and harrowing yet inspiring hope, this museum within the headquarters of the International Committee of the Red Cross is devoted to documenting human kindness and compassion, as well as the cases of cruelty and suffering that the Red Cross has sought to alleviate since its foundation in 1863. The building, a glass-and-concrete bunker, is designed to allow natural light to illuminate the rooms.

The museum initiates visitors into contemporary humanitarian action with an interactive exhibition designed around three zones, each by an internationally renowned architect: *Defending Human Dignity* (Gringo Cardia, Brazil), *Reconstructing the Family Link* (Diébédo Francis Kéré, Burkina Faso) and *Refusing Fatality* (Shigeru Ban, Japan). Within each zone, visitors "live through" an intense emotional experience, with the aim of raising awareness of an issue.

Historical and background information is then provided. The "On the Spot" area shows the latest news from the field on an interactive globe.

Quartier Des Bains

A4 **2, 19, 35** **quartierdes bains.ch**

This vibrant district in the city's west end centres on an independent and private grouping of 18 galleries and photography studios. Set in a stretch between the Rhône and the Arve, the collective frequently shares themed exhibitions, and are dedicated to promoting the latest in contemporary art, ranging from installations to sculpture. A number of cool bars and restaurants are nearby.

 HIDDEN GEM
Bains des Pâquis

Jutting out into Geneva's lake are the Bains des Pâquis *(www.bains-des-paquis.ch)*, public baths with hot tubs, Turkish baths, good food and enough shoreside towel space for (almost) everyone in the city.

Palais des Nations

F5 **14 Avenue de la Paix** **Apr-Jun: 10am-noon & 2-4pm daily; Jul & Aug: 10am-4pm daily; Sep-Mar: 10am-noon & 2-4pm Mon-Fri** **unog.ch**

Built in 1929–36 the Palais des Nations is the focal point of Geneva's international area. It began as the headquarters of the League of Nations, which has been founded in 1920. In 1946 the League was replaced by the United Nations and in 1966 the Palais des Nations became the official Geneva headquarters of the UN. Some 3,000 people from all over the world now work here.

Parts of the palace are open to the public, with guided tours (bring identification) available in 12 languages. Tours take in the Salle du Conseil (Council Chamber), whose walls and ceiling are decorated with allegorical paintings by the Catalan artist Josep Maria Sert, depicting, among other things, a vision of a future free of conflict. Visitors can also see the Salle des Assemblées (Assembly Hall). With seating for 2,000 people, it is the largest of the United Nations Office's 30-something conference rooms.

← International Red Cross and Red Crescent Museum exhibit

The Parc des Nations, which surrounds the UNO, is planted with trees and decorated with interesting sculptures.

---

12 Parc des Bastions

📍4C 🚊12, 17 🚌3, 5, 20, 25

Created in the 18th century, the Parc des Bastions lies just outside the ramparts on the south side of the city. Along the eastern edge of the park is the Mur des Réformateurs (Reformation Wall), which was erected in 1909 to mark the 400th anniversary of the birth of Jean Calvin and the 350th anniversary of the foundation of Geneva's Academy, the city's famous Protestant school. The monument takes the form of a wall 100 m (330 ft) long on which stand 5-m- (16-ft-) tall statues of four of the leaders of the Reformation in Geneva: Guillaume Farel, Jean Calvin, Théodore de Bèze and John Knox. Flanking the monument are memorials to Martin Luther and Ulrich Zwingli.

13

Bodmer Foundation

📍5F 🏠Route Martin Bodmer 19-21, Cologny 🚌A 🕐2-6pm Tue-Sun 🌐fondationbodmer.ch

Just north of the city centre is a large villa with a unique mission: to be a museum of the human mind. The 150,000 items include ancient Egyptian papyrus books of the dead and pages bearing the

handwritten scribblings of William Shakespeare. Also on view are a Gutenberg Bible and Gottfried Liebnitz's copy of Sir Isaac Newton's *Principia Mathematica*, complete with his cramped margin notes.

14

CERN

📍F5 🏠Esplanade des Particules 1, Meyrin 🚊18 🕐8am-6pm Mon-Sat 🌐home.cern

The European Organization for Nuclear Research, better known by its French acroynm, CERN, since 1954 has been trying to explore all laws and theories related to particles, which make up the entire universe. In 2010 it first opened its doors to visitors.

The research centre's various exhibitions look at the origins of the universe. The highlight is the Big Bang show, a multimedia extravaganza that takes place every hour in a futuristic globe known as the Universe of Particles. Other exhibits include a scale model of CERN's Large Hadron Collider (LHC), the world's largest particle accelerator, which includes real pieces of equipment. This model explores the technical challenges and ingenious engineering solutions that went into the LHC's construction.

EAT

Café-Restaurant de l'Hôtel de Ville
Exceptional traditional Genevois fare.

📍C4 🏠Grand-Rue 39 🌐hdvglozu.ch

Ⓢ Ⓢ Ⓢ

Fiskebar
Expect fabulous, seasonal seafood here.

📍C2 🏠Quai de Mont Blanc 11 🌐geneva-fiskebar.com

Ⓢ Ⓢ Ⓢ

15

MEG (Ethnographic Museum of Geneva)

📍A5 🏠Blvd Carl-Vogt 65 🚌2, 19 🕐11am-6pm Tue-Sun 🌐ville-ge.ch/meg

Opened in 2014, MEG has already won awards, both for its innovative architecture and for its theme of human diversity – amply exhibited by costumes, folk music and workshops.

→ The sleek modern building of the MEG (Ethnographic Museum of Geneva)

A SHORT WALK
OLD TOWN

Distance 1.5 km (1 mile) **Nearest bus stop**
Place de Neuve **Time** 25 minutes

Set on elevated ground on the south bank of
the Rhône, the Old Town (Vieille Ville) clusters
around the cathedral and Place du Bourg-de-
Four. This atmospheric district, whose main
thoroughfare is the pedestrianized Grand-Rue,
has narrow cobbled streets lined with historic
limestone houses. While the southern limit of
the Old Town is marked by the Promenade des
Bastions, laid out along the course of the old
city walls, its northern side slopes down to the
quay, which is lined with wide boulevards and
the attractive Jardin Anglais.

Did You Know?

Place du Bourg-de-
Four is the oldest
square in Geneva,
dating back to
Roman times.

Maison Rousseau,
the birthplace of the
18th-century writer
and philosopher
Jean-Jacques
Rousseau, is at
Grand-Rue 40.

START

RU

GRAND-RUE

RUE DES GRANGES

FINISH

RAMPE DE LA TREILLE

The Hôtel de Ville
is where the first
Geneva Convention
was signed in 1864.

PR

Outdoor cafés
in Place du Bourg-
de-Four in Geneva ↓

Locator Map
For more detail see p112

↑ The ornate interior of Geneva's
  majestic Cathédrale St-Pierre

Maison Tavel (p125), *the oldest
house in the city, was built in 1334.
It is now a museum documenting
daily life in Geneva through the ages.*

Cathédrale St-Pierre (p120),
*completed in the 13th century,
stands on the site of several earlier
buildings, including a bishop's
palace, whose mosaic floor survives.*

CALVIN

UITS-ST-PIERRE

RUE DE L'HÔTEL DE VILLE

RUE DE LA FONTAINE

RUE VERDAINE

REILLE

PLACE DU BOURG-
DE-FOUR

RUE DES CHAUDRONNIERS

RUE É DUMONT

*The central square of
Place du Bourg-de-Four
(p124) was used as a
marketplace in the Middle
Ages. It is still lined with
old inns, as well as modern
cafés and restaurants.*

| 0 metres | 60 |
| 0 yards | 60 |

N
↑

WESTERN SWITZERLAND

Bordered by France, French-speaking western Switzerland is known as Suisse Romande, or Romandie. The region was settled by Gallic Celts, around 450 BC, and annexed by the Christianized Burgundians in the 5th century AD. The Burgudians' language, customs and architecture were swiftly adoped throughout the region, and the French-Swiss cultural identity remains strong to this day. Although western Switzerland was taken over by the German Savoy in the 1100s, the French connection was such that the borderlands region of Vaud was placed under the protection of the governing body in Paris following the French Revolution. It was only in 1806 that Vaud become a canton of Switzerland, with Lausanne as its capital. With relatively easy countryside to navigate, western Switzerland has attracted those escaping European conflict. During the Protestant Reformation, refugees flooded Jura, setting in motion the country's now world-famous watchmaking industry. During the two World Wars, the region again became a safe harbour for refugees who made it across Kilometre Zero at the France-Swiss border. Today these same sunny hillsides serve as a gateway into this winemaking region's more mountainous landscapes.

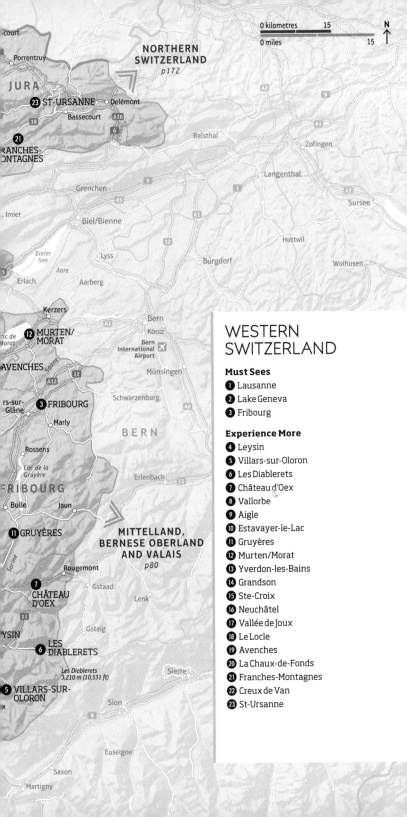

NORTHERN
SWITZERLAND
p172

WESTERN SWITZERLAND

Must Sees

1. Lausanne
2. Lake Geneva
3. Fribourg

Experience More

4. Leysin
5. Villars-sur-Oloron
6. Les Diablerets
7. Château d'Oex
8. Vallorbe
9. Aigle
10. Estavayer-le-Lac
11. Gruyères
12. Murten/Morat
13. Yverdon-les-Bains
14. Grandson
15. Ste-Croix
16. Neuchâtel
17. Vallée de Joux
18. Le Locle
19. Avenches
20. La Chaux-de-Fonds
21. Franches-Montagnes
22. Creux de Van
23. St-Ursanne

MITTELLAND,
BERNESE OBERLAND
AND VALAIS
p80

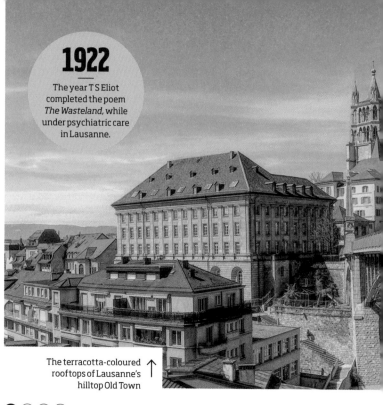

1922

The year T S Eliot completed the poem *The Wasteland*, while under psychiatric care in Lausanne.

The terracotta-coloured rooftops of Lausanne's hilltop Old Town ↑

1 🍴 🍷 🛍️

LAUSANNE

🅰 B4 🏛 Vaud 🚉 🚆 9 Place de la Gare; www.lausanne-tourisme.ch

Nestled within the outstandingly beautiful the north shore of Lake Geneva, Lausanne is one of Switzerland's finest cities. A Roman lakeshore settlement in the 1st century, its inhabitants later moved to higher ground. This area is now the city's Old Town. Lausanne became a bishopric in the late 6th century, and its Fondation Académie was founded here in 1537. Today the city remains a centre of the cultural and economic life of French-speaking Switzerland. Its importance is evident – it is the location of the Federal Supreme Court and the International Olympic Committee.

← The figure of Justice crowning the 16th-century Fontaine de la Justice

① ⚒

Place de la Palud

Ⓜ Riponne M. Béjart
🚌 1, 2, 7, 8

Lausanne's 17th-century town hall, a fine arcaded building, dominates the south side of this square. On 10 April 1915, the founder of the modern Olympics, Pierre de Coubertin, ratified the establishment of the International Olympic Committee here and moved the headquarters to the city.

At the centre of the square is the 16th-century Fontaine de la Justice, with a figure of Justice. The covered wooden stairs beyond, known as the Escaliers du Marché, lead to Rue Viret, from where further steps lead up to the cathedral.

The square is a popular meeting area. A street market takes place here twice a week on Wednesday and Saturday, and once a month the square is filled with a crafts fair.

②

Tour Bel-Air and Salle Métropole

📍 1 Place Bel-Air
Ⓜ Lausanne-Flon
🚌 1, 2, 3, 4, 6, 7, 8, 9, 16, 17
📞 021 345 00 29

Set on a steep slope, at the foot of the Old Town, the Tour Bel-Air was Switzerland's first high-rise structure. It contains offices, residential apartments and the Salle Métropole theatre. Completed in 1931, the building was initially considered "an insult to good sense and taste", but quickly became a beloved landmark. Inspired by the cityscape of New York, the building gives the town's skyline.

The theatre has become one of the city's cultural hubs and has hosted some of the best in the performing arts. In its heyday, audiences flocked here to see dancer Josephine Baker and trumpeter Louis Armstrong. These days the Métropole's programme still features highly acclaimed talents, among them the Ukrainian Classical Ballet and the musician Alain Chamfort. The Lausanne Symphony Orchestra also makes its home here.

> 🏞 GREAT VIEW
> ### Across the Rooftops
>
> Built on a hill, the lower and higher parts of the city are connected by a series of steps. Take the market stairs up to the cathedral, then climb all the way into the belfry, which is the highest point in the city, to soak up stunning views across the roofs of old Lausanne to the green steeple of St-François church, the lake and the mountains beyond.

③
Place St-François

M Lausanne-Flon ▥ 1, 2, 4, 6, 7, 8, 9, 12, 13, 16, 17

At the centre of this square stands the Église St-François, built in the 13th and 14th centuries as the church of a Franciscan monastery that was later dissolved during the Reformation. The streets leading off Place St-François are among the city's smartest. Rue du Bourg, which is lined with old houses, contains swanky jewellers' shops and bijou boutiques, as well as bars and jazz clubs.

④
Église St-Laurent

⌂ Rue St-Laurent
M Riponne M. Béjart ▥ 1, 2, 3, 4, 6, 7, 8, 9, 16, 17 **W** saint laurenteglise.eerv.ch

Amid the well-preserved houses of the Old Town stands the Protestant Église St-Laurent. Completed in 1719, on the

INSIDER TIP
Jazz Nights

You can catch the latest young talents from Lausanne's renowned jazz school performing at various venues across the city. Chorus, an atmospheric cellar near the city centre *(www. chorus.ch),* is one of our favourites. Some gigs are free.

ruins of a 10th-century church, its façade was added in the latter half of the century. Free choral concerts, with an aperitif, are offered round the year.

⑤
Musée Historique

⌂ 4 Place de la Cathédrale
M Bessières ▥ 22, 60
🕑 11am–6pm daily
W lausanne.ch/vie-pratique/culture/musees/mhl

Lausanne's museum of history fills the restored rooms of the former bishop's palace, which

The streets of the popular Flon district pulsing with energy after dark ↑

dates from the 11th century. The museum's collections provide a detailed account of the city's history from its inhabitation by Celtic tribes to the present day. Don't miss the fascinating model of Lausanne as it was in 1638.

⑥
Palais de Rumine

⌂ 6 Place de la Riponne
M Riponne M. Béjart ▥ 1, 2, 7, 8 **🕑** 10am–5pm Tue–Sun
W palaisderumine.ch

Built in 1896–1906, the Neo-Renaissance Palais de Rumine once housed the University of Lausanne. It now contains several museums covering archaeology and history, fine art, geology, zoology and numismatics (the study of currency) – all with the same hours and a shared admission fee. Of particular

←

The steps of the Église St-Laurent, a popular place to meet on a sunny day interest is the Musée Cantonal des Beaux-Arts, on the ground floor, which has a fine collection of Swiss paintings from the 18th to the 20th centuries. The museum of history and archaeology, on the sixth floor, displays artifacts unearthed in local excavations. The exhibits range from the Bronze Age to the medieval period, and one of the finest is a gold bust of Marcus Aurelius, discovered at Avenches in 1939.

Château St-Maire

🏠 Place du Château
Ⓜ Riponne M. Béjart
🚌 7, 22, 60

Although it's closed to visitors, you should still seek out this former bishop's palace. The massive edifice was built in 1397–1427 for the bishops of Lausanne, who ruled the city. When they were overthrown by Bernese forces, the château became the residence of new overlords, the bailiffs of Bern. The fight for the independence of Lausanne and the canton of Vaud was led by the notary turned soldier Jean Davel, who was beheaded in 1723 on the orders of the Bernese authorities after he led an abortive separatist movement. A monument to his memory stands in front of the château. The building is now the seat of the cantonal authorities of Vaud.

Flon

Ⓜ Lausanne-Flon 🚌 18

Once the city's main industrial district, Flon was built on a river of the same name that was filled over in the 19th century. If you look down, you can still see water running in a narrow channel under the pavement. These days the area has thrown off its grubby past to become an entertainment district, its former warehouses converted into shops, bars, restaurants, galleries, a cinema complex and the buzzing MAD nightclub. The main pedestrian square hosts a jungle-themed pop-up bar in summer and an ice rink in winter.

SHOP

Blondel
An institution since 1850, Blondel's sumptuous window displays and the delectable whiff of chocolate wafting out the door make it impossible to pass by this shop without going in.

🏠 Rue de Bourg 5
🌐 blondel.ch

Cocooning
Pick up soaps, creams and other cosmetics here. They are hand-made using natural ingredients – you can pick up a body butter made with the Swiss national flower – edelweiss – for instance.

🏠 Rue Grand-Saint-Jean 16 🌐 cocooning.ch

Collection de l'Art Brut

🏛 11 Avenue des Bergières
🚌 2, 21 🕐 Jul & Aug: 11am–6pm daily; Sep–Jun: 11am–6pm Tue–Sun; free adm 1st Sat of the month
🌐 artbrut.ch

Art Brut ("Raw Art") is the name that the French painter Jean Dubuffet (1901–85) gave to art created by people living on the fringe of society, such as criminals, patients at psychiatric hospitals or institutions, and spiritualist mediums, who had no artistic training. The ideas behind their art were free from established cultural influences and the history of a fine arts tradition. In 1945 Dubuffet began to amass a private collection, which he presented to the city in 1971. The Collection de l'Art Brut opened in 1976.

The exhibits are laid out over four floors in converted stables at the 18th-century Château de Beaulieu, northwest of the city centre. These works have a striking force and spontaneity. Alongside each exhibit is a short biography of the artist, providing insights into the circumstances in which these works were created.

← *Run Up* by Nag Arnoldi at the Olympic Museum, overlooking Lake Geneva

Olympic Museum

🏛 1 Quai d'Ouchy Ⓜ Jordils
🚌 24 🕐 9am–6pm Tue–Sun
🌐 olympic.org/museum

Set in peaceful parkland planted with Mediterranean trees and shrubs, the well-presented Olympic Museum illustrates the fascinating history of the Olympic movement. Everything from the athletes of Ancient Greece to the Olympic Games of today is explored via interactive stations, photographs, videos, archive film footage and multimedia presentations. With its excellent facilities for school groups, the museum draws over 200,000 visitors a year. There are many displays specifically geared towards younger visitors, such as "All Different, All Winners" where games investigate themes such as fair play and diversity.

Fondation de l'Hermitage

🏛 2 Route du Signal 🚌 16
🕐 10am–6pm Tue–Sun
(to 9pm Thu) 🌐 fondation-hermitage.ch

The imposing Neo-Gothic villa set in magnificent grounds north of Lausanne was built in 1842–50 by Charles-Juste Bugnion, a wealthy banker, and donated to the city by his descendants. Now known as the Fondation de l'Hermitage, it is a gallery with an impressive collection of Impressionist and Post-Impressionist paintings, as well as the works of Vaudois artists from the 20th century. Every year the Fondation also stages two or three large-scale temporary exhibitions.

The Parc de l'Hermitage, the extensive grounds in which the villa is set, is landscaped with exotic trees. Towards its northern extremity is the Signal de Sauvabelin, a hill which rises to a height of 647 m (2,120 ft) and offers views of Lake Geneva and the Alps. Beyond the hill are woodland and the Lac de Sauvabelin, where there is a reserve for ibexes, marmots and other alpine animals.

_____

⑫
Parc Mon-Repos

🏠 Avenue Mon-Repos
Ⓜ Ours 🚌 13

This landscaped park is the most elegant of all the city's gardens. At its centre is a Neo-Classical villa, once inhabited by the 18th-century French writer Voltaire. The villa was later home to the Olympics revivalist Baron Pierre de Coubertin (1863–1937), who believed that sport plays an essential role in the development of citizens and nations. In 1894, he established the International Olympic Committee (IOC), and two years later the first modern Olympic Games were held in Athens. Until the 1970s this was also the IOC's headquarters. At the north end of the park stands Switzerland's supreme court buildings.

💬 INSIDER TIP
Lakeside Pop-ups

All throughout the summer, lively pop-up bars and restaurants take over the lakeshore. Join the locals by taking a dip in the lake followed by an apéro and some tasty nibbles at Jetée de la Compagnie *(www.jeteedelacompagnie.ch)*.

⑬ 🍴 🍽 🛍
Ouchy

🏠 On Lake Geneva, 2 km (1 mile) S of central Lausanne Ⓜ Ouchy Olympiade

Once a fishing village, Ouchy is now a popular lakeside suburb of Lausanne. It has a beautiful setting with views of the surrounding mountains, and a tree-lined promenade. Cruises on the lake depart from here.

A tower is all that remains of the 12th-century castle that once defended the harbour. It forms part of the Neo-Gothic Château d'Ouchy, which was built in the 1890s. The château is now a hotel and restaurant. A short walk along the lakeshore will take you to the Hôtel d'Angleterre. This is the house where Lord Byron stayed during his visit to Lausanne and where he wrote *The Prisoner of Chillon*, a poem which details the imprisonment of a Genevois monk, François Bonivard.

_____

⑭ 🚲 Ⓜ
Musée Romain

🏠 24 Chemin du-Bois-de-Vaux 🚌 25 🕐 Jul & Aug: 11am–6pm daily; Sep–Jun: 11am–6pm Tue–Sun
🌐 museeromain.ch

About ten minutes' walk west of Ouchy are the remains of Lousonna and Vidy, two Roman towns that flourished from 15 BC to the 4th century AD. Finds uncovered during an excavation here, including glassware and fine mosaics, are on show in the Musée Romain nearby.

> Beyond the hill are woodland and the Lac de Sauvabelin, where there is a reserve for ibexes, marmots and other alpine animals.

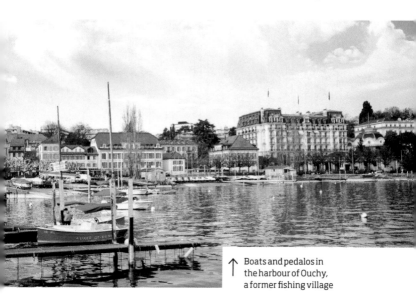

↑ Boats and pedalos in the harbour of Ouchy, a former fishing village

⑮ ⌨

CATHÉDRALE
NOTRE-DAME

🏛 1 Place de la Cathédrale 🚇 Riponne M. Béjart 🚌 16
🕐 Church: 9am–5:30pm daily (to 7pm Apr–Sep); tower: hours vary, check website 🌐 cathedrale-lausanne.ch

At the centre of Lausanne towers the magnificent Cathédrale Notre-Dame. Begun in the mid-12th century and completed in the 13th, it is the finest Gothic building in Switzerland.

The cathedral is built on the site of a Roman camp and overlies the foundations of Carolingian and Romanesque basilicas. With a central nave flanked by aisles, an ambulatory and a transept over which rises a tower and an apse, the cathedral's design and decoration show the influence of the French Gothic style. The southern arm of the transept is lit by a 13th-century rose window with stained glass depicting the seasons, the elements and signs of the Zodiac. Consecrated by Pope Gregory X in 1275, Notre-Dame has been a Protestant cathedral since the Reformation. The top of the southwest tower provides a spectacular view of the city and Lake Geneva.

Illustration of Lausanne's majestic Gothic Cathédrale Notre-Dame ↓

The north tower contains the Chapelle St-Maurice.

The west entrance is known as the Montfalcon Portal.

The tower was completed in the 19th century.

1 One of Switzerland's most visited sights, the Cathédrale Notre-Dame attracts over 400,000 visitors every year.

2 The cathedral has multiple decorative stained-glass windows, such as this one.

3 An ornate crucifix, standing in the cathedral's central nave. Notre-Dame is a working cathedral with regular services.

Rose window

Carved decorative details, including human figures, fill the vaulting.

The vestibule is decorated with late-Gothic murals dating from the early 16th century.

This Bernese pulpit is topped by a canopy with intricate wooden tracery from 1666.

INNOVATIVE ORGAN

The cathedral's striking organ was the first in Europe to be built by an American, although it was made to Italian Giorgetto Giugiaro's design, and the first to feature four styles: Romantic, Classical French, Symphonic French and Baroque. Most impressive is that it can be played remotely, by any other organist playing an organ in another part of the world, thanks to a cutting-edge interface system.

2

LAKE GENEVA

⬚ A5–B5   ⬚ Geneva and Vaud   🛈 Lausanne, 60 Avenue d'Ouchy   ⬚ lake-geneva-region.ch

Lying in an arc bordered by the Jura mountains to the west, the French Alps to the south and the Mittelland to the northeast, Lake Geneva is the largest lake in the Alps. While most of the lake's southern shore is French territory, the greater part of the lake lies within Switzerland. With the mountains reflected in its still blue waters, it is one of Switzerland's most spellbinding sights. Pretty towns dot the shores and many of these serve as departure points for boat trips – an ideal way to experience the lake's serenity. Another way to take in the sights is to walk the shore path, a 42-km- (26-mile-) long trail that weaves its way around the water.

① 🎨 🍷

Vevey

⬚ Vaud   🚆🚌   🛈 5 Rue du Théâtre, Montreux   ⬚ montreuxriviera.com

With Montreux, Vevey is one of the two best-known holiday resorts of the Swiss Riviera – the stretch of land on the shore of Lake Geneva between Lausanne and Villeneuve. The region's climate and culture attracted English Romantics Lord Byron and Mary Shelley in the 19th century, and later Charlie Chaplin, who spent the last 25 years of his life in Vevey.

Known in Roman times as Viviscus, Vevey was once Lake Geneva's main port. By the 19th century it was the first industrial town in the Vaud canton. It was here, in 1867, that Henri Nestlé set up the powdered milk factory that revolutionized baby foods. Nestlé still has its international headquarters in Vevey.

One of the most attractive parts of Vevey is its Grande Place (also known as Place du Marché). On Tuesday and Saturday mornings this square is filled with a market, and in summer regional growers offer wine tastings. A folk arts market is also held here on Saturday mornings in July and August.

Chaplin's World, a museum dedicated to the comedian's life and work, is in Le Manoir-de-Ban, Chaplin's former home. It features personal items, an interactive studio and re-created film sets.

East of the train station is the **Musée Jenisch**, housing paintings and sculptures by Switzerland's prominent 19th and 20th-century artists, as well as the vast Fondation Oskar Kokoschka, which

→
A statue of Charlie Chaplin in Vevey

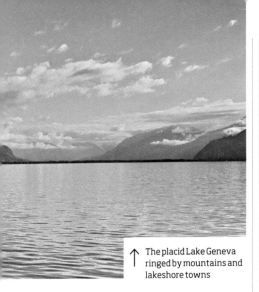

↑ The placid Lake Geneva ringed by mountains and lakeshore towns

Did You Know?

The bottled water brand Evian is sourced from Évian-les-Bains, on Lake Geneva.

contains 800 paintings by the Austrian artist. Also here is Europe's largest collection of lithographs by Rembrandt.

Chaplin's World

⊛ ⊚ 🏠 2 Route de Fenil, Le Manoir-de-Ban ⏰ Jan–mid-Apr & Nov–Dec: 10am–5pm daily; mid-Apr–Jun, Sep & Oct: 10am–6pm daily, Jul & Aug: 10am–7pm daily 🌐 chaplinsworld.com

Musée Jenisch

⊛ 🏠 2 Avenue de la Gare ⏰ 11am–6pm Tue–Sun (to 8pm Thu) 🌐 musee jenisch.ch

EAT

Denis Martin

This Michelin-starred restaurant serves inventive fare. Opt for the tasting menu.

🏠 Rue du Château 2, Vevey 🌐 denismartin.ch

$$$

Le Brasserie J5

Locally sourced ingredients feature on the French menu here. Order the beef tartare.

🏠 Avenue de Casino 32, Montreux 🌐 brasseriej5.ch

$$$

Oasis

A cheap and cheerful spot in Villeneuve. Try the local fish.

🏠 Rue de Quai 6, Villeneuven 🌐 restuarantoasis.ch

$$$

Crémières
Jongny
Nyon 58 km (36 miles)
Chardonne
Saint-Légier-La Chiésaz
Rivaz
St-Saphorin
Corseaux
Corsier
Blonay
Vevey ①
Brent
La Tour-de-Peilz
Chailly
Lake Geneva (Lac Léman)
Clarens
Chernex
Sonzier
Montreux ③
Gilon
Territet
Veytaux
Château de Chillon ⑤

metres 1

N ↑

143

② St-Saphorin

Vaud

Overlooked by vineyards, this picturesque winemaking village's cobbled streets have little changed over the centuries. Its landmark church was founded around AD 590 and is dedicated to Symphorian of Autun, an early Christian martyr for whom the village is now named. The current Gothic church, featuring a bell tower, dates from the 1520s, but the ruins of a Roman villa can still be seen in the church grounds.

Today, St-Saphorin is best known for its wine, producing everything from dry, white chasselas to fruity, red pinot noirs. Many footpaths wind their way from the village to the vineyards set above it.

③ Montreux

Vaud **5 Rue du Théâtre; www.montreux riviera.com**

The jewel of the Swiss Riviera, Montreux is famous for its annual jazz festival. The town began to develop as an international tourist resort in around 1815, and its golden age lasted until the outbreak of World War I in 1914.

Montreux has several belle époque hotels. The most well known of them is the Montreux Palace on Grand Rue, located west of the town centre. Opposite this hotel is the Centre des Congrès, housing the Auditorium Stravinsky, a concert hall built in 1990 and dedicated to Igor Stravinsky (1882–1971), who composed *The Rite of Spring* while in Montreux. Montreux's other famous musical connection is to Freddie Mercury, vocalist in the band Queen, who made the town his second home and famously proclaimed that "if you want peace of mind, come to Montreux". On the lakeshore, you'll see a bronze statue of the singer.

④ Nyon

Vaud **Avenue Viollier 8** **lacote-tourisme.ch**

Surrounded by vineyards, the small town of Nyon is

200,000

The average number of people who attend the annual Montreux Jazz Festival.

best known today as the home of European football's governing body, UEFA. The town was founded by the Romans as the settlement of Noviodunum around AD 30, and three columns from the original Roman forum, found during construction work in the 1950s, still stand on the leafy Esplanade des Marronniers.

A short walk away is the town's defining feature, its Romanesque castle. First built in the 12th century, and greatly extended between 1574 and 1583, the **Château de Nyon** is now home to a museum displaying exquisite porcelain, produced in the town between 1781 and 1813, as well as contemporary ceramics. The collection also

← Narrow street lined with boutiques and alfresco café tables in Nyon

includes works by local artists and the extensive Louis and August Kunz collection, two pioneers of early photography. The pedestrian streets behind the castle are packed with rows of elegant shops, cafés and restaurants.

The **Lake Geneva Museum** in the lower town tells the story of the lake's formation, its wildlife and the lives of those who live on its shores.

Château de Nyon
⊛ ⓘ 🅰 Place du Château
🅞 Apr-Oct: 10am-5pm Tue-Sun; Nov-Mar: 2-5pm Tue-Sun 🆆 chateaude nyon.ch

Lake Geneva Museum
⊛ ⓘ 🅰 Quai Louis-Bonnard 8 🅞 Apr-Oct: 10am-5pm Tue-Sun; Nov-Mar: 2-5pm Tue-Sun 🆆 museeduleman.ch

DRINK

Lavaux Vinorama, Rivaz
Sample some of Switzerland's finest wines, including the locally grown and subtly fruity Chasselas blanc, at this terraced vineyard and tasting room in Rivaz.

🅰 Route du Lac 2, Rivaz 🆆 lavaux-vinorama.ch

───

Le Vins de Pierre et Michel Anex
Take a two-hour guided walk through the Ollon vineyards of Pierre and Michel Anex, tasting a range of their splendid white, rosé and red wines along the way. Tours by appointment only.

🅰 Chemin de la Monnaie 2, Ollon 🆆 anexvins.ch

───

Domaine des Faverges
Soak up the views of Lake Geneva, framed by terraced vines, at this St-Saphorin winery, before taking a tour of the domain's 19th-century stately home, the Grande Maison. By appointment only.

🅰 Route de Vevey 11, St-Saphorin 🆆 vignobles deletat.ch

← Montreux, an idyllic waterside town on Lake Geneva

⑤ ⌖ 🖈 💻 🛍

CHÂTEAU DE CHILLON

🅰B3 🏠21 Ave de Chillon, Veytaux, Vaud 🚆Veytaux-Chillon 🚌From Montreux 🕐Jan-Mar: 10am-5pm Tue-Sun (Apr-Dec: to 6pm daily) 🗓1 Jan and 25 Dec 🌐chillon.ch

This enchanting medieval castle, set on a rocky spur on the eastern shore of Lake Geneva, is one of Switzerland's most evocative sights and attracts hordes of visitors each year.

Built for the Dukes of Savoy, the castle's origins probably go back to the 11th century; however, its present appearance dates from the 13th century. In 1536, the castle was captured by the Bernese, and from then until 1798 it was the seat of the region's Bernese bailiffs. Following the Vaudois Revolution of 1798, the castle became national property and has belonged ever since to the canton of Vaud. Throughout its history the castle was the centre of court life, and it was also used as a prison. Its most famous captive was François Bonivard, imprisoned there from 1530 to 1536. Today, the castle's many guided tours (by reservation only) are a great way to explore its history.

IMPRISONMENT OF FRANÇOIS BONIVARD

Born in 1493, François Bonivard was the prior of St Victor, a monastery just outside Geneva. Following his opposition to the Duke of Savoy's infringements against the liberties of the city of Geneva, he was held prisoner at Chillon for six long years. Bonivard was finally freed in 1536, when the Bernese attacked and gained control of the castle. He was later immortalized by Lord Byron in the long narrative poem *The Prisoner of Chillon*, which he wrote in Ouchy while travelling with fellow authors Percy Bysshe and Mary Shelley, in 1816.

Two bedchambers are located here.

Aula Nova, a former banqueting hall, now contains a museum.

The spectacular Castellan's Hall has a wooden ceiling resting on columns that support arches. The walls are richly decorated with paintings.

The covered bridge was originally a drawbridge.

Illustration of the Château de Chillon, a popular historical sight ↑

Did You Know?

The castle's damp, dark dungeons are cut into the bedrock of the island itself.

Heraldic Hall

The Grand Ducal Hall has chequered walls and a 15th-century wooden ceiling.

The Ducal Chamber, also known as the Camera Domini, has a wooden beamed ceiling and contains Gothic furniture.

The chapel, dedicated to St George, is in the early Gothic style, with a rib-vaulted ceiling. The walls and ceiling are covered with frescoes.

The vaulted underground chambers were once used as a prison.

Bergfrieg, the tower that was the castle's final defence, is one of its oldest elements.

1 Built on a rocky island, the castle was also defended by thick walls and three semicircular turrets.

2 Soft light pours out upon one of the castle's four cobblestoned courtyards.

3 This bedroom, named the Bernese Chamber, features wall paintings and period-appropriate furnishings.

Did You Know?

The Pont de Berne, built in 1653, is the city's last remaining covered wooden bridge.

The River Sarine flowing under the Ponte de Berne at Fribourg ↑

❸
FRIBOURG

🅐 B4 🚉 Fribourg 🚌 🛈 1 Place Jean-Tinguely; www.
fribourgtourism.ch

**With steep cobbled streets, immaculately preserved
Gothic houses and numerous fountains, Fribourg
(known as Freiburg in German) is one of the most
attractive towns in Switzerland.**

Set on a rocky peninsula within a bend of the River Sarine (the
Saane in German), Fribourg was founded in 1157 by Berthold IV
of Zähringen, and joined the Swiss Confederation in 1481.
Despite the Reformation, Fribourg remained Catholic, and
a Catholic university was founded here in 1889. The town's
historic core has plenty to interest visitors. Just north of the
Gothic Cathédrale St-Nicolas is the Éspace Jean Tinguely–Niki
de Saint-Phalle, a vast gallery with works by Fribourg-born Jean
Tinguely and his wife, Niki de Saint-Phalle. Next to it, set in a
restored granary, is the Gutenberg Museum, showcasing the
history of printing. South of the cathedral is the short Rue d'Or,
worth a quick visit for its row of Gothic houses. The peninsula
is connected to the river's south bank by the Pont de
Berne, which leads to the Place des Forgerons,
with a pretty Renaissance fountain
and vestiges of the old
town fortifications.

↑ The city's 1899 funicular,
one of the last in Europe
to run on waste water

The Musée d'Art
et d'Histoire

The Franciscan Église
des Cordeliers, with
art and carvings
dating from the
13th century onwards

Éspace Jean
Tinguely–Niki
de Saint-Phalle

Gutenberg
Museum

Basilique
Notre-
Dame

Tilleul de Morat,
the descendant
of a linden tree
planted to mark
a 1476 victory
over Charles
the Bold at
Murten (Morat)

Cathédrale
St-Nicolas,
dating from
1283–1490

RUE DE MORAT

PLACE
NOTRE-
DAME

RUE DU PONT–MURE

RUE DES ÉPOUSES

GRAND-RUE

RUE DU PONT-SUSPENDU

RUE DES CHANOINES

The elegant
Hôtel de Ville
(1522), with a
fountain depict-
ing St George
and the dragon

The Baroque Maison de
Ville, designed by Hans
Fasel and built in 1730–31

↑ Illustration
showing Fribourg's
historic core

EXPERIENCE MORE

4

Leysin

🅰B5 🏔Vaud �︎🚌 ℹPlace Large; www.leysin.ch

Lying at an altitude of 1,260 m (4,135 ft), Leysin enjoys an unusually dry and sunny climate. Once a centre for the treatment of tuberculosis, the village is now a ski resort. Cable cars carry visitors up to the Tour de Mayen (2,326 m/ 7,631 ft) and to Berneuse (2,037 m/6,683 ft).

5

Villars-sur-Oloron

🅰B5 🏔Vaud 🚂🚌144

Popular with families, the ski resort of Villars-sur-Ollon sits on a sunny plateau, from where a cogwheel train transports visitors to Col-de-Bretaye at 1,800 m (6,000 ft).

Up here, golfers can enjoy an 18-hole course with a view of Mont Blanc; come winter the whole area is taken over by skiers. There are gentle slopes, making it a decent resort for beginners, while the chairlift links to nearby Gryon and Les Diablerets mean

more experienced skiers have plenty of challenging runs to keep them entertained.

6

Les Diablerets

🅰B5 🏔Vaud and Valais 🚂🚌 ℹRue de la Gare; www.diablerets.ch

Set among meadows in the Ormonts valley, the ski resort of Les Diablerets offers many attractions including the Alpine Coaster, the world's highest bobsleigh on rails, and the Monster Snowpark. There's also the narrow Peak Walk – the world's first suspension bridge to link two mountain

↑ The revolving panoramic restaurant at the top of Berneuse, above Leysin

peaks, the Scex Rouge and Glacier 3000. At 2,987 m (9,800 ft), it is also the second-highest suspension bridge in the world after Titlis Cliff Walk in Obwalden.

7

Château d'Oex

🅰B5 🏔Vaud 🚂🚌175 ℹPlace du Village 6; www.chateau-doex.ch

Pretty Château d'Oex is immediately identifiable from

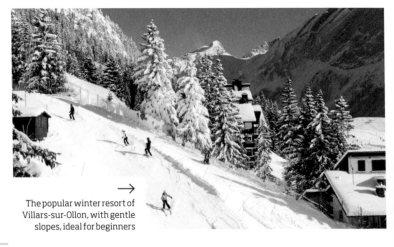

→ The popular winter resort of Villars-sur-Ollon, with gentle slopes, ideal for beginners its 15th-century church, which sits on a hill in the centre of the village. An attractive, sleepy place, the village is known for its special microclimate which is favourable to hot-air ballooning. Flights are available all year, and it's especially worth visiting in late January when it hosts the nine-day International Balloon Festival.

---

⑧ Vallorbe

Ⓐ A4 Ⓒ Fribourg �俄🚌 ℹ 11 Rue des Grandes-Forges; www.vallorbe-tourisme.ch

This small industrial town lies near the Franco-Swiss border. From the Middle Ages until recently, the town was an iron-smelting centre. It was also at Vallorbe that the tunnel under the Jura was built, thus creating the Paris–Istanbul rail route.

The history of both the Swiss iron and railway industries is reflected in the **Musée du Fer et du Chemin de Fer** (Iron and Railway Museum), which sits on the bank of the River Orbe.

About 3 km (2 miles) southwest of Vallorbe are the **Grottes de Vallorbe**. These are caves with spectacular stalactites and stalagmites. The caves form a tunnel over the Orbe's passage, which surges through a gorge.

Musée du Fer et du Chemin de Fer

⊛ ⊛ Ⓐ 11 Rue des Grandes-Forges Ⓒ Apr–Oct: 10am–6pm Tue–Sun; Nov–Mar: 1–5pm Tue–Fri, 10am–5pm Sat & Sun 🅦 museedufer.ch

Grottes de Vallorbe

⊛ Ⓒ Mar & Nov: 1:30–4pm daily; Apr & May: 9:30am–4:30pm daily; Jun–Aug: 9:30am–5:30pm daily; Sep & Oct: 9:30am–4:30pm daily 🚫 Dec 🅦 grottesde vallorbe.ch

---

⑨ Aigle

Ⓐ B5 Ⓒ Vaud 🚉🚌 ℹ 5 Rue Colomb; www.aigle-tourisme.ch

Aigle is the capital of the Chablais, a winegrowing region that lies southeast of Lake Geneva and produces some of Switzerland's best wines. Set among vineyards covering the foothills of the Alpes Vaudoises, the town is dominated by the turreted Château d'Aigle. Built in the 12th century by the Savoyards, it was severely damaged in the 15th century and later rebuilt as the residence of the region's bailiffs. The castle now houses the **Musée de la Vigne et du Vin**, whose exhibits illustrate the age-old methods of vine cultivation and winemaking. Opposite this museum is the **Musée International de l'Etiquette**, which documents the history of wine labels.

Musée de la Vigne et du Vin and Musée International de l'Étiquette

⊛ Ⓐ Château d'Aigle, 1 Place du Château ☎ 024 466 21 30 Ⓒ Jan–Mar & Nov–Dec: 10am–5pm Tue–Sat; Apr–Jun & Sep–Oct: 10am–6pm Tue–Sat; Jul & Aug: 10am–6pm daily 🅦 museeduvin.ch

→
The turreted Château d'Aigle, now a museum of wine and winemaking

10

Estavayer-le-Lac

AB4 **A**Fribourg ▭
i16 Rue de l'Hôtel de Ville;
www.estavayerpayerne.ch

On the southern shore of Lake Neuchâtel, this town lies within an enclave of the canton of Fribourg. A popular yachting centre, Estavayer-le-Lac is also a pleasant medieval town with arcaded streets. Its focal point is the Château de Cheneaux, a fine Gothic castle that is now the seat of local government.

The **Musée des Grenouilles** (Frog Museum), housed in a 15th-century mansion, boasts an unusual curiosity, namely a collection of 108 stuffed frogs (grenouilles) and other animals arranged in poses that parody the social life of the mid-19th century. The scenes, including dinner parties and playing pool, were created by François Perrier, an eccentric resident of Estavayer who served in the Vatican's Swiss Guard and who put together this somewhat bizarre display in the 1860s.

Musée des Grenouilles

⊘ **A** 13 Rue du Musée
C Mar-Dec: 1-6pm Tue-Sun
C Jan & Feb **w** museedes
grenouilles.ch

 11

Gruyères

AB4 **A**Fribourg ▭
i26 Place des Alpes,
Bulle; www.la-gruyere.ch

The well-preserved medieval village of Gruyères is a popular destination for visitors, and is often crowded in summer. As its only street is pedestrianized, vehicles must be left in the parking areas below.

The village has medieval-era houses and is crowned by an 11th-century castle, the **Château de Gruyères**. It was inhabited by the counts of Gruyères until the mid-16th century, when the bankrupted 19th count fled and his lands were divided between the lords of Bern and Fribourg.

Gruyères is also famous for its cheese. At the dairy La Maison du Gruyère (www.lamaisondugruyere.ch), visitors can watch it being made.

Château de Gruyères

⊘ ⊛ **A** 8 Rue du Château
C Apr-Oct: 9am-6pm daily;
Nov-Mar: 10am-5pm daily
w chateau-gruyeres.ch

ALPINE CATTLE DESCENTS

Each autumn after several happy months munching on alpine flowers on the high mountain pastures, it's time for the cows to come home to the valley for the winter. Many villages, including Charmey, near Gruyères, host a day-long celebration with plenty of local wine, cheese and bell-ringing as the cows and their farmers parade through the streets.

 12

Murten/Morat

AB4 **A**Fribourg
C ▭ **i** Französische
Kirchgasse 6; www.
murtentourismus.ch

The resort town of Murten (Morat in French) lies on the eastern shore of Murtensee (Lac de Morat). It has strong historical associations. It was

Sampling cheesy dishes at La Maison du Gruyère's restaurant, Pringy

at Murten, on 22 June 1476, that the forces of the Swiss Confederation crushed the army of Charles the Bold, Duke of Burgundy, killing 12,000 of his soldiers, while losing only 410 of their own. According to legend, a messenger ran 17 km (10 miles) from Murten to Fribourg with news of the victory, dropping dead with exhaustion on his arrival. His sacrifice is commemorated by an annual run between Murten and Fribourg that takes place on the first Sunday in October.

The town was founded by the Zähringer dynasty in the 12th century, and is still encircled by walls dating from the 12th to the 15th centuries. Hauptgasse, the main street through the old town, is lined with 16th-century arcaded houses with overhanging eaves. The rampart walk, reached from several points along Deutsche Kirchgasse, offers views of Murtensee, the

↑ The château at Estavayer-le-Lac seen from Lake Neuchâtel

castle and of the Old Town's brown-tiled houses. At the western end of the town is a 13th-century castle, with a courtyard that provides a fine view over the lake. At the eastern end stands Berntor (or Porte de Berne), a striking Baroque gatehouse with a clock dating from 1712. The **Musée Historique**, in a disused mill on the lakeshore, displays prehistoric finds from local archaeological excavations, and Burgundian War artifacts. It also stages frequent temporary exhibitions.

Musée Historique

⊛ ⌂4 Ryf, Murten
🕐Apr-Dec: 2-5pm Tue-Sat, 10am-5pm Sun 🕐Jan-Mar
🌐museummurten.ch

---

⑬
Yverdon-les-Bains

🅰B4 ⌂Vaud 🚍 ℹ1
Avenue de la Gare; www.yverdonlesbainsregion.ch

Situated at the southwestern extremity of Lake Neuchâtel, Yverdon-les-Bains is Vaud's second town after Lausanne. The Romans built thermal baths here to take advantage of the hot sulphurous springs. Yverdon's town centre overlies the Roman settlement. The focal point is the **Château d'Yverdon**, a 13th-century castle built by Peter II of Savoy.

Part of the castle now houses a museum of local history, with a collection of Gallo-Roman finds and other exhibits.

Place Pestalozzi, opposite the castle, is dominated by the Hôtel de Ville, the town hall built in 1768–73 on the site of a former market hall. The collegiate church on the west side of the square dates from 1757. The arched pediment of its Baroque façade features an allegory of Faith. To the east, the otherworldly **Maison d'Ailleurs** (House of Elsewhere) is of interest to science fiction fans. This museum presents temporary exhibits related to science fiction, utopian worlds and fantasy.

Yverdon's thermal baths, the **Centre Thermal**, is one of Switzerland's largest and most modern spa centres, with indoor and outdoor pools, saunas and physiotherapy.

Château d'Yverdon

⊛ 🕐Jun-Sep: 11am-5pm Tue-Sun; Oct-May: 2-5pm Tue-Sun

Maison d'Ailleurs

⊛ ⌂Place Pestalozzi
🕐11am-6pm Mon, 2-6pm Tue-Fri 🕐Sat & Sun 🌐ailleurs.ch

Centre Thermal

⌂22 Avenue les Bains🕐 8am-10pm Mon-Sat, 8am-8pm Sun & public hols 🌐cty.ch

⓮ Grandson

🗺 B4 🚉 Vaud 🚌 ⓘ 13 Rue Haute; www.yverdon lesbainsregion.ch

Dominated by its medieval castle, the town of Grandson is associated with a momentous event in the history of the Swiss Confederation: the defeat of Charles the Bold, Duke of Burgundy, at the Battle of Grandson on 2 March 1476.

In February 1476, the duke's army laid siege to Grandson and its castle, eventually securing the surrender of the garrison, which was put to death. After raising an army of 18,000, the Confederates marched on Grandson to wreak revenge on the duke and his army. The Burgundians fled, abandoning their arms and horses, as well as the ducal treasury. The trove is now displayed in Bern's Historisches Museum (p77).

Built between the 11th and 14th centuries, the **Château de Grandson** rises proudly from the magnificent shores of Lake Neuchâtel. It contains a model of the battlefield and a diorama illustrating the town's history from the Middle Ages to the present day. In the basement is an automobile museum with a white Rolls-Royce that belonged to Greta Garbo and Winston Churchill's Austin Cambridge.

Château de Grandson
⊘ 🅿 Place du Château
☎ 024 445 29 26 🕐 Apr–Oct: 10am–6pm daily; Nov–Mar: 10am–5pm daily

---

GREAT VIEW
Sea of Fog

The elevated terrace at Ste-Croix enjoys panoramic views from Santis, in the Alpstein massif, to Mont Blanc on clear days, but even on cloudy days it's worth the trip here for the chance to see the Swiss plateau blanketed in a thick sea of fog.

⓯ Ste-Croix

🗺 A4 🚉 Vaud 🚌 ⓘ 10 Rue Neuve; www.sainte-croix-les-rasses-tourisme.ch

Appropriately known as the Balcony of the Jura, the town of Ste-Croix lies at an altitude of 1,092 m (3,583 ft) and commands a wide view of the Alps, the Swiss Upland and the Jura mountains.

Since the early 19th century Ste-Croix has been the world capital of musical-box manufacture. Two local museums are devoted to this art. In the town centre, the **Musée du CIMA** (Centre International de la Méchanique d'Art) has every mechanical toy and device imaginable, while the **Musée Baud**, in the village of L'Auberson, features music boxes collected by the Baud family, as well as singing birds and animated figures.

← An exhibit from the museum of mechanical devices in Ste-Croix

Musée du CIMA
⊘ ⊗ 🅿 2 Rue de l'Industrie 🕐 By guided tours only; see website for times 🌐 musees.ch

Musée Baud
⊘ ⊗ 🅿 23 Grand-Rue, L'Auberson 🕐 By guided tour and reservation only at 2pm & 3:30pm daily; call 024 454 24 84 🌐 museebaud.ch

---

⓰ Neuchâtel

🗺 B3 🚉 Neuchâtel 🚉 🚌 ⓘ Hôtel des Postes; www. neuchateltourisme.ch

Lying on the northwestern shore of Lake Neuchâtel, Neuchâtel is a graceful town with a strikingly Gallic atmosphere. Its main attractions are its castle, early Gothic church (the Église Collégiale) and Renaissance market hall. It also has two museums of note. The Musée d'Art et d'Histoire displays paintings by some of the Swiss and French Impressionists, as well as fascinating automata.

Once a year the town's century-old Grape Harvest Festival celebrates the bounty from the region's vineyards.

↑ The Fête des Vendanges
(Grape Harvest Festival),
in late September, Neuchâtel

⓱

Vallée de Joux

 A4 ⌂ Vaud 🚆🚌

The Jura may not be as dramatic as the Alps, but its moderate peaks and valleys offer a more accessible way to make the most of the great outdoors. One of the loveliest places in the Swiss Jura is the Vallée de Joux and its centrepiece, Lac de Joux, the largest lake in the Jura.

At 1,004 m (3,300 ft) altitude, the lake sometimes freezes in the coldest weeks, creating the largest natural ice rink in Europe. In summer, the lake is a playground for boaters, swimmers and windsurfers, while hikers and cyclists take to the surrounding trails, including the hike up Mont Tendre – at 1,679 m (5,500 ft) it's the highest peak in the region, but a mere hillock compared to the Alps.

⓲

Le Locle

 B3 ⌂ Neuchâtel 🚆🚌
🌐 lelocle.ch

The town of Le Locle is renowned the world over as being the birthplace of Swiss watchmaking, and has been awarded World Heritage status by UNESCO. In 1705 the young watchmaker Daniel Jeanrichard arrived from Neuchâtel to settle in Le Locle, where he set up a workshop. The apprentices that he trained then established workshops of their own in La Chaux-de-Fonds, thus launching the now-famous Swiss watchmaking industry.

The Musée d'Horlogerie, which occupies a stately 18th-century mansion (the elegant Château des Monts), presents a large collection of timepieces from around the world, as well as several elaborate automata.

⓳

Avenches

 B3 ⌂ Vaud 🚌 🛈 3 Place
del'Église; avenches.ch

Originally the capital of the Helveti, the Celtic tribe that once ruled this part of the country, Avenches was conquered by the Romans in the 1st century BC. Named Aventicum, it became the capital of the Roman province of Helvetia. Vestiges of the Roman city can still be seen to the east of the medieval town centre. The most complete of these remains is the amphitheatre, with seating for 6,000. Other features include the Tornallaz, a tower that is the only surviving part of the old city walls, the forum, the baths and a 12-m (40-ft) Corinthian column known as the Tour du Cigognier. The **Musée Romain**, set within the amphitheatre, contains an impressive display of Roman artifacts discovered during excavations at Aventicum. The exhibits range from items of daily life to statues of Roman deities, mosaics and wall paintings. Avenches is famous for its music festivals, including an eclectic rock festival that has drawn international artists for nearly 30 years to perform in the Roman amphitheatre each August.

Musée Romain
🎟️ 📍 Tour de l'Amphithéâtre
🕐 Apr-Sep: 10am-5pm Tue-Sun; Oct, Feb & Mar: 2-5pm Tue-Sun; Nov-Jan: 2-5pm Wed-Sun 🌐 aventicum.org

---

EAT

Ananda Café-Boutique
Himalayan food
in a vintage setting.

📍 Fbg de l'Hôpital 31,
Neuchâtel 🌐 ananda-online.ch

 🅢🅕 🅢🅕 🅢🅕

KJU
Mediterranean dishes
served with a twist.

📍 Quai Perdonnet 22,
Vevey 🌐 q-vevey.ch

 🅢🅕 🅢🅕 🅢🅕

← Ornate clocks at the Musée International d'Horlogerie at La Chaux-de-Fonds

La Chaux-de-Fonds

⚑B3 **⊙Neuchâtel** **🚆🚌**
**🛈1 Rue Espacité; 032 889
68 90**

If Le Locle is the birthplace of the Swiss watchmaking industry, La Chaux-de-Fonds may be regarded as its cradle. The largest town in the canton of Neuchâtel, La Chaux-de-Fonds lies in the Jura at an altitude of 1,000 m (3,280 ft). Introduced to the town in the early 18th century, watchmaking was initially a cottage industry. In time it was industrialized, and La Chaux-de-Fonds became the leading centre of Swiss watchmaking. The industry reached its peak in the late 18th and 19th centuries.

After it was destroyed by a fire in 1794, the town was rebuilt to a grid pattern, with long, wide avenues. It is now dotted with a number of modernist buildings.

The illustrious past of La Chaux-de-Fonds is celebrated in the magnificent **Musée International d'Horlogerie**. The museum's collection of

some 3,000 pieces from around the world illustrates the history of timekeeping from its beginnings in antiquity to state-of-the-art instruments able to record time lapses of infinitesimal fractions of a second. Many of the most impressive-looking pieces on display were made in La Chaux-de-Fonds during the town's apogee. Musical, astrononomical, atomic and quartz clocks are also on display. The museum has audiovisual facilities, a library and a restoration workshop for antique clocks and watches. At the entrance is a tubular steel carillon that sounds every 15 minutes.

La Chaux-de-Fonds is also the birthplace of the Modernist architect Charles-Édouard Jeanneret (1887–1965), known as Le Corbusier, from the French word "le corbeau" or "the raven". Before he moved to Paris in 1917, Le Corbusier built several houses here, and an itinerary taking in buildings that he designed and places associated with him is available from the town's tourist office.

Musée International d'Horlogerie

⊛ 🏛29 Rue des Musées
🕐10am–5pm Tue–Sun
🌐chaux-de-fonds.ch/
musees/mih

Did You Know?

Watches produced in Switzerland account for 53 per cent of the worldwide market by value.

Franches-Montagnes

⚑B3 **⊙Jura** **🚆🚌**
**🛈Saignelégier, 6 Place
du 23 Juin; www.jura
tourisme.ch**

The part of the Jura mountains that lies within the canton of Jura itself are known as the Franches-Montagnes. The area received its name in the 14th century, when the prince-bishop of Basel, who owned the territory that now makes up the canton of Jura, granted its inhabitants a *franchise*, or exemption from taxation, to encourage migration to this sparsely populated region.

The Franches-Montagnes lie at an altitude of 1,000–1,100 m (3,300–3,600 ft). With spruce and fir forests, undulating pastures and prettily picturesque low houses, this outstandingly beautiful plateau has extensive hiking trails, and cycling and cross-country skiing routes. It is also famous for its sturdy breed of horses.

The region's principal town is Saignelégier. Every year, in

→ The Creux de Van, Western Switzerland's "Grand Canyon"

the second week of August, it hosts the Marché Concours National des Chevaux, a showpiece for the area's unique breed of Franches-Montagnes horses.

 22

Creux de Van

🅰B4 🔲 Neuchâtel

This horseshoe-shaped rock formation in the Jura is sometimes nicknamed Western Switzerland's "Grand Canyon" (the Rhine gorge stakes its claim for the east of the country). That may be a bit of a stretch, but still, the 160-m- (525-ft-) high cliffs are impressive and offer far-reaching views of the Jura mountains and the lush valley below – if you dare look over the vertigo-inducing edge. The easiest way to access it is to drive up the road to the restaurant near the top, though it's much more satisfying to earn the views by hiking up the steep path through the woods from the village of Noiraigue. To descend, take an alternative path down through the centre of the horseshoe. You'll pass by the *fontaine froide*, a natural spring where the water is a chilly 4° C (39° F) year-round. It's a peaceful, isolated spot with a mythical status – during the century that absinthe was banned in Switzerland, covert drinkers would come here to enjoy it in secret, preparing it in the traditional way, by slowly adding water, a process known as "troubling".

ABSINTHE

Absinthe may be the preferred tipple of anguished poets and painters in Paris, but the Green Fairy *(right)* actually comes from the canton of Neuchâtel *(p154)*. The spirit was banned for a century, though many continued to distil it in secret, creating colourful anecdotes of clandestine activity that are told in the Maison de l'Absinthe in Môtiers *(www.maison-absinthe.ch)*. Walk or cycle the Absinthe Trail, which connects distilleries, restaurants and even a chocolate shop that uses absinthe in its products.

 23

St-Ursanne

🅰B3 🔲 Jura 🚌 ℹ️ Place Roger Schaffter; www. juratourisme.ch

A charming medieval walled town with fortified gates, St-Ursanne is set in a deep canyon washed by the River Doubs. The town grew up around the hermitage that Ursicinus, a disciple of St Columba, established here in the early 7th century.

The focal point of the town is its beautiful Romanesque and Gothic church. It has a fine Romanesque portal, with statues of the Virgin and St Ursicinus. There are many fine old medieval houses, as well as graceful arched stone bridge, built in 1728 across the River Doubs on the south side of St-Ursanne, which provides a good view of the town and its setting. The bridge features a statue of St John Nepomucene, who is often considered the patron saint of bridges.

ZÜRICH

Capital of the densely populated canton of the same name, the city of Zürich lies on the north shore of Zürichsee at the point where the River Limmat flows north out of the lake. By the 1st century BC, a Celtic settlement, Turicum, had been established on the Lindenhof. A Carolingian palace was built on this hill, now in the heart of the old city, in the 9th century, and a trading settlement developed at its base. Briefly under the control of the Zähringen dynasty, Zürich passed to the Holy Roman Empire in 1218 and joined the Swiss Confederation in 1351.

By the early Middle Ages, the silk, wool, linen and leather trades had already brought Zürich's merchants great wealth. This merchant class was overthrown and replaced by disgruntled guilds, who in turn held power until the late 18th century.

In the 16th century, Zürich embraced the Reformation, thanks to Ulrich Zwingli, who preached from the Grossmünster, the city's great cathedral. The city then fell into a period of relative obscurity until the 19th century, when Zürich underwent rapid industrial growth. As a result of Switzerland's neutrality, the city emerged from the aftermath of both world wars as a major centre of finance, which it continues to be to this day.

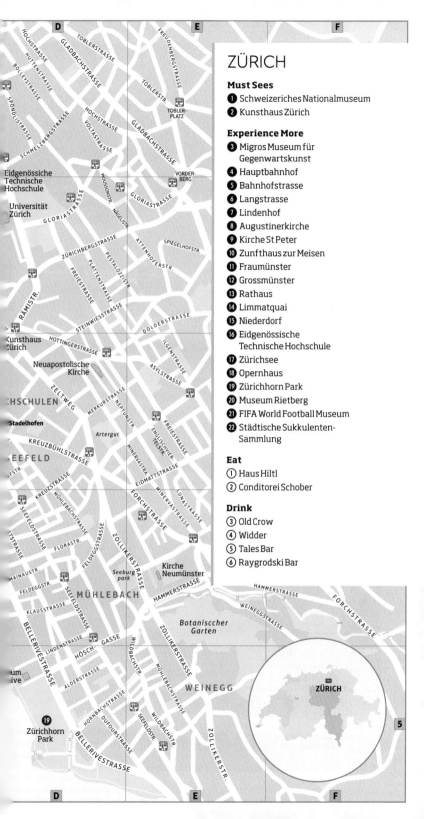

ZÜRICH

Must Sees
❶ Schweizeriches Nationalmuseum
❷ Kunsthaus Zürich

Experience More
❸ Migros Museum für Gegenwartskunst
❹ Hauptbahnhof
❺ Bahnhofstrasse
❻ Langstrasse
❼ Lindenhof
❽ Augustinerkirche
❾ Kirche St Peter
❿ Zunfthaus zur Meisen
⓫ Fraumünster
⓬ Grossmünster
⓭ Rathaus
⓮ Limmatquai
⓯ Niederdorf
⓰ Eidgenössische Technische Hochschule
⓱ Zürichsee
⓲ Opernhaus
⓳ Zürichhorn Park
⓴ Museum Rietberg
㉑ FIFA World Football Museum
㉒ Städtische Sukkulenten-Sammlung

Eat
① Haus Hiltl
② Conditorei Schober

Drink
③ Old Crow
④ Widder
⑤ Tales Bar
⑥ Raygrodski Bar

←

1 People sitting in Bürkliplatz.

2 A yacht on Lake Zürich.

3 Admiring a sculpture in Zürichhorn Park.

4 The Grossmünster looming over Zürich.

3 DAYS

in Zürich

Day 1

Morning Jump straight into the city's (and Switzerland's) past with a visit to the Schweizerisches Nationalmuseum *(p164)*, where local history is revealed through fascinating exhibits on home design and fashion. Mull it all over with lunch at Spitz, the museum restaurant.

Afternoon Cross the Walchbrücke and explore the pedestrianized warren of Niederdorf *(p171)*. Detour down narrow Napfgasse and into Conditorei Schober *(p169)* for irresistible pastries and drinking chocolate made by Lindt to Herr Schober's own specification. Meander on to the city's largest church, the Grossmünster *(p171)*, where the Protestant reformer Ulrich Zwingli preached.

Evening Stroll down Bahnhofstrasse *(p168)*, which ends at Bürkliplatz, then nip into the Arboretum and Belvoirpark with its huge collection of irises and daylilies. After, enjoy fresh fish dishes at a restaurant overlooking the water.

Day 2

Morning Have breakfast at Confiserie Sprüngli *(www.spruengli.ch)*. A meeting place for Zürich's well-to-do since 1859, it is now renowned for its Bircher muesli with seasonal berries. Cross the Limmat to visit Zürich's Kunsthaus *(p166)*, home to one of the city's most important collections of art. Its highlight is Rudolf Koller's *Gotthard Post* (1873), a vivid painting of a postal coach scattering cows; it was voted Switzerland's most popular piece. Stop for lunch at Hiltl *(p169)*, the world's first vegetarian restaurant, opened in 1898.

Afternoon Take in another side of the city with a train trip, from Hauptbahnhof *(p168)* to Üetliberg, Zürich's "mountain". A path from the station leads through the woods to Hotel Uto Kulm's *(www.utokulm. ch)* delightful café terrace. After a coffee, climb the 179 steps of the communications tower for splendid views over the city.

Evening Return to the city centre for an evening cruise on Zürichsee *(p172)* from the pier at Bürkliplatz. Afterward, walk along the riverside into the Old Town for cocktails at Old Crow *(p170)*.

Day 3

Morning Dip into the city's best-known area of urban regeneration, Zürich West. This former *Industriequartier* has been transformed into a vibrant area of independent bars, restaurants and shops selling everything from Tunisian textiles to electric bikes. Nearby is the iconic Freitag shop *(www.freitag.ch)*, housed inside a stack of 19 shipping containers.

Afternoon After a lunch of pan-Pacific cuisine at hip Steinfels microbrewery *(www.steinfels-zuerich.ch)*, wander through Zürichhorn Park *(p173)*, which stretches all the way to Zürichsee. The park is dotted with sculptures by modern artists, including *Heureka*, a kinetic sculpture created by artist Jean Tinguely for Expo 64 in Lausanne *(p134)*.

1 ⬡ ⬡ ⬡ ⬡

SCHWEIZERISCHES NATIONALMUSEUM

📍C1 🏛Museumstrasse 2 🚉Zurich HB 🚊4, 6, 8, 11, 13, 14 🚌46
🕐10am–5pm Tue–Sun (7pm Thu) 🌐landesmuseum.ch

Housed in an 1898 fairy-tale mansion and an adjoining contemporary wing on the banks of the River Limmat, the Swiss National Museum's eclectic collections take visitors on a time-travelling turn through the highlights of Switzerland's history.

The collections of the Swiss National Museum illustrate the country's history and culture from prehistoric times to the present day. The museum has outposts at various locations around the country – the Château de Prangins in Vaud and the Forum of Swiss History in Schwyz – but its headquarters are in Zürich, which have the largest collection of objects illustrating the cultural history of Switzerland.

Highlights include artifacts from Switzerland's rich archaeological past, displays of costumes and Swiss handicrafts. A wing of exposed concrete, connected to the original 1898 building and designed by Swiss architects Christ & Gantenbein, opened in 2016. This striking, angular edifice houses a permanent collection of Swiss archaeology, temporary exhibition spaces, a library and an auditorium.

The museum was extensively renovated in 2020 and new attractions were added. These include "A Magic Carpet Ride Through History", which transports children into the past through interactive exhibits.

↑ A globe by Jost Bürgi (1552–1632), one of the scientific instruments on display at the museum

↑ The stark exterior of the museum's 2016 extension, and the exhibition "Ideas of Switzerland" *(inset)*

GALLERY GUIDE

The west wing houses the Collections Gallery, which showcases a cross-section of objects from the museum's collection and focuses on their history and how they were made. Items include altarpieces and tapestries from the Middle Ages, and fashion and jewellery. The first and second floors contain the History of Switzerland galleries, though parts of these floors are closed for renovation until fall 2019. The southern wing has Swiss archaeology on the first floor. There are temporary exhibition spaces on all floors.

1 The altarpiece with Saint Eligius in the smithy was painted around 1495, by Hans Leu the Elder.

2 Visitors take in a Renaissance bust in the extension wing.

3 Young people engage with interactive displays in the Middle Ages section.

2

KUNSTHAUS ZÜRICH

EXPERIENCE Zürich

⚐ D3 ⌂ Heimplatz 1 ⊟ Stadelhofen ⊞ 3, 5, 8, 9, 11 ⊞ 31, 33 ⊕ 10am-6pm Tue, Fri-Sun, 10am-8pm Wed & Thu ⊞ kunsthaus.ch

Switzerland's greatest art gallery, the Kunsthaus Zürich contains major works of art, from medieval religious paintings and Dutch Old Masters to Impressionist and Post-Impressionist artworks. The gallery's holdings also exemplify the art movements of the 20th century.

Highlights of this superb collection include paintings by the 19th-century Swiss artists Ferdinand Hodler and Albert Anker, the largest assemblage of work by Edvard Munch outside Scandinavia, paintings by Marc Chagall, and paintings and sculpture by Alberto Giacometti. In 2021, the Sammlung E G Bührle collection of Impressionist and Post-Impressionist paintings moved into an extension of the Kunsthaus.

HIDDEN GEM
The Gates of Hell

Before you go into the museum, take a moment to admire *The Gates of Hell*, next to the entrance. Created by French sculptor Rodin, this intricate pair of bronze doors depicts a version of hell inspired by Dante's *Inferno*. It features almost 200 figures all clustered around a single man - a small-scale version of Rodin's famous *Thinker*.

Did You Know?

The gallery is home to three sculptures by renowned British artist Henry Moore.

GALLERY GUIDE

The first and second floors of the gallery are dedicated to the museum's permanent collections, while the ground floor houses a shop, café, cloakroom and information desk. On the first floor, European, American, Swiss and contemporary works are exhibited. The second floor has displays of early 19th-century French art, modern art and photography. The museum's temporary exhibitions are usually situated on the ground and first floors of the museum.

1 Visitors admire the work of German artist Sigmar Polke on display at the gallery.

2 *Wilhelm Wartmann* (1923) is one of several works by Edvard Munch on display in the permanent collection.

3 *Falstaff in the Laundry Basket* was painted by Swiss artist Johann Heinrich Füssli in 1792.

↑ The grand building within which sits the impressive fine arts gallery

EXPERIENCE MORE

Migros Museum für Gegenwartskunst

Q B1 **A** Limmatstrasse 270 **A** Wipkingen **T** 4, 6, 8, 13 **O** 11am–6pm Tue–Sun (to 8pm Thu) **W** migros museum.ch

Several galleries with dynamic programming have made Zürich a leading international centre of contemporary art. One such gallery is the Migros Museum für Gegenwartskunst, which is located in the former Löwenbräu brewery. It specializes in organizing exhibitions of current art by Swiss and foreign artists. The museum provides an interactive space for reflection and viewing the works on display.

Hauptbahnhof

Q B1 **A** Bahnhofplatz **A** Zurich HB **T** 4, 6, 8, 11, 13, 14 **B** 46

Zürich's Neo-Renaissance train station is one of the city's greatest icons. Completed in 1871, it is well preserved and the original structure of the main hall remains unaltered.

The clean, well-kept concourse is filled with stalls throughout the year, and it is also used for seasonal fairs and markets. Beneath the concourse is a modern shopping centre.

From the concourse ceiling hangs an eye-catching statue, its vibrant, almost garish colours contrasting with the sobriety of the surroundings. This is *Guardian Angel* by the French sculptor Niki de Saint Phalle (1930–2002).

Bahnhofstrasse

Q B2 **T** 6, 7, 10, 11, 13

Running north to south from Bahnhofplatz to the edge of Zürichsee, Bahnhofstrasse is a long avenue that lies on the course of the medieval city's moat. Mostly pedestrianized, with tramlines running along it, this the centre of Zürich's commercial activity. It is lined with restaurants and shops, as well as the headquarters of several major Swiss banks.

Between Bahnhofstrasse (east) and Löwenstrasse (west) and Schweizergasse and Sihlstrasse (to the north and south) are Zürich's main department stores, Globus

and Jelmoli, offering exclusive brands and upscale cafeteria-style dining. Beneath Beyer, a watch and jewellery shop, is the Uhrenmuseum Beyer, a clock museum containing a collection of timepieces ranging from simple sundials to elegant modern watches.

At Fraumünster, the street opens onto Paradeplatz on its western side. Once a military parade ground, the square is now lined with large buildings including the headquarters of Sprüngli, the Swiss chocolatier. Bahnhofstrasse ends at Bürkliplatz. Facing onto Zürichsee, this square is the departure point for boat trips on the lake.

Langstrasse

Q A1 **T** 8 **B** 31, 32

Once a seedy red light district, "Long Street" is today a trendy if not chic, area that features mostly inexpensive boutiques and Zürich's best selection of ethnic food stands. It is the most vibrant area of town at night. In July the four-day Latin music festival Caliente, Europe's biggest Latin festival, takes over the street.

Parallel to the main railway line, and intersected by

←

Trams plying along the Bahnhofstrasse, Zürich's main shopping street

↑ Panoramic views from the Lindenhof over the River Limmat and the Old Town

Langstrasse, is Europaallee, a new district of Zürich currently under construction. The name has changed three times and completion by 2020 is not guaranteed. It promises a heady mix of culture, cutting-edge technology and the kind of modish shops and eateries already found on Langstrasse.

7

Lindenhof

 C2   7, 10, 11, 13

This tree-covered hill rises on the west bank of the Limmat. Its strategic position made it an ideal location for a Celtic settlement and later for a Roman fort. In the 10th century, an imperial palace stood here. No buildings remain, but an observation platform offers a view of the surrounding rooftops and the university buildings. There's also a giant chess-board for open-air games.

8

Augustinerkirche

C2 Augustinerhof 8
7, 10, 11, 13 10am-7pm daily christkath-zuerich.ch

This beautiful early Gothic church was built in the late

13th century for a community of Augustinian monks. When the monastery was dissolved during the Reformation, the church was deconsecrated and stood unused for almost 300 years. The interior was restored in the 1840s, and in 1847 the church was reconsecrated as a Roman Catholic church.

9

Kirche St Peter

C2 St-Peter-Hofstatt 6
4, 15 8am-6pm Mon-Fri, 10am-4pm Sat, 11am-5pm Sun kirche-zh.ch

The most distinctive feature of the Church of St Peter is its clockface. With a diameter of 8.7 m (28 ft), it is the largest church clockface in Europe. The oldest surviving vestiges are those of a handsome late Romanesque church erected in the early 13th century. They include the simple rectangular presbytery, which is lit by a semicircular window with an intricate frame. The presbytery is crowned by a mid-15th-century tower.

The main body of the church dates from 1705 to 1716. It takes the form of a galleried basilica with a striking Baroque interior. The dark panelling contrasts with the red columns of the nave and the brilliant white stucco decoration.

10

Zunfthaus zur Meisen

C3 Münsterhof 20
4, 15 By appt Mon-Sat
zunfthaus-zur-meisen.ch

This elegant late Baroque house contains a collection of 18th-century faïence and porcelain, including pieces by Meissen and Sèvres. There are also locally made items produced by Schooren and other Swiss manufacturers.

EAT

Haus Hiltl
Try the saffron gnocchi at this pioneering vegetarian buffet.

B2 Sihlstrasse 28
hiltl.ch

Conditorei Schober
Impossible-to-resist hand-made chocolates tempt at this lavish cakebox of a café.

C2 Napfgasse 4
cafe1842.ch

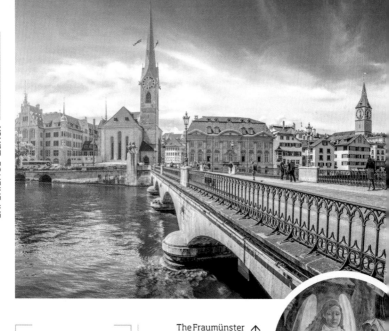

The Fraumünster church and one of its Bodmer frescoes in the cloisters *(inset)*

DRINK

DRINK

Old Crow
Expertly mixed cocktails in an elegantly intimate setting.

📍 C2 🏠 Schwanengasse 4 🕐 Mon & Sun 🌐 oldcrow.ch

Widder
An extensive wine list served with an innovative menu.

📍 C2 🏠 Widdergasse 6 🌐 widderhotel.com

Tales Bar
Creative and bespoke cocktails, plus live music.

📍 B2 🏠 Selnaustrassse 29 🕐 Mon, Sun 🌐 tales-bar.ch

Raygrodski Bar
This cocktail bar buzzes with a hipsterish vibe.

📍 A2 🏠 Sihlfeldstrasse 49 🕐 Sun 🌐 raygrodski.ch

⑪

Fraumünster

📍 C3 🏠 Am Münsterhofplatz 🚋 4, 15 🕐 Nov–Mar: 10am–5pm daily; Apr–Oct: 10am–6pm daily 🌐 fraumuenster.ch

The history of the Women's Minster goes back to 853, when King Ludwig the German made his daughter Hildegard the abbess of a convent here. The convent was dissolved during the Reformation, and the site is occupied by the Stadthaus, a Neo-Gothic building that is now used for exhibitions.

The church, however, survives. It has a mid-13th-century presbytery in the late Romanesque style, an early Gothic transept and a nave that has been remodelled several times. The Neo-Gothic façade was added in 1911.

The presbytery is lit by five stained-glass windows designed by Marc Chagall (1887–1985) and made in 1970. They depict biblical themes, and a different colour predominates in each. The central window, where green is the prevailing colour, depicts scenes from the life of Christ. It is flanked by a blue window with a design inspired by the visions of Jacob, and a yellow window known as the Zion Window, which features King David and the New Jerusalem. The rosette in the south transept, illustrating the Creation, was also designed by Chagall. The north transept has a window with a giant vision of Paradise created by Augusto Giacometti and installed in 1940.

The Romanesque cloisters on the south side of the church are decorated with frescoes executed by Paul Bodmer in 1923–32. They tell the story of the convent's foundation and illustrate the lives of Felix and Regula, the patron saints of Zürich, and of the city's legendary links with Emperor Charlemagne. The emperor is said to have founded Zürich when he discovered the graves of Felix and Regula, who deserted a Roman legion in the Valais and who were martyred for their Christian faith.

12

Grossmünster

📍 C3 🏛 Grossmünsterplatz 🚋 4, 15 🕐 Mar–Oct: 10am–6pm daily; Nov–Feb: 10am–5pm daily 🌐 gross muenster.ch

The tall twin towers of the Grossmünster, or Great Minster, dominate Zürich's skyline from the east bank of the Limmat. According to legend, Charlemagne founded a church here in the late 8th to early 9th century, on the graves of Felix and Regula. After they were killed at the site of the Wasserkirche, these martyrs are said to have carried their heads up the hill to the spot now marked by the Grossmünster.

Construction of the present basilica began in about 1100, and the west towers were eventually completed in the late 15th century.

DADA

The avant-garde artistic movement Dada came to prominence in Zürich in around 1916, as an anarchic reaction to the senseless carnage of World War I. The focus of the movement was the Cabaret Voltaire in Zürich and among its main exponents were Tristan Tzara, Hans Arp and Francis Picabia. Dada's aim was to flout convention and the traditions of the artistic establishment through irony.

It was from the pulpit of the Grossmünster that the humanist Ulrich Zwingli preached the Reformation. In line with reformist ideals, the minster was stripped of its furnishings and decoration, so that the interior is now almost completely bare. However, vestiges of Gothic frescoes as well as the fine Romanesque capitals of the nave survive.

The Grossmünster's large crypt contains a 15th-century statue of Charlemagne, which originally graced the south tower. (The present statue on the tower is a replica.) Other notable features are its Romanesque portal, with a bronze door (1935), and stained-glass windows by Augusto Giacometti (1932).

13

Rathaus

📍 C2 🏛 Limmatquai 55 🚋 4, 15 🕐 By guided tour: only Mon (book one month in advance) 🌐 kantonsrat.zh.ch

Zürich's town hall was built on piles driven into the riverbed, and the waters of the Limmat flow beneath the platform on which it stands. The two-storey building dates from 1694–8.

The Rathaus's façade is ornamented with friezes featuring masks, the windows crowned with broken pediments filled with busts. The marble doorway has gilt decoration. One of its most impressive rooms is the Baroque council chamber.

14

Limmatquai

📍 C2 🚋 4, 15

This pleasant riverside boulevard snakes along the east bank of the Limmat, running between the Bellevueplatz in the south

and the Bahnhofbrücke in the north. The most interesting stretch of Limmatquai is its southern section, lined with guild houses, which have been converted into trendy shops or restaurants offering alfresco dining.

Among the finest of these houses are Haus zur Saffran at No 54, dating from around 1720; Haus zur Rüden at No 42, dating from the 17th century; and the adjoining Haus zur Zimmerleuten, an 18th-century building with a colourful oriel window.

15

Niederdorf

📍 C2 🚋 4, 15

Consisting of a dense network of cobbled alleys leading towards Limmatquai, this small district constitutes the heart of the Old Town's eastern section. The main artery through this historic district is Niederdorfstrasse, a pedestrianized thoroughfare that turns into Münstergasse to the south. Niederdorf's narrow alleys are lined with antiques shops and art galleries, as well as small hotels, cafés, restaurants, beer halls and fast-food outlets.

↑ A narrow cobbled street in the picturesque old quarter of Niederdorf

16

Eidgenössische Technische Hochschule

Q D2 **🚋** 6, 9, 10
🏠 Rämistrasse 101
W ethz.ch

The Federal Institute of Technology, or ETH, opened in 1855, and today it is one of the most highly regarded universities in the world. It occupies a Neo-Renaissance building designed by Gottfried Semper, a prominent German architect who was also the institute's first professor of architecture.

The architecture of the building is of interest in its own right, as is the displays from the eclectic Graphische Sammlung (Graphic Collection) of drawings and graphic art, and the temporary exhibitions that often fill its corridors. The ETH also owns the **Thomas-Mann-Archiv**, in a building nearby. The archive is the entire literary legacy of this great German writer, who died in Zürich in August 1955.

The terrace of the ETH building commands a magnificent view of the city. Located just to the north of the ETH is the upper station of the Polybahn, a funicular that runs down to Central, a large square on the east side of the Bahnhofbrücke.

STREET PARADE

The city's single biggest event, drawing over a million fans, the Street Parade *(www.street parade.com)* is the biggest techno music festival in the world. It takes place every second Sunday in August. The theme is "culture of tolerance". There are 30 mobile stages and 8 concert platforms. There is even an "Antiparade" for techno fans who think the main festival has sold-out of the music's core values.

Thomas-Mann-Archiv
Schönberggasse 15 **Q** 10am–5pm Mon–Fri **W** tma.ethz.ch

17

Zürichsee

Q C4 **🚋** 2, 4, 5, 8, 9, 11, 15
🚌 912, 916

This beautiful glacial lake stretches in a 40-km (25-mile) arc from Zürich to the foot of the Glarner Alps, at its eastern tip. Many boat trips, run by such companies as **ZSG**, depart from the city. Ranging from short trips to half- and full-day cruises, they take in several lakeshore towns and villages. Zürichsee's clear blue waters are unpolluted and there are numerous beaches and swimming areas along the shoreline.

ZSG
🏠 Mythenquai 333 **W** zsg.ch

18

Opernhaus

Q C3 **🏠** Falkenstrasse 1
🚉 Stadelhofen **🚋** 2, 4
W opernhaus.ch

Zürich's Neo-Baroque opera house stages a world-class

The beautiful blue waters of serene Zürichsee ↑

programme of operas and ballets. It was designed by the Viennese architects Hermann Helmer and Ferdinand Fellner and completed in 1891. The elegant façade is fronted by two tiers of columns and a balcony framed by porticoes.

19
Zürichhorn Park
D5 912, 916

This pleasant park contains sculptures by well-known modern artists. At the southern end is a large kinetic sculpture that Jean Tinguely created for Expo 64 in Lausanne; entitled *Heureka*, it is set in motion from April to October at 11.15am and 5.15pm daily.

In the eastern part of the park high walls enclose the **Chinagarten**. This Chinese garden, laid out in 1994, was a gift from the city of Kunming, and is filled with plants, buildings and objects typical of a Chinese formal garden.

Bordering the park, on Höschgasse, is the **Atelier Hermann Haller**, the studio of this Swiss sculptor. Designed by Haller (1880–1950), it is a rare example of wooden Bauhaus architecture. Next to it is the Pavillon Le Corbusier, closed for restoration until summer 2019.

Chinagarten
Mid-Mar-mid-Oct: 11am-7pm daily.

Atelier Hermann Haller
Höschgasse 6 044 383 42 47 Jul-Sep: noon-6pm Fri-Sun.

20
Museum Rietberg
B4 Gablerstrasse 15 5 10am-5pm Tue-Sun (to 8pm Wed) rietberg.ch

The vast assemblage of ethnographic pieces and artifacts that make up the collections of this museum is displayed in two villas (covered by a single entry ticket) linked by extensive underground exhibition areas. Villa Wesendonck, a Neo-Classical mansion in which the composer Richard Wagner once stayed, houses the main collection. This consists of wooden, bronze and ceramic objects from Africa, India, China, Japan, and other Southeast Asian countries. The neighbouring Park-Villa Rieter is devoted to Asian art. Two floors of the house are filled with changing selections of Indian, Chinese and Japanese prints and paintings.

21
FIFA World Football Museum
B4 Seestrasse 27 5, 6, 7, 8, 10 10am-8pm Tue-Sun fifamuseum.com

Zürich has been the home of FIFA, world football's governing body, since 1932. This excellent museum, which opened in 2016, offers an in-depth look at football's past and hints at its future. Exhibits here feature FIFA's founding documents, rare team shirts, unique photos, balls used in historic matches and the actual World Cup trophy. There is also a special kids' trail, with

↑ Exhibits on display at the Villa Wesendonck, Museum Rietberg

interactive games, and a cinema showing films on the game's history.

22
Städtische Sukkulenten-Sammlung
B5 Mythenquai 88 161, 165 9am-4:30pm daily stadt-zuerich.ch/sukkulenten

Comprising more than 8,000 species of cactuses, spurges, agaves, aloes and other succulents, this collection, founded in 1931, is one of the largest of its kind in Europe. Amazing succulents from every arid region of the world, from giant agaves to the tiniest cactuses, are found here in a fascinating display.

> INSIDER TIP
> **Thermalbad and Spa Zurich**
>
> Bathe in wooden vats in this former brewery, turned spa, not far from Museum Rietberg (www.thermalbad-zuerich.ch). The water is drawn from the legendary "Aqui" springs.

NORTHERN SWITZERLAND

Bordered by the Rhine to the north and the Jura to the southwest, this relatively flat area was settled by the Celts around 450 BC. By 44 BC, the Romans, attracted by the trade opportunities opened by the Rhine, founded the town of Augusta Raurica, in the area east of what is now Basel, and soon spread westwards. On the banks of the Rhine, this port town soon became a centre of commerce, developing a wealthy merchant class. At the behest of a Papal bull, Basel Council established Switzerland's oldest university here, in 1460, to educate its wealthy sons. Around this time, Baden, to the east, had become an *ad hoc* capital city for the expanding Swiss Confederation, and the regular meeting place for the executive council. A popular spa town since Roman times, thanks to its natural thermal springs, Baden's reputation as a resort began to spread in the 15th century. Refugees of the War of Religion brought trade and industry to the flourishing northern cantons throughout the 1500s, and, by the 19th century, northern Switzerland was industrialized, and had become the country's most populated region.

NORTHERN SWITZERLAND

Must Sees

1 Basel
2 Baden
3 Winterthur

Experience More

4 Riehen
5 Augusta Raurica
6 Zofingen
7 Dornach
8 Aarau

9 Muri
10 Kloster Königsfelden
11 Wettingen
12 Regensberg
13 Kaiserstuhl
14 Eglisau

↑ Basel's riverside Old Town under the towering presence of the cathedral

1 🍴 🖥 🛍

BASEL

🗺 C2 🚉 Basel 🚊 ℹ️ Stadtcasino, Barfüsserplatz; Steinenberg 4, Bahnhof Basel SBB train station, www.basel.com

Mention the city of Basel and most people today will think of industry or art. Straddling the Rhine, this city of contrasts is the country's only port and as such is a major centre of industry, with a long history of pharmaceutical expertise. The city is also one of Switzerland's most cultured cities, hosting Art Basel, the world's largest contemporary art fair. It is also famous for its festivals, the largest of which, Fasnacht, is an exuberant masked carnival.

1 🎨 🎭 🛍

Jüdisches Museum der Schweiz

🏠 Kornhausgasse 8 🚋 3 🚌 30, 34 🕐 1-4pm Mon-Fri, 11am-5pm Sun 🌐 juedisches-museum.ch

Through a variety of artifacts dating back to the 13th century, including liturgical objects, the museum illustrates Jewish religion and customs, and the history and daily life of this community. It is the only Jewish museum in Switzerland. The Jewish population in Basel is the second largest in Switzerland after Geneva. The first Zionist Congress took place in Basel, in 1897.

2

Universität

🏠 Petersplatz 1 🚋 3 🚌 30, 34

Founded in 1460, Basel's university is the oldest in the country. Among the illustrious figures with whom it is associated are the humanist Erasmus of Rotterdam (1466–1536), the mathematician Jakob Bernoulli (1654–1705) and the philosopher Friedrich Nietzsche (1844–1900). The present university building is the Kollegienhaus, a great Modernist edifice on the east side of Petersplatz, completed in 1946. The entrance to the building is embellished with mosaics depicting the university's founders, and the main hall has stained-glass windows.

3

Spalentor

🏠 Spalenvorstadt 🚋 3 🚌 30, 33

This monumental Gothic gate stands at the entrance to

↑ The Gothic crenallated turrets framing the old city gates, the Spalentor

Spalenvorstadt, a narrow alley lined with picturesque shuttered houses, on the west side of the Old Town (Altstadt). Built in 1370, the Spalentor formed part of the defensive walls that once encircled Basel. The tower consists of a pair of crenellated turrets framing a square central section, which has a pointed roof laid with glazed red, black and white tiles. The gate, which has wooden doors and a portcullis, is embellished with sculptures and on its west side it bears the arms of the city.

④ 🎨 🎭 🍽 🛍

Spielzeug Welten Museum Basel

🏛 Steinenvorstadt 1
🚊 3, 6, 8, 11, 14, 15, 16, 17
🕙 10am–6pm Tue–Sun (daily in Dec) 🌐 spielzeug-welten-museum-basel.ch

With more than 6,000 items laid out on four floors, the Toy Worlds Museum in Basel is the largest of its kind in Europe. Most of the exhibits date from the late 19th to the early 20th centuries, although there are also some contemporary pieces displayed as well. All the doll's houses and miniature shops on display are meticulously decorated and furnished. The collection also includes mechanical models, teddy bears and a variety of other stuffed animals made by leading toymakers of today and yesterday.

Even if you don't have time to go in, the museum is always worth a visit – the spectacular window displays are an event in themselves.

↑ A mannequin and a bicycle on display in the Spielzeug Welten Museum Basel

⑤ 🖫 🖫
Pharmazie-historisches Museum Basel

📍 Totengäslein 3 🚊 6, 8, 11, 14, 15, 16, 17 🕐 10am–5pm Tue–Sun 🌐 pharmazie museum.ch

Appropriately for one of the world's centres of the pharmaceuticals industry, Basel has a museum devoted to the history of medicinal chemistry. Among its collection are instruments and medicines used by apothecaries through the ages, and it is located in the house where Erasmus and Paracelsus once lived. There are also reconstructions of a pharmacy and a laboratory.

⑥ 🖫 🖫 🍽 🖫
Antikenmuseum

📍 St Alban-Graben 🚊 1, 2, 15 🕐 10am–5pm Tue–Sun (to 10pm Thu & Fri) 🌐 antikenmuseum basel.ch

Basel's museum of antiquities covers over 5,000 years of history, and is devoted to the four great early civilizations of the Mediterranean basin – ancient Greece, Etruria, Rome and Egypt. The Greek pieces include a fine collection of vases from the Archaic to the Classical periods, marble sculpture, bronze figurines, pottery, coins and jewellery. The collections of Etruscan pottery and Roman and Egyptian art are equally impressive.

⑦ 🍽 🖫 🖫
Marktplatz

📍 Kornhausgasse 8 🚊 3, 6, 8, 11, 14, 15, 16, 17 📞 061 261 95 14 🕐 7am–2pm Tue–Thu (to 6pm Fri & Sat)

Every weekday morning, Marktplatz is filled with the stalls of a produce market, and on public holidays it becomes the hub of Basel's seasonal festivals. The square is lined with fine buildings dating from the late 19th to the early 20th centuries.

Just to the northeast of the Marktplatz is Mittlere Rheinbrücke. Near the bridge is a curious, bearded figure, the Lällekönig (Tongue King), which has become the symbol of Basel. It is a static replica of an amusing 19th-century mechanical figure that rolled its eyes and stuck out its tongue at passersby. The original figure is in the Historisches Museum.

⑧
Leonhardskirche

📍 Kohlenberg 🚊 3 🕐 9am–4pm daily

The church of St Leonard overlooks the city from its hilltop location. It stands on the site of an 11th-century

> **Every weekday morning the Marktplatz is filled with the stalls of a produce market, and on public holidays it becomes the hub of Basel's seasonal festivals.**

Basel's bustling Marktplatz, with stalls setting up for market day ↑

church, whose Romanesque crypt survives. After the 1356 earthquake that destroyed much of Basel, the church was rebuilt in the Gothic style. The interior features 15th- and 16th-century Gothic paintings and a rood screen from 1455.

Historisches Museum

Barfüsserplatz 3, 6, 8, 11, 14, 15, 16, 17 10am-5pm Tue-Sun hmb.ch

The headquarters of three separate history museums, this collection occupies the Barfüsserkirche, a former Franciscan church. The Historisches Museum traces Basel's history from its beginnings as a Celtic settlement. Exhibits include pottery, silver-mounted vessels, wooden chests and Gothic, Renaissance and Baroque liturgical vessels, as well as other items from the cathedral treasury. There are also tapestries, altarpieces and weapons on display.

Kunsthalle

Klostergasse 5 1, 2, 3, 8, 10, 11, 14, 15, E11 11am-6pm Tue, Wed & Fri, 11am-8:30pm Thu, 11am-5pm Sat & Sun kunsthallebasel.ch

Thanks to the Kunsthalle, Basel is a well-established forerunner in the world of modern art. One of the city's most prominent cultural institutions, the Kunsthalle hosts a rolling programme of exhibitions of work by leading contemporary artists. The Kunsthalle is located opposite the Theater Basel, another institution in the city's cultural hub. Between the two buildings stands a fountain that incorporates several of Jean Tinguely's kinetic sculptures with moving elements, created in a style known as metamechanics.

BASEL FASNACHT

Starting in early morning darkness, Basel gets turned upside down for *die drey scheenschte Dääg* ("the three most beautiful days") of the year. During Switzerland's biggest carnival, a sea of illuminated lanterns and thousands of costumed music-makers and masked *Fasnächtler* (participants) pour through the city streets for parties, parades and music.

Architekturmuseum

Steinenberg 7 11am-6pm Tue, Wed & Fri, 11am-8:30pm Thu, 11am-5pm Sat & Sun sam-basel.org

The Kunsthalle also houses Switzerland's museum of architecture. This museum seeks to expand people's perceptions of architecture and urban development, concentrating primarily on the architecture of the early 20th century onwards, with an array of well-considered displays in Neo-Baroque rooms. The Architecture Museum also hosts temporary exhibitions, usually four per year, which showcase the work of Swiss architects, and of international architecture, as well as related subjects such as architectural photography, the effect of acoustics on the design of a building and the links between art and architecture. There is also a programme of public workshops and lectures.

Haus zum Kirschgarten

Elisabethenstrasse 27-29 1, 2 Summer: 11am-5pm Wed-Sun (winter: Tue-Sun) hmb.ch

This Rococo mansion, built in 1775–80, was the residence of J R Burckhardt, the owner of a silk mill. Furnished in period style, it now houses a museum that illustrates patrician life in the 18th and 19th centuries. On the first and second floors there are elegantly furnished drawing rooms, a dining room, a music salon and a kitchen. The top floor contains a display of rocking horses and other toys. The ground floor and basement are filled with a superb collection of ceramics, including Italian faïence, clocks and fine porcelain made at major European factories.

←

Ornately decorated 18th-century clock in the Haus zum Kirschgarten

↑ A visitor looking at a Papua New Guinean mask of initiation at the Museum der Kulturen

Augustinergasse

🚊 6, 8, 11, 14, 15, 16, 17

Augustinergasse is an alley that runs north from Münsterplatz, along the escarpment on the south side of the Rhine. As well as a Renaissance fountain with a figure of a basilisk, the street contains several 14th- and 15th-century houses.

The handsome Neo-Classical building at No 2 houses the **Naturhistorisches Museum**, which contains an extensive collection of minerals, and has

sections devoted to zoology and palaeontology. Around the corner is the **Museum der Kulturen**, set in a building crowned with a shimmering fishscale roof that was designed by Basel architects Herzog & de Meuron. This anthropology museum examines cultures from around the world. Among the finest pieces are wooden reliefs from Tikal, the ancient Mayan site in Guatemala.

Naturhistorisches Museum
🔲 Augustinergasse 2 ⏰ 10am–5pm Tue–Sun (to 8pm first Wed of month) 🌐 nmbs.ch

Museum der Kulturen
🔲 Münsterplatz 20 ⏰ 10am–5pm Tue–Sun 🌐 mkb.ch

Rathaus

🔲 Marktplatz 9 🚊 6, 8, 11, 14, 15, 16, 17

The main feature of Basel's Marktplatz is the Rathaus, the Gothic town hall with a bright red façade. The central arcaded section of the building dates from 1504–21, while the tower and annexe date from the 19th century. The inner courtyard is painted with frescoes from the 16th century, though they are

heavily restored. Tours in many languages, including English, can be arranged through the tourist office.

St Alban

🚊 3

The district of St Alban takes its name from the church of a former Benedictine monastery founded in the 11th century. The canal that runs through this attractive district was used to power the monastery's mills. One of these, the **Basler Papiermühle**, now houses a museum of paper, writing and printing. Visitors can watch paper being made by hand. The **Museum für Gegenwartskunst** (Museum of Contemporary Art), a short distance from the mill, showcases contemporary art.

Basler Papiermühle
🔲 St Alban-Tal 37 ⏰ 11am–5pm Tue–Fri & Sun, 1–5pm Sat 🌐 papier museum.ch

Museum für Gegenwartskunst
🔲 St Alban-Rheinweg 60 ⏰ 11am–6pm Tue–Sun 🌐 kunst museumbasel.ch

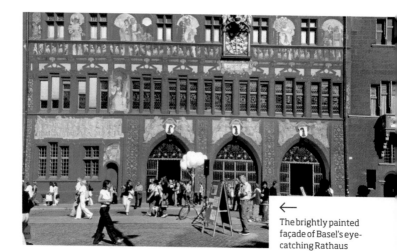

← The brightly painted façade of Basel's eye-catching Rathaus

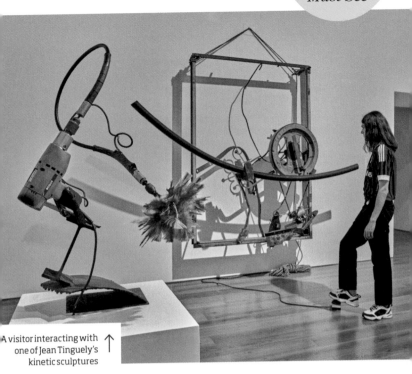

A visitor interacting with one of Jean Tinguely's kinetic sculptures

Kleinbasel

🚋6, 8, 14, 15, 17 🚌31, 34, 38

The first permanent bridge over the Rhine at Basel was built here in 1226. A small fortress was subsequently established on the north bank, and the settlement that grew up around it became part of the city in the late 14th century. For centuries, Kleinbasel – which translates as "Lesser Basel" – was inhabited mainly by the poorer sector of the

> 💬 INSIDER TIP
> **Museum Pass**
>
> Valid for a full year, the Museum Pass is a good option if you plan to visit a few of Basel's 37 museums. The pass also gets you into castles, museums, gardens and parks across Germany, France and Switzerland.

city's population. In recent years, however, the area has been gentrified and it now buzzes with trendy galleries, cafés and restaurants.

Museum Tinguely

📍 Paul-Sacher Anlage 2
🚌31, 36, 38, 42 ⏰11am–6pm Tue–Sun 🌐 tinguely.ch

This pale pink sandstone building, designed by the Swiss architect Mario Botta, stands in Solitude Park, on the banks of the Rhine. The museum is devoted to the work of Jean Tinguely, famous for his kinetic sculptures and interactive drawing machines.

Born in Fribourg in 1925, he was educated in Basel. He later settled in New York in 1960, but in 1968 he returned to his native country, where he lived until his death in 1991. The nucleus of the collection consists of works by Tinguely,

> **Did You Know?**
>
> Jean Tinguely created his first piece of kinetic art when he was 12 years old.

donated by his wife, the artist Niki de Saint-Phalle. These pieces, along with many later gifts, bequests and purchases, allow visitors to trace Tinguely's artistic development.

While various engine-driven contraptions that visitors can set in motion occupy the mezzanine, the upper floor is home to various items associated with Tinguely. The central exhibit on the ground floor is a huge sculpture, Tinguely's *Grosse Méta Maxi-Maxi Utopia* (1987). The museum also stages exhibitions concentrating on aspects of Tinguely's work, including its Dadaist roots.

⑱ ⓂⓈ

BASEL MÜNSTER

🏠 Rittergasse 3 🚋 1, 2, 15 🕐 Apr-Oct: 10am-5pm Mon-Fri (to 4pm Sat),
11:30am-4pm Sun; Nov-Mar: 10am-4pm Mon-Sat (from 12:30pm Sun)
🌐 baslermuenster.ch

Set on a hill above the Rhine, Basel's monumental cathedral is
a conspicuous and majestic presence in the city. With dark red
sandstone walls and patterned roof tiles, it is a vivid monument
to Romanesque and Gothic architecture.

The church that originally stood on this site was
built in the 8th century, but the present cathedral
was begun in the 12th century. Partly damaged
by an earthquake in 1356, it was rebuilt in the
Gothic style, although elements of the earlier
building were also incorporated into the structure.
In the 16th century, as a result of the Reformation,
the cathedral was stripped of almost all its furnishings and decoration. However, some fine
Romanesque and Gothic sculptures survive, as
does the church's 19th-century stained glass
and the beautiful 14th-century frescoes in the
crypt. On the south side of the cathedral are
peaceful Gothic cloisters, with several tombs
and epitaphs that give this part of the complex
its dignified, contemplative character.

The ambulatory is lit by
19th-century stained-glass
windows depicting the
Nativity, Crucifixion and
Resurrection of Christ.

Carved elephants
adorn the win-
dows of the choir.

The magnificent
Romanesque Galluspforte
portal has carvings depicting Judgment Day and
works of mercy.

↑ A fine Nativity scene among the
frescoes on the ceiling of the crypt

↑ The church's exterior, with its patterned
roof atop sturdy sandstone walls

On the south side of the cathedral
are peaceful Gothic cloisters, with
several tombs and epitaphs that
give this part of the complex its
dignified, contemplative character.

Did You Know?

The hill on which the church is located was a Celtic *oppidum* (fortified town) in the 1st century BC.

The Georgstrum features a figure of St George. The whiter stonework at its lower levels formed part of the 11th-century church.

The Martinstrum culminates in a decorative fleuron completed in 1500.

The roof is decorated with green and yellow tiles.

Intricately carved, the 1486 font is an outstanding example of late Gothic sculpture.

The late Romanesque Panel of the Apostles in the north aisle shows six of the apostles.

↑ The Basel Münster, a heritage site of national significance

⑲ 🛡️ 🚳 🍴 🛍️

KUNSTMUSEUM BASEL

🏛️ St Alban-Graben 16 🚊 1, 2, 15 🕐 10am–6pm Tue–Sun (to 8pm Wed)
🌐 kunstmuseumbasel.ch

The prestigious Kunstmuseum Basel is the largest art museum in Switzerland, with an impressive collection of paintings and sculpture spanning the early 15th century to the modern day.

Ranging from 17th-century Dutch and Flemish paintings, through 19th-century works by Delacroix and Pissarro, to 20th-century art, including works by Rousseau, Picasso and Dalí, the Kunstmuseum Basel's collection is vast. The galleries on the first floor of the museum's main building are hung with works of art from the 15th to 19th centuries, while the second floor is devoted to 20th-century art. Located across the street from the original 1930s building, a concrete minimalist extension (connected to the main building by an underground passageway) hosts special exhibitions and changing displays from the permanent collection.

Entry to the museum is free on the first Sunday of every month and also between 5 and 6pm on Tuesday, Wednesday, Friday and Saturday. There are regular guided tours, including some in English.

ART BASEL

Each year, members of the art world gather in the city for Art Basel. This internationally renowned art fair – and an absolute highlight of the art calendar – is a week-long celebration of top modern and contemporary works from around the globe.

① Auguste Rodin's evocative bronze *Burghers of Calais* sculpture is on display in the Kunstmuseum's inner courtyard.

② The modernist façade of the Kunstmuseum Basel was designed by Basel-based architect Rudolf Christ.

③ Dating from 1627, *David Presenting Saul with the Head of Goliath* is a small-scale painting of the well-known biblical story; it is one of Rembrandt's earlier works.

Did You Know?

The museum contains the largest collection of Holbein paintings in the world.

↑ Inside the Kunstmuseum Basel, with its colourful stained-glass windows

A SHORT WALK
OLD TOWN

Distance 2 km (1 mile) **Nearest tram** Schifflände **Time** 30 minutes

The nucleus of Basel's medieval Old Town, or Altstadt, lines the escarpment of the south bank of the Rhine. The hub of the Old Town is Barfüsserplatz, a buzzing square lined with cafés and crossed by trams, and its major landmarks are the Basler Münster, Basel's great Romanesque-Gothic cathedral, and the unmistakable Rathaus, the brightly painted town hall on Marktplatz. With shopping streets, several churches, steep alleyways and leafy courtyards, this is Basel's busiest district. As many streets in the Old Town are closed to motor traffic, it is a pleasant area to explore on foot.

Dating from the 14th century, **Martinskirche** *is the oldest parish church in Basel.*

Marktplatz (p180) *has for centuries served as a market-place. It is also the hub of the city's festivals.*

The **Rathaus** (p182) *has a brightly and elaborately painted façade and a clock surmounted by figures.*

Mittlere Rheinbrücke, *a stone bridge spanning the Rhine, links Grossbasel, on the south bank, to Kleinbasel, a district on the north bank.*

MARKTGASSE

EISENGASSE

START

RHEINS

MARKT-PLATZ

MARTINS

GERBERGASSE

Barfüsserplatz, *named after the Discalced, or barefooted, Franciscans, is surrounded by buildings dating mostly from the 19th and 20th centuries.*

FALKNERSTRASSE

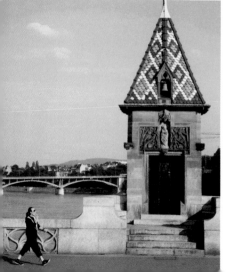

← Walking along Mittlere Rheinbrücke, with its decorated towers

→ The medieval Basler Münster, looming over Munsterplatz

FINISH

Basel's ethnographic museum, **Museum der Kulturen** (p182), contains an extensive collection, including some oustanding examples of Pre-Columbian South American sculpture.

Augustinergasse (p182), a street lined with picturesque houses and mansions, runs along the excarpment on the south bank of the Rhine.

Did You Know?

Basler Münster was destroyed by the Basel Earthquake in 1356 and later rebuilt.

Basler Münster (p184), Basel's magnificent medieval cathedral, dominates the city from an elevated terrace above the Rhine.

AUGUSTINERGASSE

MÜNSTER–PLATZ

RITTERGASSE

TREITGASSE

MÜNSTERGASSE

Münsterplatz, the cathedral square, overlies the site of a Roman camp.

Housed in a former Franciscan church, the **Historisches Museum** (p181) illustrates the history of Basel, with particular emphasis on life in the city during the Middle Ages.

| 0 metres | 75 |
| 0 yards | 75 |

N ↑

Autumnal view across the terraces from the ruins of Baden's castle

BADEN

D2 **Aargau** **Bahnhofplatz 1; www.baden.ch**

One of Switzerland's oldest health resorts, Baden (meaning "baths") is a peaceful, stately town. The therapeutic properties of its hot sulphur springs, which the Romans knew as Aquae Helveticae, have been exploited since ancient times. From the Middle Ages, Baden's location on the River Limmat has contributed to its becoming an important centre of trade, and its beautiful Old Town is the legacy of this historical status. Today, Baden is still a popular spa centre, with facilities for large numbers of visitors, as well as a thriving industrial town. A good place to begin exploring Baden's Old Town is the east bank of the Limmat. From here, the rest of the Old Town is reached by crossing a wooden bridge.

① Ruine Stein

The ruins of a castle look eastwards towards the Old Town from the top of a rocky promontory, beneath which runs a road tunnel. Originally built in the 10th century, the castle passed through the hands of several noble families before being inherited by the Habsburgs in 1264. It was rebuilt in the 13th century as an arsenal and fortress for Austrian forces, when Baden and the surrounding area fell under *Vorderösterreich* (Further Austria). In 1712, the castle was destroyed during conflicts between Protestant and Catholic cantons. Today these ruins are wreathed by green spaces, making it a pleasant place for a stroll. The hilltop offers a splendid view over the curving passage of the River Limmat and of the picturesque Old Town laid before it.

② Stadtturm

Schlossbergplatz 3 **056 200 87 87**

This tall four-sided tower was built in the 15th century to guard the Old Town. It is set with four corner turrets, and its steep roof of red, black and white tiles is crowned by a belfry. The tower also features a clock framed by frescoes.

③ Pfarrkirche Mariä Himmelfahrt

Kirchplatz **056 222 57 15**

Baden's parish church, the Church of the Assumption, was built in the centre of

> 💬 **INSIDER TIP**
> **Spanisch Brötli**
>
> A light, flaky pastry, filled with a tasty mix of roasted and crushed hazelnuts and apricot jam, this baked treat is a Baden specialty. Enjoy it warm from the oven with a cup of coffee as a delicious morning snack.

original Gothic outline, and is topped by a pointed spire. The church treasury, with a collection of liturgical objects, is open to visitors by appointment only.

 he Old Town between 1457 nd 1460. Although it was emodelled on several ccasions, acquiring Baroque eatures in the 17th century nd Neo-Classical elements the early 19th, it retains its

④ Ⓜ

Stadthaus

🏠 Rathausgasse 1 🕐 8am-noon Mon-Fri 🌐 baden.ch

The Stadthaus, Baden's town hall, located north of the church, contains a thoughtfully restored council chamber, the Tagsatzungssaal. It was here that the Swiss Diet, an early version of Switzerland's parliament, sat from 1426 to 1712. This well-preserved chamber is lined with wood panelling and beautifully carved wooden adornments. The striking stained-glass windows, which feature the emblems of 13 of the Swiss cantons, are copies of those created by the Zürich glass painter Lukas Zeiner; each was donated to the Stadthaus by ten towns across the canton in 1500.

Historisches Museum Baden

🏠 Landvogteischloss 🕐 1–5pm Tue, Wed, Fri & Sat, noon–7pm Thu, 10am–5pm Sun 🌐 museum.baden.ch

The massive Gothic castle on the east bank of the Limmat was built in the 15th century, and from 1415 to 1798 was the residence of Baden's bailiffs. The castle keep now houses a museum of local history. Its archaeological section includes Roman pottery, coins and other objects found in Baden. There are also displays of weapons, traditional costumes of the Aargau region and rooms decorated in the style of different historical periods. A wing, which extends along the riverbank, contains displays of objects relating to Baden's more recent history. The interactive displays will keep older children busy, while younger visitors will love exploring the castle with Frank the Bat.

↑ A bust of the Roman goddess Juno at the Historisches Museum

⑥ Spa Quarter

A short distance north of the Holzbrücke, along the Limmat's left bank, Baden's 18 thermal springs spout warm mineral-rich waters that are especially effective in curing rheumatism and respiratory ailments. The quarter has several hotels with their own pools and wellness areas. A new public complex opened in 2018, with thermal pools and treatment areas.

↑ Colourfully shuttered houses lining the streets of Old Town near the Holzbrücke

⑦ Holzbrücke

Spanning the Limmat from the base of the Historisches Museum Baden, this pretty wooden bridge is covered by a ridge roof. It was built across this narrow stretch of the river to connect the Landvogteischloss (Bailiff's Castle) to the lower-lying east bank in the 13th century. The current bridge, built in 1810 on 17th-century abutments, had at least five predecessors, each destroyed over the centuries by either natural calamity, such as flood, fire or ice drift, or in an effort to save the town in times of war.

AD 14

The year the Romans discovered the naturally warm springs in the bend of the Limmat.

The Holzbrücke stretching across the River Limmat towards the Old Town ↑

Museum Langmatt

📍 Römerstrasse 30
🕐 Mar–early Dec: 2–5pm Tue–Fri, 11am–5pm Sat & Sun 🌐 langmatt.ch

On Römerstrasse, a short walk westwards from the spa area, stands a charming villa that was once the home of the industrialist and art connoisseur Sidney Brown-Sulzer (1865–1941) and his wife, Jenny. The Art Nouveau villa was built in 1900–1901 by Karl Moser; a few years later a wing was added, which, like the house itself, contains an exquisite art collection. The nucleus of the collection consists of French Impressionist paintings, with works by Corot, Pissarro, Renoir, Monet, Sisley, Degas and Cézanne. The collection also includes rare ceramics and a series of 18th-century Venetian *veduta*, several works by Fragonard

and Watteau, and paintings by Van Gogh and Gauguin. Some of the rooms contain 17th- and 18th-century French furniture.

The Brown-Sulzers filled their house with artists and musicians, and in keeping with this tradition, there are regular formal and informal events that bring together art, literature and music in interesting ways to discuss a selected theme. Also regularly held are special events to introduce children to Impressionist art.

↑ A display of toys engaging visitors of all ages at the Schweizer Kindermuseum

Schweizer Kindermuseum

📍 Ländliweg 7
🕐 2–5pm Tue–Sat, 10am–5pm Sun 🌐 kinder museum.ch

Housed in an old mansion, this museum contains an expansive collection of toys and everyday objects from around the world that illustrate various aspects of childhood, including children's mental development and education. Younger visitors are actively encouraged to touch, examine and play with many of the exhibits.

BADENFAHRT

Taking place once every 10 years, this themed party seems to defy what might be expected of a visit to Switzerland. The cobblestoned town swells to 10 times its normal population as attendees flood in to chug beer, chow down on street food, dance to Swiss-German rap music till the wee hours and go for a spin on carnival rides. It's a rare opportunity to see the Swiss really let their hair down.

3

WINTERTHUR

E2 **Zürich** **Winterthur Hauptbahnhof; winterthur-tourismus.ch**

Now associated chiefly with textiles and mechanical engineering, Winterthur is the second-largest city in the canton of Zürich. Despite its industrial character, this is a pleasant town, with leafy streets, open green spaces and a fully pedestrianized historic core. It also has several outstanding art galleries that can be explored via the museum bus, which circles the town every hour, stopping at the main museums and galleries.

① Kunsthalle Winterthur

Marktgasse 25 **Noon-6pm Wed-Fri, noon-4pm Sat & Sun** **kunsthalle winterthur.ch**

The former Waaghaus (Weigh House) has been converted into a spacious exhibition hall, the Kunsthalle Winterthur, which organizes shows of contemporary art by local and internationally renowned artists every year. Marktgasse, the Old Town's pedestrianized main artery and its principal shopping street, is lined with several other historic buildings, including the 1717 Haus zur Geduld (Patience House).

② Rathaus

Marktgasse 20 **052 267 51 51** **2-5pm Tue-Sat, 10am-noon & 2-5pm Sun**

Winterthur's Neo-Renaissance town hall was built in 1874 on the site of a former Gothic structure. In 1878, the ground floor was converted into a shopping arcade. The upper floors have remained intact and include the stuccoed Festsaal, and former offices and residential quarters. The town hall passage, which connects Marktgasse with Stadthausstrasse, is decorated with opulent ceiling frescoes and hosts shops and a café.

A two-minute walk away, at Stadthausstrasse 4a, stands the imposing Neo-Renaissance Stadthaus, it was designed by Gottfried Semper, who lectured at Zürich's Technical University, and completed in 1869. Once the seat of the city council, it now houses the town's main concert hall.

③ Fotomuseum

Grüzenstrasse 44 **11am-6pm Tue-Sun (to 8pm Wed)** **foto museum.ch**

This oustanding museum, set in a spacious and well-restored warehouse, is one of the finest of its kind in Europe. On display is a comprehensive range of images, from the early beginnings of photography to the most recent examples of the art, by international and local photographers. The museum also holds world-class exhibitions.

Tubular undulation hanging above the foyer of Technorama

④
Technorama

📍 Technoramastrasse 1
🕐 10am–5pm daily
🌐 technorama.ch

Featuring more than 500 fascinating interactive exhibits, Switzerland's only science and technology museum is a family-friendly affair, with indoor picnic rooms and barbecue areas in the leafy park. There are daily shows on various topics.

⑤
Kunst Museum Winterthur

📍 Beim Stadthaus: Museumstrasse 52; Reinhart am Stadtgarten: Stadthausstrasse 6
🕐 10am–5pm Tue–Sun (Beim Stadthaus to 8pm Tue, Reinhart am Stadtgarten to 8pm Thu)
🌐 kmw.ch

In 2017, the Kunstmuseum and Museum Oskar Reinhart merged to form the Kunst Museum Winterthur, with two main locations in town.

The Kunst Museum Beim Stadthaus has an excellent collection of 19th- and 20th-century works by a range of artists, including Monet, Van Gogh, Picasso, Rodin, Miró and Mondrian. The building also houses the Naturmuseum (a natural history museum) and the Kindermuseum.

Across Museumstrasse stands the Classical-style building of the Kunst Museum Reinhart am Stadtgarten. Oskar Reinhart (1885–1965), who was born in Winterthur, amassed one of the greatest private art collections of the 20th century. He bequeathed part of it to the town, and the rest to the Swiss nation.

Must See

The collection here has German, Austrian and Swiss Romantic and Realist works from the late 18th to the early 20th centuries.

⑥
Sammlung Oskar Reinhart am Römerholz

📍 Haldenstrasse 95
🕐 10am–5pm Tue–Sun (to 8pm Wed) 🌐 roemerholz.ch

From 1926 until his death, the art collector Oskar Reinhart lived in this lovely country villa. It holds about 200 works from his extensive collection. Reinhart juxtaposed various styles, hanging Goya with Renoir, in an effort to establish continuities across time and to reveal the quintessence of art.

Did You Know?

The name of the town is thought to be a compound of the Celtic words *uito* (willow) and *durōn* (gate).

An exhibition at Riehen's modern-art museum, the Fondation Beyeler

EXPERIENCE MORE

 4

Riehen

C2 **Basel** **riehen.ch**

The charming town of Riehen, northeast of Basel, is filled with smart villas and old country houses, and has much to interest visitors.

Wettsteinhaus, once the home of a 17th-century mayor, now houses the **Muzeum Kultur & Spiel Riehen**. This superb toy museum contains exhibits ranging from toy trains and tin cars to dolls and board games, some dating from the 19th century. Also here are the Dorfmuseum, which documents daily life in Riehen in 1900, and the Rebbaumuseum, devoted to the local winemaking industry.

Riehen's largest museum is the exceptional **Fondation Beyeler**. It was set up by Hilda

> **INSIDER TIP**
> **Take a Trip**
>
> Fancy a French break? Take tram 10, one of the few municipal transport routes in the world to cross an international border, from Dornach to Rodersdorf. The penultimate stop on the line, Leyman, is in France.

and Ernst Beyeler, prodigious art collectors who acquired some 200 pieces. These were put on public display in 1997, in a building designed by the Italian architect Renzo Piano. Most of the paintings in the collection date from the late 19th and 20th centuries. Among them are Impressionist paintings by Monet, works by Cézanne, Van Gogh, Picasso and Matisse, and canvases by Miró, Mondrian, Bacon, Rothko, Warhol and other major artists of the 20th century. A selection of artifacts from other parts of the world, including Africa and Oceania, complements the paintings.

Muzeum Kultur & Spiel Riehen

Baselstrasse 34 **11am–5pm Mon & Wed–Sun** **muks.ch**

Fondation Beyeler

Baselstrasse 101 **10am–6pm daily (to 8pm Wed)** **fondationbeyeler.ch**

 5

Augusta Raurica

C2 **Augst, Basel** **augustaraurica.ch**

The Roman town of Augusta Raurica lies 11 km (7 miles) east of Basel, at the confluence

of the Ergolz and the Rhine. It was founded in 27 BC and at its height in about AD 200 it had a population of 20,000 people. By about AD 350, the town had been largely destroyed by the Alemani, a northern tribe.

Carefully excavated, Augusta Raurica is now a large and fascinating open-air museum. The site includes restored temples, amphitheatres, baths and sewers, as well as a forum and numerous houses.

Some of the many objects unearthed during excavations are displayed in the excellent **Römermuseum**. They include a hoard of late antique silver discovered at the foot of the town's fortress. The reconstruction of a Roman house furnished with pieces found at the site illustrates daily life in the town.

Römermuseum

Giebenacherstrasse 17, Augst **061 816 22 22** **10am–5pm daily**

 6

Zofingen

D3 **Aargau** **Kirchplatz 26; www.zofingen.ch**

Zofingen, in the canton of Aargau, is a charming town with a history that goes back to the 12th century. Its well-preserved old town is surrounded by a green belt laid out along the course of the former fortifications. Almost all the town's sights are clustered around three neighbouring squares, Alter Postplatz, Kirchplatz and Niklaus-Thut-Platz.

In the centre of Alter Postplatz is a historic arcaded market hall that is still used for a weekly market today.

Kirchplatz (Church Square) takes its name from the Stadtkirche, a parish church built in the Romanesque style but with later Gothic and Renaissance elements added.

Niklaus-Thut-Platz is marked by a fountain with a statue of the eponymous Thut, hero of the Battle of Sempach fought in 1386, when the Confederates routed the Austrians. Among the fine buildings surrounding the square are the Metzgern-Zunfthaus (butchers' guild house), dating from 1602, and the Baroque town hall with a council chamber furnished in the Neo-Classical style.

 7

Dornach

🚆C2 🚊Solothurn 🚌🚐
🌐dornach.ch

The small town of Dornach, on the southern outskirts of Basel, is the location of the world centre of anthroposophy. Founded in about 1912 by the Austrian-born social philosopher and educator Rudolf Steiner (1861–1925), anthroposophy holds that one's spiritual development, nourished by myth-making and other creative activities,

is of prime importance to their humanity. Steiner was strongly influenced by the writing of the German author Johann Wolfgang von Goethe and his ideas live on in the world-wide network of Waldorf schools.

The **Goetheanum**, a huge concrete building overlooking Dornach, is the seat of the Anthroposophical Society, which advocates the freedom of the individual. Constructed in line with the principles of this philosophy, it has no right angles, and is widely regarded as the epitome of Expressionist architecture.

Goetheanum
🏛️🕐 🚏Rüttiweg 45
🕐9am–6:30pm daily
🌐goetheanum.org

8

Aarau

🚆D2 🚊Aargau 🚌🚐
🏠Metzgergasse 2; www.aarauinfo.ch

Aarau has a scenic location on the River Aare. The old part of the town is built on terraces that rise steeply from the riverbank.

Briefly the capital of the Helvetic Republic, Aarau

became the capital of the canton of Aargau in 1803. Its wealth is derived from the textiles industry.

The town's highest point is marked by Schlössli, a castle thought to date from the 11th century, which now houses a museum of local history. Other notable buildings are the 16th-century town hall with a Romanesque tower and the 15th-century Stadtkirche. Some houses lining the narrow streets of Aarau's old districts have stepped gables and are decorated with floral motifs.

The town also has a decent art gallery, the **Aargauer Kunsthaus**, with a collection of modern paintings, and a museum of natural history.

Aargauer Kunsthaus
🏛️🕐🚏🏠 🚏Aargauerplatz
🕐10am–5pm Tue–Sun (to 8pm Thu) 🌐aargauer
kunsthaus.ch

The Goetheanum in Dornach, seat of the Anthroposophical Society ↑

⑨

Muri

📍 D3 🚉 Aargau 🚌🚃
ℹ Marktstrasse 10; www.
muri.ch

The splendidly restored Benedictine monastery in Muri constitutes this town's main attraction. **Kloster Muri** was founded by Ita von Lothringen and Count Redebot von Habsburg in 1027 and was inhabited by a community of monks until 1841. It then fell into disrepair and was gutted by fire in 1889. In 1960, after it had been meticulously restored, a small group of Benedictine monks returned to the monastery, where they ran a hospice.

The oldest surviving parts of the monastery's church include its Romanesque presbytery, crypt and transept. Some Gothic elements also survive. The main body of the church, however, is in the Baroque style. Built to an octagonal plan and topped by a dome, it dates from the 17th century. Most of the church furnishings were made in the late 17th and 18th centuries.

The cloisters adjoining the church are the burial place of the hearts of Emperor Karl I and his wife, Zita. An exhibition of paintings by the Swiss artist Caspar Wolf and items from the monastery's treasury are also displayed here.

Kloster Muri

📍 Marktstrasse 4 ⏰ Summer: 11am–5pm Tue–Sun; winter: 11am–4pm Tue–Sun

---

⑩

Kloster Königsfelden

📍 D2 🏛 Museumstrasse, Windisch, Aargau 🚉
⏰ Apr–Oct: 10am–5pm Tue–Sun; Nov–Mar: by request
🌐 klosterkoenigsfelden.ch

The Franciscan Abbey of Königsfelden lies between the quaint villages of Brugg and Windisch. It was founded in 1308 by Elizabeth von Habsburg to mark the spot where her husband Albrecht I was murdered by Duke Johann of Swabia. The monastery was later given to a community of Franciscan monks and nuns of the Order of St Clare. After Elizabeth's death, building work on the abbey was continued by her daughter Agnes of Hungary.

During the Reformation these religious communities were dissolved and in 1804 the monastery buildings were converted into a psychiatric hospital. When the hospital moved to new premises later in the 19th century, most of the monastery buildings were dismantled.

The church, however, survives. Built in 1310–30, it takes the form of a monumental Gothic basilica with a wooden ceiling. In the aisles are wooden panels with depictions of knights and coats of arms. The 11 stained-glass windows in the presbytery are some of the country's finest. Made between 1325 and 1330 and restored in the 1980s, they show scenes from the lives of Christ, the Virgin Mary, the Apostles and various saints.

The splendidly restored Kloster Muri, with its highly decorative Baroque interior (inset)

The medieval village of Regensberg attractively set on a hill among vineyards

⑪ Wettingen

 D2 ⚑ Aargau 🚉
🛈 Seminarstrasse 54;
www.wettingen.ch

Set among hills bordering the Limmat valley, Wettingen is a town with a stunning Cistercian abbey, **Zisterzienserkloster**. The monastery was dissolved in 1841, and now serves as a school. Its church and the cloisters are open to visitors.

The abbey church was founded in 1227. Although the Renaissance stalls survive, the church's interior is decorated in Baroque style. The Gothic cloisters now contain a display of stained glass.

Zisterzienserkloster

🕭 ⚑ Klosterstrasse 11
📞 056 437 24 03 🕙 Church: Mar-Oct: 9am-5pm Mon-Sat; cloisters: Mar-Oct: 9am-5pm Sat & Sun

⑫ Regensberg

 D2 ⚑ Zürich
🚌 From Dielsdorf

The attractive winegrowing village of Regensberg lies on a minor road off the highway between Zürich and Waldshut. Set on a hillside amid vineyards, it is one of the best-preserved medieval villages in Switzerland. Its main square and oldest streets are lined with half-timbered houses. The history of Regensberg goes back to 1245. The oldest building in the town is the castle's circular crenellated keep; the castle itself dates from the 16th and 17th centuries. Also of note is the 16th-century parish church, overlying the foundations of a medieval building.

---

⑬ Kaiserstuhl

 D2 ⚑ Aargau 🚉🚌
🌐 kaiserstuhl.ch

Set on a hillside on the bank of the Rhine, Kaiserstuhl is a beautiful old town. Its historic centre, which is contained within an irregular triangle, is a listed conservation area.

The upper corner of the triangle is marked by Oberer Turm (Upper Tower), a medieval bastion that once formed part of the town's fortifications. From Kaiserstuhl, a bridge over the Rhine leads to Hohentengen, where there is a 13th-century castle, Schloss Rötelen.

---

⑭ Eglisau

 E2 ⚑ Zürich 🚉
🛈 Untergass 7; www.eglisau.ch

Eglisau straddles the River Rhine and is surrounded by gentle hills covered in vineyards. Its origins go back to medieval times, when it was established at what was then a ford across the river, on an ancient route south to Zürich.

When a hydroelectric dam was built across the Rhine, the picturesque houses that once stood on the riverbank were engulfed by water. Eglisau's historic covered bridge was also lost. The higher part of the old town, with its 18th-century domed church, now stands just above water level. This historic centre is filled with half-timbered houses, some of which are decorated with colourful murals.

CENTRAL SWITZERLAND AND TICINO

The cradle of the Swiss Confederation and the birthplace of the legendary hero William Tell, central Switzerland is at both the geographical and the historical heart of the country. Bordering the east and south shores of Lake Lucerne, Schwyz, Uri and Unterwalde, known as the Waldstätte, or Forest Cantons, formed an alliance in 1291 that marked the foundation of the Swiss Confederation. Champion of the people William Tell became the stuff of legend by inciting the peasant rebellion, in 1307, that would go on to overthrow Habsburg rule, but it wasn't until the latter half of the 15th century that he appears in a collection of folk tales.

While William Tell was reputedly leading uprisings to the north, the dukes of Milan were fighting over what is now the southern canton of Ticino. Separated from its northern neighbours by the Alps, this Mediterranean-influenced region is bordered on almost all other sides by Italy. It was annexed by the Swiss Confederates in the early 16th century, but it only joined the Confederation as a free canton in 1803. This large, Italian-speaking canton in the sunny foothills of the southern Alps has a pace of life that's markedly more relaxed than elsewhere in Switzerland.

NORTHERN
SWITZERLAND
p172

7 Baar
7 ZUG

Z U G

Pfäffikon
Lachen

Sihlsee

3 KLOSTER
EINSIEDELN

Näfels

Arth

Goldau

IGI

12 SCHWYZ

S C H W Y Z

*Wägitaler
See*

Glarus

VITZNAU

Brunnen
Muotathal

Linthal

13 URNERSEE

Flüelen

ALTDORF **15**

14 BÜRGLEN

*Klausen
Pass*

U R I

Erstfeld

*Gross Scharhorn
3,295 m (10,810 ft)*

*Gross-Spannort
3,198 m (10,492 ft)*

*Gotthard Base
Tunnel*

Vassen

Göschenen

Andermatt

Sedrun

Disentis

Rhein

Chur

Flims

Breil

Ilanz

Lenzerheide

Thusis

**EASTERN
SWITZERLAND AND
GRAUBÜNDEN**
p238

Zillis

Savognin

Gotthard Tunnel

24 MUSEO SASSO SAN GOTTARDO

23 ST GOTTHARD PASS

22

Quinto

AIROLO

Valle Leventina

Olivone

Splügen

San Bernardino

Chiggiogna

21 VALLE DI
BLENIO

Fusio

L BAVONA

20

T I C I N O

Sonogno

Giornico

Malvaglia

Mesocco

Madesimo

Bignasco

Maggia

Brione

Biasca

Soazza

Chiavenna

Stampa

Cevio

ALLE MAGGIA **19**

18 VALLE
VERZASCA

Maggia

Vogorno

San
Vittore

Novate Mezzola

CENTOVALLI **16**

5 LOCARNO

6 BELLINZONA

I T A L Y

alagnedra

ASCONA **17**

Vira

Domaso

Brissago

Mezzovico

Ticino

Piantedo

Morbegno

Mezzovico

Bioggio

Lugano

*Lago
di Como*

Fraccia

*Lago
Maggiore*

Luino

4 LAKE
LUGANO

*Monte Generoso
1,704 m (5,590 ft)*

Lecco

San Pellegrino
Terme

Verbania

Mendrisio

Chiasso

Stresa

Varese

Como

LUCERNE

 D3 Lucerne Zentralstrasse 5; www.luzern.com

Central Switzerland's largest town, Lucerne (Luzern in German) lies on the western shore of Lake Lucerne. From its origins as a small fishing village, it grew into an important staging point when the St Gotthard Pass was opened in 1220. Easily explored on foot, the medieval Old Town lies on the north bank of the River Reuss and can be reached by crossing over the Chapel Bridge. The town's newer 20th-century suburbs climb the hills to the northeast and southwest, and stretch out along the banks of the lake.

①
Chapel Bridge

This 14th-century covered footbridge spanning the Reuss at an angle formed part of the town's early fortifications, protecting its citizens against attack from the direction of the lake. Near the centre of the river, the bridge joins the iconic Wasserturm, an octagonal tower that has served as a lighthouse, a prison and a treasury. In the 17th century, the bridge's roof panels were painted with scenes from the history of Lucerne and episodes in the lives of the martyrs St Leodegar and St Mauritius, who became the town's patron saints.

The oldest wooden bridge in Europe, Chapel Bridge (Kapellbrücke) has become the symbol of Lucerne. In 1993 the bridge was partly destroyed by a fire but it has since been rebuilt and most of its historic paintings have been restored.

KKL

Europaplatz 1 kkl-luzern.ch

With its cantilevered roof, the Kultur- und Kongresszentrum Luzern (Luzern Culture and Convention Centre), or the KKL, is a strikingly modernist glass-and-steel building that juts out over Lake Lucerne. It was designed by the French architect Jean Nouvel and was opened in 1998. The building contains both intimate and capacious theatres, concert and conference halls, and the Kunstmuseum, displaying contemporary art. Lounge areas, a range of restaurants and bars, and a seasonal ice rink also add to the appeal.

Did You Know?

The town hosts the Lucerne Festival of Classical Music with three annual events.

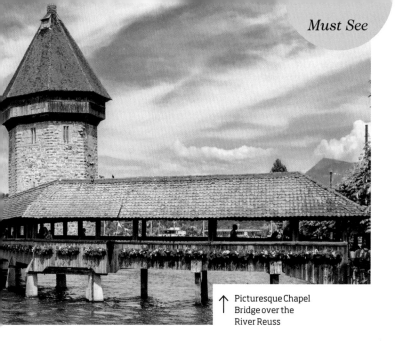

↑ Picturesque Chapel Bridge over the River Reuss

③ 🏃 🖥 🏛
Kunstmuseum

🚌 KKL ⏰ 11am-6pm
Tue-Sun (to 7pm Wed)
🌐 kunstmuseumluzern.ch

The vast collections of the Kunstmuseum are displayed in about 20 rooms on the topmost floor of the KKL building. The gallery has a fascinating permanent collection of 18th- and early 20th-century Swiss painting, and presents a rotating pro-gramme of exhibitions of the work of international contemporary artists. On the same floor, and accessible to the general public, is the Kunstmuseum's Art Library which has an interesting collection of various art books and magazines as well as an archive of previous exhibition catalogues.

④ Spreuerbrücke

This wooden covered bridge spans the Reuss at the western edge of the Old Town. It was built in 1408 and incorporates a small chapel. The bridge's roof is lined with panels painted by Kaspar Meglinger in 1626–35. Depicting the Dance of Death, they run in sequence from the north bank and culminate with Christ's triumph over Death at the south bank.

The Nadelwerk, a device that controls floods, stands downstream of the bridge.

Did You Know?

Of the original 67 paintings in the Spreuerbrücke Dance of Death, 45 are preserved on the bridge.

⑤ Franziskanerkirche

 Franziskanerplatz

This Franciscan church was built in the Gothic style, but over the centuries has been transformed with ornate Renaissance choir stalls and Baroque ceiling paintingsr.

⑥ Jesuit Church

🏛 Bahnhofstrasse 11

A major landmark on the south bank of the Reuss, the great Jesuitenkirche, the Jesuit church of St Francis Xavier, was built in 1666–73, however, its onion-domed twin towers were not completed until the 19th century. The Baroque interior is richly and colourfully decorated with intricate stuccowork and beautiful ceiling paintings depicting the apotheosis of St Francis Xavier.

⑦ Historisches Museum

 📍 Pfistergasse 24 🕙 10am–5pm Tue–Sun 🌐 historischesmuseum.lu.ch

Lucerne's history museum occupies the former arsenal, a Renaissance building dating from 1597. Also named the Depot, the museum has been brought up to date with interactive displays, barcodes and hand-held scanners in place of traditional information boards and audio guides.

Thousands of fascinating historical objects on display include weaponry, costumes, and folk art and crafts, as well as early advertising material from the Swiss manufacturing and tourism industries. Actors in period costume dramatize scenes from history in daily performances at the museum.

In the adjacent building is the Naturmuseum. Its displays focus on various aspects of natural history, in particular zoology and geology.

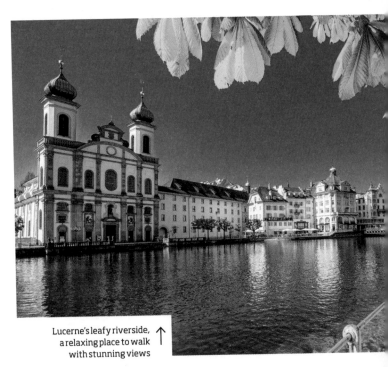

Lucerne's leafy riverside, a relaxing place to walk with stunning views ↑

The mournful Lion Monument, carved into the wall of a former sandstone quarry

Löwendenkmal

Denkmalstrasse

his massive figure of a dying lion pierced by a spear is a startling monument to the Swiss Guards of Louis XVI of France. On 10 August 1792, the guards defended the Palais des Tuileries, in Paris, when it was stormed by revolutionaries. Those who survived the attack were

arrested and guillotined on the night of 2–3 September. The Löwendenkmal, or Lion Monument, was designed by the Danish sculptor Bertel Thorwaldsen, and carved out of the sandstone cliff face by Lukas Ahorn. The sculpture was unvieleved in 1821 and is 10 m (33 ft) long and 6 m (20 ft) high. Reflected in the waters of a small pond, the monument has great drama and pathos.

⑨

Naturmuseum

🏠 **Kasernenplatz 6**
🕐 **10am-5pm Tue-Sun**
🌐 **naturmuseum.ch**

The Natural History Museum is an easy ten-minute stroll from the Old Town, southwest across the Spreuerbrücke. With a variety of live animals and interactive displays, this is a popular choice with children and is one of the country's most family-friendly museums. Hallways are lined with stuffed animals, and there is a full-time guide on hand to explain the exhibits in detail. There is plenty to keep adults engaged, too, such as the topographical representation of the Alps in prehistoric times. Various flora and fauna from central Switzerland, including a brightly coloured exhibit of butterflies, are displayed on rotating panels.

⑩

Rathaus

🏠 **Kornmarkt 3** 📞 **041 417 03 10** 🕐 **By arrangement**

The present town hall, built in a grand Renaissance style, was completed in 1606. Of the 14th-century town hall that stood on the same site, only a tower remains. The council chamber inside is lined with finely carved wood panelling.

⑪

Kapellplatz

🕐 **St Peterskapelle: 7:30am-6:15pm Mon-Wed & Fri, 7:30am-9pm Thu, 7:30am-5pm Sat, 8:30am-8pm Sun**

This square buzzes with life, particularly on market days. In the centre lies the Fritschi Fountain, adorned with allegorical figures depicting Brother Fritschi, a figure of Swiss legend who features in Lucerne's Carnival tradition.

Kapellplatz takes its name from the 18th-century chapel, St Peterskapelle, which stands on the site of a 12th-century church, the earliest to be built in Luzern. The chapel contains a 14th-century Gothic crucifix.

> 💬 INSIDER TIP
> **Lucerne's Markets**
>
> Although a relatively compact town, the markets in Lucerne are dazzling in their array of goods. Small farmers markets generally occur on Tuesdays whereas on weekends you'll find a selection of unique handicrafts, locally produced food and vintage gems. The squares of Weinmarkt and Kapellplatz are two of the key hotspots.

Admiring a rich selection of Picasso's work in the private Rosengart Collection

EAT

Luz

A perfect pit-stop, this tiny coffee joint serves delicious snacks and fabulous lake views.

Landungsbrücke 1
luzseebistro.ch

SF SF SF

Taube

The go-to place for delicious local Lucerne dishes, cooked just like your grandmother would do.

Burgerstrasse 3
taube-luzern.ch

SF SF SF

 13

Rosengart Collection

Pilatusstrasse 10
Apr-Oct: 10am-6pm daily; Nov-Mar: 11am-5pm daily rosengart.ch

The Rosengart Collection (Sammlung Rosengart) is a private collection of over 300 modernist paintings that was formed over several decades by the art dealers Siegfried Rosengart and his daughter, Angela. As well as 125 works by Paul Klee, the museum also has a fabulous collection of watercolours and sculptures by Pablo Picasso, many of them from the former Picasso Museum. The collection also includes Impressionist paintings, with canvases by Cézanne and Monet, as well as art works by Chagall, Matisse and Kandinsky.

 14

Gletschergarten

Denkmalstrasse 4
Apr-Oct: 10am-6pm daily; Nov-Mar: 10am-5pm daily gletschergarten.ch

This attractive garden is an oasis of tranquillity, as well as being the setting for a fascinating natural phenomenon. In 1872 an enormous rock, complete with 32 potholes and well-sized holes, was excavated here. Formed by glacial abrasion, the rock was shown

by research to date from the Ice Age. The garden was made to conserve this geological feature, which is protected by a tent-roof that allows visitors to view the rock from the sides.

The site includes a museum, an exhibition on the geological processes involved in creating

---

 12

Bourbaki Panorama

Löwenplatz 11 Apr-Oct: 10am-6pm daily; Nov-Mar: 10am-5pm daily
bourbakipanorama.ch

One of the world's few surviving panoramas, this giant circular mural depicts the march of the French army through Switzerland under General Bourbaki, during the Franco-Prussian War (1870–71). In a stone building now housed in a glass shell, it is 112 m (370 ft) long and 10 m (33 ft) high, and was painted by Edouard Castres. Sound effects, a spoken narrative (in several languages) and a smartphone app help bring the characters depicted to life and turn this early form of storytelling into an incredibly immersive experience with a digital narrative. The building hosts a variety of cultural events and contains a museum, a cinema and a small art gallery, as well as bars and a restaurant.

the holes and the fascinating Mirror Maze of more than 90 mirrors in the royal style of Granada's Alhambra fortress.

---

⑮ Weinmarkt

Lined with historic houses, this square is one of the most attractive features of the Old Town. In the centre stands the Weinmarktbrunnen, a Gothic fountain which is a close copy of the original that now stands in the quiet courtyard of the Ritterscher Palast, on pretty Bahnhofstrasse. The houses around both this square and the adjacent Hirschenplatz have painted façades, ornate doorways and oriel windows. Many of these buildings were once guildhouses, and Passion Plays enacting Christ's last days were performed in this iconic location in the late Middle Ages. These plays grew famous across Europe.

 PICTURE PERFECT
Fancy Frescoes
Each building lining the Weinmarkt is uniquely and intricately painted. Pay attention to the details of these beautiful frescoes that often tell a story and be sure to take a snapshot of the square.

⑯

Richard Wagner Museum

🏠 Richard-Wagner-Weg 27
🕐 Apr–Nov: 11am–5pm Tue–Sun 🔲 richard-wagner-museum.ch

The German Romantic composer Richard Wagner was a regular visitor to Lucerne. It was here that he wrote the third act of his opera *Tristan und Isolde*. Two complete operas, *Die Meistersinger von Nürnberg* and *Siegfried*, date from this period, and Wagner also started work here on *Götterdämmerung*.

The tranquil Villa Tribschen, where Wagner and his wife and son lived from 1866 to 1872, is devoted to this particularly happy period. Its rooms, with original furniture, are filled with memorabilia of the composer's life, including paintings, letters and musical instruments. Overlooking the lake, the museum's setting is very tranquil and there is also a little café outside in the summer months.

← A group of visitors looking at the brightly coloured frescoes of Weinmarkt's buildings

⑰ 🛴 🏍 🍴 🛍

VERKEHRSHAUS DER SCHWEIZ

📍 Lidostrasse 5 🕐 Apr-Oct: 10am-6pm daily; Nov-Feb: 10am-5pm daily 🌐 verkehrshaus.ch

The Swiss Museum of Transport celebrates one of humankind's most fundamental longings: the urge to travel across our planet and beyond it. Planes and spacecraft hang overhead in its lofty galleries while the floors are filled with more earthbound means of transport.

Almost every mode of mechanized transport, from the earliest bicycle to the latest spacecraft, is displayed at Lucerne's Swiss Museum of Transport, Switzerland's most visited museum. Vintage cars and steam locomotives are part of the exhibitions on road and rail transport, while the tourism section highlights the ingenuity of rack railways and cable cars. Water transport, aviation and space travel are also showcased. Among the museum's interactive features are three flight simulators, as well as a range of activities for young visitors. The museum also boasts the country's largest planetarium and the Swiss Chocolate Adventure, which immerses visitors in the delicious world of one of Switzerland's principal exports.

Did You Know?

The first Swiss railway company was called Spanisch Brötli Bahn, literally "Spanish bread roll railway".

GALLERY GUIDE

The rooms to the left of the main entrance are devoted to rail transport. Opposite the main entrance is the Road Transport Hall. The other main rooms contain aviation and space travel exhibits. The museum's Filmtheatre has the largest screen in the country, while the planetarium and the Swiss Chocolate Adventure are fun as well as educational.

↑ A hands-on exhibit that allows families to play a game involving Geneva Airport

↑ Eye-catching transport signs covering the exterior of the museum

Exhibits, including a colourful ↑
paraglider, on display at the
Swiss Transport Museum

A SHORT WALK
OLD TOWN

Distance 1 km (0.5 miles) **Nearest bus stop**
Hirschengraben **Time** 20 minutes

Lucerne's historic Old Town (Altstadt) is set on
a shallow bend of the Reuss at the point where
the river turns from Lake Lucerne. From the Middle
Ages the town was defended by ramparts on its
northern side and by Chapel Bridge, which spans
the river on its eastern side. The Old Town's ancient
layout survives, and the façades of its fine historic
houses, particularly around Hirschenplatz and
along Weinmarktgasse, are painted with frescoes
or covered with sgraffito decoration. This historic
district of Lucerne is also a bustling urban centre,
with plenty of shops, restaurants and cafés.

Did You Know?

The Chapel Bridge
(Kapellbrücke) is the
oldest covered wooden
bridge in Europe.

*Many of the paintings on
the façades of the houses in
Lucerne's Old Town are full
of symbolism and allusions.*

*The central square of **Weinmarkt**
(p209), where wine was once sold,
has several fine houses, many of
which were guildhalls.*

ROSSLIGASSE

WEGGISGA

EISENG

KORNMARKT-
PLATZ

WEINMARKT

UNTER DER EGG

*The narrow alleys off
Weinmarkt are lined with
tall houses, some with colourfully painted shutters.
Many of these houses have
been converted into hotels,
or contain boutiques
and restaurants.*

▶ START

*Completed in 1606, the lat
Renaissance **Rathaus** (p207
has an ornate façade*

↑ The elaborate façades of Lucerne's medieval buildings on Weinmarkt

The fountain in **Kapellplatz** (p207) is crowned by a figure of Fritschi, a legendary character associated with spring and joy. He is celebrated at Fasnacht, Lucerne's great spring festival.

A relief showing Christ and his disciples in the Garden of Gethsemane is set into the chapel of **St Peterskapelle**'s south wall.

The covered **Chapel Bridge** (p204) has become the symbol of Lucerne. Originally built in the 14th century, the footbridge was partly destroyed by fire in 1993 and has been reconstructed.

FINISH

STERNEN–PLATZ

KAPELL–PLATZ

APELLGASSE

FURRENGASSE

RATHAUSQUAI

0 metres   30
0 yards   30

N ↑

→ Pretty Chapel Bridge, stretching over the Reuss

❷
PILATUS

🅐 D3   🏠 Obwalden, Nidwalden and Lucerne   �æ From Alpnachstad

The rugged outlines of Pilatus, whose highest peak reaches an altitude of 2,132 m (7,000 ft), rise on the southwestern side of Lake Lucerne. Various legends shroud the mountain, including claims that it is both home to a dragon and that its heights are haunted by Pontius Pilate, who unleashes violent storms.

The massif has plenty to entertain visitors, including walking trails to its various peaks, a rope park and paragliding, as well as plenty of restaurants and two hotels. Getting to the summit is an adventure in itself. The first stage is a boat or train ride from Lucerne to Alpnachstad, near the foot of Pilatus, from where you can either take the cogwheel railway, a gondola or a cable car called the "Dragon Ride" *(www.pilatus.ch)* from Schlossweg 1 to Pilatus Kulm, the upper station. The magnificent views from Pilatus' summit reward the journey.

← Walking up a signposted trail to the marker on Oberhaup peak

COGWHEEL RAILWAY

Completed in 1889, the cog railway that climbs from Alpnachstad to Pilatus Kulm is, at an average gradient of 48 per cent, the steepest in the world. Designed by engineer Eduard Locher, the railway is almost 5 km (3 miles) long, and the journey takes 30 minutes. Originally driven by steam locomotives, the railway was electrified in 1937. One of the original steam railcars can be seen at the Swiss Museum of Transport in Lucerne *(p210)*.

Gondolas take visitors over the lush forest from Kriens to the top of Pilatus, offering panoramic views.

A variety of restaurants are found at Pilatus's summit.

Built in 1890, Hotel Pilatus-Kulm is a luxurious lodge with a beautiful restaurant.

 INSIDER TIP
Flora Path

Follow the easy, well-marked flower trail at the top of Pilatus for an insight into the many colourful flowers that dot the hillside; some, like the Alpine dwarf orchid, can only be found at this altitude.

↑ A cable car descending from the Pilatus terminal, passing breathtaking scenery

215

3

KLOSTER EINSIEDELN

📍 D2 🏠 Hauptstrasse 85, Einsiedeln, Schwyz
🚉🚌 Einsiedeln 🕐 Church: 6am–9pm Mon–Sat (from 7am Sun); Grosser Saal: 1:30–6pm daily; library: 2pm daily or by appointment 🌐 kloster-einsiedeln.ch

Completed in 1735, the Benedictine abbey at Einsiedeln is one of the finest examples of Baroque architecture in the world. The abbey has been a place of pilgrimage since 948 when, according to legend, a miracle occured during the consecration of the church, and now more than one million pilgrims come here each year.

The history of the abbey goes back to 835, when Meinrad, a monk, chose the spot for his hermitage. In 934 a monastery was founded on the site, and it soon flourished as a place of learning, printing and music. Its library became renowned for its extensive collection of manuscripts. In the 13th century the pilgrimage to the abbey became known as the "Einsiedeln tradition". The abbey was left alone during the Reformation in the 16th century, despite the fact Protesant Reformist Ulrich Zwingli preached here during this time. The church and monastery were rebuilt in the 18th century, to a grand Baroque design. Most of the paintings, gilding and stuccowork are by the Bavarian brothers Cosmas Damian and Egid Quirin Asam. Today 60 monks continue to work and follow the Benedictine tradition.

Did You Know?

In the abbey's library is *Versus de scachis*, with the earliest known mention of chess in Western literature.

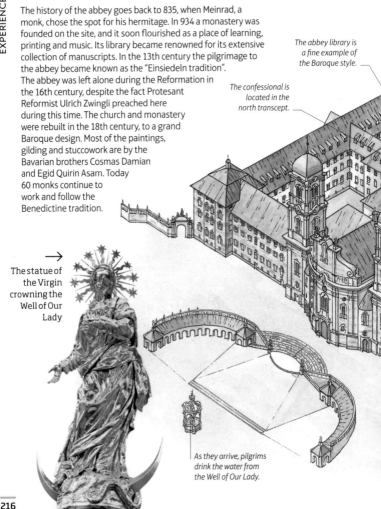

The abbey library is a fine example of the Baroque style.

The confessional is located in the north transcept.

→ The statue of the Virgin crowning the Well of Our Lady

As they arrive, pilgrims drink the water from the Well of Our Lady.

1 The Benedictine abbey glistens under a layer of snow, flanked by the Mythen mountains.

2 The 15th-century wooden figure of the Madonna, reputed to have miraculous powers, stands in gilt surroundings.

3 An intricately carved statue stands guard in front of the abbey.

The walls, ceiling and ceiling and domes of the church are covered with frescoes and gilt stuccowork.

← The 18th-century abbey complex, built in typically opulent Baroque style

The lavishly decorated Grosser Saal, or Great Hall, is still used for official ceremonies.

The organ is bedecked with figures of putti playing instruments.

The spacious nave is decorated with Baroque frescoes.

Figures of angels and the symbols of the Four Evangelists decorate the gilt pulpit.

> 💬 INSIDER TIP
> **Christmas Time**
>
> Every December a Christmas market sets up along the town's main street and on the abbey square. With more than 150 stalls, it is one of the country's largest. Be sure to sample the gingerbread (it's a tasty local speciality).

4 🍴 🥤 🛍️

LAKE LUGANO

E6 🚉 Ticino 🚌 Lugano 🛈 Lugano train station, Riva Giocondo Albertolli; 091 913 32 32

Nestling between steep alpine slopes, this sheltered, glacial lake is one of Ticino's most beautiful natural features. Although most of it lies in Swiss territory, the southwestern shore, northeastern branch and a small central enclave belong to Italy.

A gateway to the Alps, Lake Lugano (Lago di Ceresio in Italian) endured a medieval tug-of-war between different Italian, and later, Swiss factions. It was only in 1752, when the Italian-Swiss border was fixed, that control of the lake was settled, and it remains largely unchanged to this day.

A road bridge crosses the lake at Melide, leading up to the St Gotthard Tunnel, but the best way of exploring it is by boat, from the town of Lugano or several other points along the lakeshore. The lake's shape is unusual, twisting into branches dotted with villages and semitropical parks which cling to its rugged shoreline, and is best understood from above. Fortunately, a funicular from Lugano up Monte Brè and a cogwheel railway from Capolago up Monte Generoso allow just that, carrying passengers into the mountains that flank the lake.

Did You Know?

Fossils dating from the mid-Triassic (around 220 million years ago) have been found around the lake.

1 The restaurant atop Monte Generoso, designed by Mario Botta, commands stunning views of the southern shores of the lake.

2 Swissminiatur, the main attraction of Melide, displays 1:25 scale models of the country's landmarks.

3 The panorama of Lake Lugano and the mountains in the distance spills away from Monte Brè, which lies north of the lake.

PICTURE PERFECT
The Pearl of Ceresio

Set sail towards pretty Morcote, dubbed the Pearl of Ceresio. The postcard-ready terraced vineyards, with the domed Captain's Tower clinging to the slopes, are best viewed from the water.

The small church of Santa Maria del Sasso overlooking the lakeside hamlet of Morcote ↑

A SHORT WALK
LUGANO

17
The number of heritage sites of national significance in Lugano.

Distance 1 km (0.5 miles) **Nearest funicular** Lugano Città **Time** 20 minutes

Lying in a shallow inlet on the north shore of Lake Lugano, this is the largest town in Ticino and one of the canton's great lakeside resorts. Lugano is also a centre of finance and banking. With piazzas, stepped streets and narrow, winding alleys, the Old Town (Centro Storico) has an Italianate character. Its hub is Piazza della Riforma, a square lined with tall shuttered buildings and filled with busy pavement cafés. Palm-fringed promenades line the quays, and the distinctive sugar-loaf outlines of Monte Brè and Monte San Salvatore rise to the east and south.

START

The 18th-century **Palazzo Riva** has decorated windows with wrought-iron balconies.

The Renaissance façade of **Cattedrale San Lorenzo** contains a rose window depicting the Madonna and Child.

VIA SAN LORENZO

VIA PESSINA

VIA MOTTA

PIAZZA DELLA RIFORMA

RIVA GIOCONDO ALBERTOLLI

Palazzo Civico, the Neo-Classical town hall built in 1844–5, features a statue of the architect Domenico Fontana from Melide.

← A pastel-coloured restaurant on the Piazza della Riforma

Filled with pavement cafés, **Piazza della Riforma** is the social and geographical hub of Lugano's historic centre.

The luxuriously decorated nave of Cattedrale San Lorenzo in Lugano, with intricate frescos

Replacing an earlier Gothic church, **San Rocco**, with its Baroque high altar, was built after the plague that swept through the city in 1528.

VIA VEGEZZI

Palazzo dei Congressi conference centre, built in 1975, is set in a park with fountains and modern statuary.

RIVA GIOCONDO ALBERTOLLI

VIA ELVEZIA

FINISH

metres 30 N

yards 30 ↑

Built in the 17th century and remodelled in the mid-19th, **Villa Ciani** is a focal point for special events.

↑ A quiet sunny day in Piazza Grande, the core of the town of Locarno

LOCARNO

E5 **Ticino** **Piazza Stazione; www.ascona-locarno.com**

With an enchanting setting at the northern tip of Lake Maggiore, Locarno lies in a wide bay in the shelter of the Lepontine Alps. It is often said to be the sunniest of all Swiss towns, and date palm, fig, pomegranate and bougainvillea thrive in its mild climate. During the Middle Ages, Locarno was the centre of a dispute between the bishops of Como and the dukes of Milan, until the Swiss Confederates gained control in 1512. The capital of Ticino from 1803 to 1878, today Locarno is a resort that attracts visitors from north of the Alps who come to enjoy its Mediterranean climate.

① Piazza Grande

This rectangular paved square, one of Switzerland's biggest, is the focus of life in Locarno. Along its north side are 19th-century buildings with arcades of shops, cafés and restaurants. There is a weekly market here selling handicrafts and local produce on Thursdays, concerts are held in July, and during the renowned International Film Festival, a ten-day extravaganza held in early August, the square becomes an open-air cinema, lined with rows of seats and a huge screen.

② Chiesa San Francesco

Via Cittadella 20

Completed in 1572, the church of St Francis stands on the site of a 13th-century Franciscan monastery. The eagle, ox and lamb on its Renaissance façade represent Locarno's aristocrats, ordinary citizens and country-dwellers respectively. The interior decoration dates mainly from the 18th century.

③ Castello Visconteo

Piazza Castello 2 **Apr-Oct: 10am-noon & 2-5pm Tue-Sun** **locarno.ch**

The origins of this castle go back to the 12th century, when it was built for the Orelli family. In 1342 ownership fell into the hands of the Milanese Visconti family. The dovetailed crenellation of the walls and the towers dates from a series of 15th-century expansions, as does the ravelin fortification, believed to be the work of Leonardo da Vinci. The surviving wing now houses an archaeology museum, which has a particularly good collection of Roman artifacts.

2,155

The average hours of sunshine Locarno enjoys every year.

romenade
ungolago Giuseppe
otta

ed with trees, plants and
rubs from around the world,
is lakeshore promenade
sembles the seafront boule-
rds of the French Riviera.
e promenade leads north-
rds to the end of the lake,
ere the Ghisla Art Collection,
mall gallery, hangs an
ectic array of abstract art.
the south, the promenade
ds towards the marina,
yond which is a sandy beach
d an impressive public pool.

)

iesa di San Vittore

Via Collegiata, Muralto

ilt in the 12th-century, the
manesque basilica of San
tore stands on the site of a
th-century church in Muralto,
st of the train station. The
silica's belfry, begun in the
th century but only com-
eted in 1932, has a charming
naissance relief of St Victor.
e austere interior bears
aces of medieval frescoes,
d below, the crypt contains
lumns with carved capitals.

)

iesa Nuova

Via Cittadella

is church, also known as
iesa Santa Maria Assunta,
as completed in 1636. Its
nstruction was funded
the architect Cristoforo
elli. It has a splendid pastel-
inted Baroque interior with
mptuous stuccowork and
intings depicting scenes
om the life of the Virgin.
acing the west front is a
ge statue of St Christopher
th unusually tiny feet for a
atue of its size. The Palazzo
istoforo Orelli, next to the
urch, now serves as the
non's office.

Must See

Casa Rusca

🏠 Piazza Sant' Antonio
🕐 10am-noon & 2-5pm Tue-
Sun 🌐 museocasarusca.ch

This elegant 18th-century
residence houses an art
gallery focussing on the work
of modern and contemporary
artists, many of whom have
donated pieces of their work
to the gallery. A highlight of
the collection is a display of
work by Hans Arp (1886–1966),
the Dadaist artist who spent
his final years in Locarno.

Santuario della
Madonna del Sasso

🏠 Via Santuario 2, Orselina
🕐 Church: 7:30am-6pm
daily; museum: Apr-Nov:
9:30am-12:30pm & 1-5pm
Fri-Sun (Jul-Nov: also on
Thu) 🌐 madonnadel
sasso.org

The pilgrimage church of the
Madonna of the Rock (Santa
Maria Assunta) overlooks the
town from the summit of a
wooded spur. Dating from
1596, the church stands on
the site of a 1487 chapel that

↑ Detail of the exquisite
ceiling of Santuario della
Madonna del Sasso

marked the spot where legend
claims the Madonna appeared
before Bartolomeo da Ivrea, a
monk in the Franciscan order.
The present church features
frescoes and oil paintings,
including an altarpiece with
the Flight into Egypt painted
by Bramantino in 1522.

⑨

Palazzo della
Conferenza

🏠 Via della Pace

It was in this *palazzo* that the
Treaty of Locarno, drawn up
between Germany and other
European countries in the
aftermath of World War I,
was ratified in 1925.

→

The 270-m-(885-ft-) long suspension bridge above Bellinzona town

❻ 🍴 ☕ 🛍️

BELLINZONA

🅰 E5 **📍 Ticino** **🚌🚆** **ℹ Palazzo Civico; www.bellinzonaturismo.ch**

Due to its strategic location between the great alpine passes, Bellinzona was a fortress town from Roman times. During the Middle Ages, the dukes of Milan built the three castles here that now form a UNESCO World Heritage Site. The town was taken over by the Swiss Confederates in the 16th century, and became the capital of Ticino in 1803.

Did You Know?

Bellinzona's annual Carnevale Rabadan (meaning "noise carnival") is over 150 years old.

①

Castelgrande

🏛 Salita Castelgrande
🕐 Apr-Oct: 10am-6pm daily (Jul & Aug: to 8pm Wed); Nov-Mar: 10:30am-4pm daily **🌐 bellinzonese-altoticino.ch**

Set on a high plateau, this is the oldest and grandest of Bellinzona's three castles. In the 12th century, the Roman fortress that already stood on the site was rebuilt and enlarged by the bishops of Como. The fortress was extended on several occasions until the late 15th century.

Today Castelgrande's main features are the Torre Bianca (White Tower) and the Torre Nera (Black Tower), which are joined by crenellated walls that form inner baileys. In the south wing, a museum traces Bellinzona's history, displaying 15th-century painted panels from the walls and ceiling of a villa from the town.

② 🍴 ☕ 🛍️

Old Town

Bellinzona's Old Town nestles in the wide Ticino valley, in the shadow of its great medieval castles. With Italianate squares, Renaissance buildings and red cobblestones peppering its winding alleys, it is a typical Lombard town. Among the town's many fine buildings are the Palazzo Civico, an elegant town hall with an arcaded courtyard, and the Chiesa Santa Maria delle Grazie, a church with 15th-century frescoes. On Saturday mornings the Old Town fills with colourful market stalls heaped with fresh produce such as cheeses and bread, plus wines and local crafts.

③

Chiesa Collegiata dei Pietro e Stefano

🏛 Piazza Collegiata

This Renaissance monastery church stands at the foot of the ramparts of Castelgrande. The interior retains an earlier set of Gothic arches, and is sublimely decorated with stuccowork and lavish fresco. Over the high altar is a depiction of the Crucifixion, painted by Simone Peterzano in 1658.

> **INSIDER TIP**
> **The Tibetan Bridge**
>
> From the Bellinzona suburbs, a funicular will carry you through chestnut woods up into Monte Carasso. A pleasant circular hike leads to the spectacular Carasc wooden Tibetan bridge, anchored with flexible cables. It hangs above the Sementina Valley, and offers sweeping views over the treetops to the town.

Castello di Montebello

🚪 Via Artore 4
🕐 Apr-Oct: 10am-6pm daily (Jul & Aug: to 8pm Wed) 🌐 bellinzonese-altoticino.ch

A 13th-century keep and a 15th-century residential palace make up this complex fortress.

The crenellated walls linking Castello di Montebello, to the east of the town, and Castelgrande, to the west, created a formidable defence system across the valley. The views from the castle are spectacular; on a clear day you can see as far as Lake Maggiore (p234). A museum, in the keep, contains archaeological artifacts from the vicinity.

Castello di Sasso Corbaro

🚪 Via Sasso Corbaro 44
🕐 Apr-Oct: 10am-6pm daily (Jul & Aug: to 8pm Wed) 🌐 bellinzonese-altoticino.ch

Castello di Sasso Corbaro is the youngest of the town's three fortresses. It was built in 1479 to the design of Benedetto Ferrini, after the Swiss had defeated the Milanese at the Battle of Giornico, thus increasing the threat to Ticino. The fortress, a quadrilateral residential tower and square ramparts, is set on an elevated headland and commands wide views across the Ticino valley all the way to Lake Maggiore.

Villa dei Cedri

🚪 Piazza San Biagio 9
🕐 2-6pm Wed & Thu, 10am-6pm Fri-Sun 🌐 villa cedri.ch

Overlooking a vineyard, this Neo-Renaissance villa is the town's art gallery. On display are 19th- and 20th-century paintings and prints, including works by Giovanni Segantini.

A fountain standing in Zug's picturesque medieval Old Town ↑

EXPERIENCE MORE

7
Zug

 E3 ❑ Zug 🚇🚌⛴
i Bahnhofstrasse;
www.zug-tourismus.ch

Zug is set on the northeastern shore of Zugersee, in the wooded foothills of the Zugerberg. It is the capital of its namesake, Zug, the smallest but also the richest of all the Swiss cantons. Having the lowest taxation in Switzerland, Zug has become the headquarters of many multinational companies.

Substantial parts of the walls, set with towers, still encircle Zug's medieval Old Town. The main hub of the Old Town is Kolinplatz, which features a fountain with a statue of Wolfgang Kolin, a standard-bearer of the Swiss army. Nearby stands the Gothic Rathaus, built in 1509.

The former bailiff's castle houses the **Museum Burg**
Zug, with small permanent collections of local history, as well as special exhibitions. Nearby is a 16th-century granary now converted into the **Kunsthaus**, a gallery with an important collection of Viennese modern art. The **Museum für Urgeschichte (n)** concentrates both on prehistory and antiquity.

Cruises on the Zugersee depart from the harbour jetty.

Museum Burg Zug
⊛ ❑ Kirchenstrasse 11
🕐 2–5pm Tue–Fri, 10am–5pm Sat & Sun 🌐 burgzug.ch

Kunsthaus
⊛ ❑ Dorfstrasse 27
🕐 Noon–6pm Tue–Fri,
10am–5pm Sat & Sun
🌐 kunsthauszug.ch

Museum für Urgeschichte(n)
⊛ ❑ Hofstrasse 15
🕐 2–5pm Tue–Sun
🌐 urgeschichte-zug.ch

8
Küssnacht am Rigi

D3 ❑ Schwyz 🚌⛴
i Unterdorf 15; www.hohlgassland.ch

The small town of Küssnacht am Rigi lies at the foot of the Rigi. This massif rises to the east of Küssnachtersee, which extends as the northern arm of Lake Lucerne.

The town is a good base for hiking and other activities in the mountains and for exploring Lake Lucerne.

Buildings of interest in Küssnacht's historic district include the Baroque town hall and the Kirche St Peter und St Paul. Another is the Engel Hotel, a half-timbered building that dates from 1552 and has been an inn for over 400 years.

9
Rigi and Vitznau

D3 ❑ Lucerne 🚂⛴
i Bahnhofstrasse 7,
Vitznau; www.rigi.ch

The Rigi massif, with views of 13 lakes and hundreds of peaks, is one of Switzerland's most popular holiday destinations. Instead of glaciers and crevasses, there are lavish resort hotels and hiking paths through woods and open pastures with more than 1,000

> 💬 INSIDER TIP
> **Trotti Bike**
>
> Ride down prepared forest trails on these stand-up scooter-like bikes with fat tyres and no seat. They are suitable for anyone aged ten and up and can be rented in Engelberg (www.titlis.ch).

→
Engelberg's thrilling
Titlis Cliff Walk, Europe's
highest suspension bridge

species of flora. The highest of the summits is called Rigi-Kulm (1,798 m/5,900 ft), less than half the height of the Matterhorn, but a lot easier to climb with children.

A popular base is Vitznau, which lies in a sheltered bay on the north shore of Lake Lucerne. Vitznau is also the base station of the oldest rack railway in Europe, opened in 1871. It leads up to just below the summit of Rigi-Kulm, offering breathtaking views.

 10

Stans

D4 **Nidwalden** 🚗🚌
i Bahnhofplatz 4; www. tourismusstans.ch

Stans is a town on the banks of the River Engelberger Aa. Above the small town rises the Stanserhorn (1,900 m/ 6,234 ft), the summit of which can be reached from Stans by funicular and the world's first double-decker cable car with an open top.

The town's charming historic district revolves around Dorfplatz. This square is dominated by a Baroque parish church, Pfarrkirche St Peter und St Paul, with a Romanesque tower, the remains of an earlier church. In the centre of Dorfplatz

STAY

Rigi Kaltbad Spa Hotel
A designer retreat high on Mount Rigi with epic views.

 D3 **Zentum 4, Rigi Kaltbad** **w** hotel rigikaltbad.ch

(SF)(SF)(SF)

Hotel & Spa Internazionale
A powder pink confection with pleasant rooms in the town centre.

 E5 **Viale Stazione 35, Bellinzona** **w** hotel-internazionale.ch

(SF)(SF)(SF)

stands a 19th-century monument to Arnold von Winkelried who sacrificed his life to help his Confederate comrades defeat the Austrians at the Battle of Sempach in 1386.

Also noteworthy in the town are the Höfli, a medieval turreted house that contains a museum of local history, and the Winkelriedhaus, a late Gothic building that houses a museum of local folk crafts and traditions.

11

Engelberg

D4 **Obwalden** 🚗🚌
i Klosterstrasse 3, www. engelberg.ch

A popular mountain resort, Engelberg lies at an altitude of 1,000 m (3,280 ft), at the foot of Titlis, whose rocky peak reaches 3,239 m (10,627 ft) to a glacier.

The village nestles around the Kloster, a Benedictine monastery. Founded in the 12th century and rebuilt in the mid-18th, it has an exquisite Rococo church, built in 1735–40. The monastery, and its working cheese dairy, are open to visitors.

Engelberg has about 80 km (50 miles) of skiing pistes. It also offers tobogganing and ice-skating facilities. Marked trails in the vicinity lead up to the summits of Schlossberg Titlis, Urirotstock and Hutstock. There are also many cycling routes. The Rotair cable car, which rotates as it travels to give passengers an all-round view, runs from Stand, above Engelberg, over the Titlis glacier. Those with a head for heights can also inch across the Titlis Cliff Walk, Europe's highest suspension bridge, at 3,040 m (9,980 ft).

⑫
Schwyz

🅰E3 🄰Schwyz 🚌🚉
🛈Zeughausstrasse 10;
www.schwyz-tourismus.ch

This quiet town, capital of the canton of the same name, lies at the foot of the twin peaks of the Mythen. It has immense importance in Swiss history and culture.

The canton of Schwyz gave Switzerland both its name and its flag. Having sworn their mutual allegiance in 1291, the joint forces of Schwyz, Uri and Unterwalden united to defeat the Habsburgs at the Battle of Morgarten (1315). Thereafter they were known as Schwyzers, and by the late 1400s, the Swiss had adopted the name Schwyzerland.

The **Bundesbriefmuseum** (Museum of the Swiss Charters) in Schwyz preserves a number of important historical documents. The most highly prized exhibit is the Charter of Confederation, written on parchment and stamped with the seals of the three Forest Cantons in 1291.

Schwyz's Old Town contains many 17th- and 18th-century buildings. Hauptplatz, the central square, is dominated by the Baroque Pfarrkirche St Martin and the Rathaus, the 17th-century town hall whose façade features a depiction of the Battle of Morgarten painted in 1891. The **Ital-Reding-Haus**, a mansion built in 1609, contains a suite of rooms with 17th- and 18th-century furnishings and decoration. Nearby is Haus Bethlehem, a wooden house built in 1287.

Did You Know?

Oscar-winning filmmaker Xavier Koller was born in Schwyz.

↑ The calm waters of Urnersee, backed by steep-sided mountains

A former granary dating from 1711 houses the **Forum der Schweizer Geschichte**, a museum of daily life.

Bundesbriefmuseum
♿ 🄰Bahnhofstrasse 20
🕙10am–5pm Tue–Sun
🅆bundesbrief.ch

Ital-Reding-Haus
♿ 🄰Rickenbachstrasse 14
🕙May–Oct: 2–5pm Tue–Fri, 10am–4pm Sat & Sun
🅆irh.ch

Forum der Schweizer Geschichte
🄰Zeughausstrasse 5
🕙10am–5pm Tue–Sun
🅆forumschwyz.ch

---

⑬
Urnersee

🅰E4 🄰Uri 🚌🚉 🛈Brunnen, Bahnhofstrasse 15; www. brunnentourismus.ch

Stunningly beautiful Urnersee forms the south-eastern arm of Lake Lucerne. Surrounded on all sides by high, steep-sided mountains, Urnersee resembles a Norwegian fjord. On an elevated promontory below Seelisberg, on the west side of the lake, is Rütli Meadow (Bergwiese Rütli), where the alliance between the cantons of Schwyz, Unterwalden and Uri was sworn in 1291 (*p57*).

The village of Seedorf, at the southern extremity of Urnersee, has a picturesque Gothic-Renaissance castle. It was built in 1556–60 and now houses a small geological museum. Flüelen, nearby, is the furthest port of call for any boats that sail across the lake from Lucerne.

→ Rathausplatz in the centre of Altdorf, in which stands the Telldenkmal

About 3 km (2 miles) north of Flüelen is the Tellsplate, a flat rock. According to legend, this is where William Tell made his leap to freedom during his journey across Lake Lucerne, on his way to imprisonment at Küssnacht. Near the rock stands the Tellskapelle, a 16th-century chapel remodelled in the 19th century.

14

Bürglen

This small town at the mouth of the Schächen valley is reputed to be the birthplace of William Tell, hero of Swiss legend. The supposed site of his house is marked by a chapel built in 1582. It is decorated with frescoes illustrating how Tell killed a Habsburg duke, triggering confederacy.

The legend of William Tell and the place it occupies in Swiss culture are illustrated through over 600 years' worth of paintings and chronicles at the fascinating **Tell Museum**. Also of interest in Bürglen are a 17th-century wooden tavern, the Adler Inn, which serves local beers, and an early Baroque church with a Romanesque tower.

Tell Museum

⊗ ⊗ 🏛 Postplatz ⏰ May, Jun, Sep & Oct: 10-11:30am & 1:30-5pm daily; Jul & Aug: 10am-5pm daily 🌐 tell museum.ch

WILLIAM TELL

Switzerland's national hero, or perhaps just a myth? Revisionist historians say William Tell *(right)* was invented more than a century after he allegedly freed his son, and his emerging country, from Habsburg feudal lords by shooting the evil bailiff Hermann Gessler in 1307. This emblematic act of courage and resistance has echoed down the ages and across the globe, thanks in part to Hollywood, Friedreich von Schiller's play and Gioachino Rossini's opera. If, as now suggested, it was all a ploy designed to forge a sense of national unity, it worked.

15

Altdorf

🅰 E4 🏛 Uri 🚌 🚆
🛈 Tellspielhaus; www.uri.info

Altdorf is said to be the town where William Tell shot an apple from his son's head. The Telldenkmal, a statue of Tell, stands on Rathausplatz, and plays of the story are are regularly performed.

16

Centovalli

🅰 E5 🚉 Ticino 🚻
🛈 Intragna; 091 780 75 00

The stunning Centovalli (Hundred Valleys) is so named for the many side valleys that cut into it. The **Centovalli Railway**, from Locarno to Domodossola in Italy, takes a spectacularly scenic route up the Centovalli. On this journey of about 40 km (25 miles), the train crosses 79 bridges or viaducts over deep canyons and passes through 24 tunnels. The first part of the journey leads along the vineyard-covered Val Pedemonte and then wends its way through rugged countryside and deep forests full of chestnut trees.

The train stops at several villages along the route. At Verscio, 4 km (2.5 miles) from Locarno, there is a performing

1995
—
The year Swiss clown Dimitri was inducted into the International Clown Hall of Fame.

arts school, founded by the famous Swiss clown Dimitri. Nearby Intragna has a Baroque church. Palagnedra has a small Gothic church decorated with 15th-century frescoes.

Centovalli Railway
🅰 Via Franzoni 1, Locarno
🔳 centovalli.ch

___

17

Ascona

🅰 E6 🚉 Ticino 🚻🚆 🛈 Via B Papio 5; www.ascona-locarno.com

A small fishing village for many centuries, Ascona developed in the early 20th century, when it became a fashionable health resort, attracting writers, painters and composers. Nearby Monte Verità (Hill of Truth) was established as a progressive colony around the same time, attracting some of Europe's leading thinkers, artists, revolutionaries and writers.

Ascona's exquisite Old Town (Centro Storico) is a maze of narrow cobbled streets, with small craft shops and art galleries. Many of the most picturesque of Ascona's historic buildings, the oldest of which date from the 14th century,

line Contrada Maggiore. Piazza San Pietro is dominated by the 16th-century Chiesa dei Santi Pietro e Paolo, which has an altarpiece painted by Giovanni Serodine, a pupil of Caravaggio. Also notable are the Collegio Papio, which has a pretty Renaissance arcaded court-yard, and Santa Maria della Misericordia, a church with colourful 15th-century frescoes. The Museo Comunale d'Arte Moderna, in a 16th-century *palazzo*, contains work by artists who flocked to the town, including Paul Klee. Piazza Motta, a pedestrianized lakefront promenade, is home to cafés and restaurants.

___

18

Valle Verzasca

🅰 E5 🚉 Ticino 🚆 🛈 Via ai Giardini, Tenero; www.ascona-locarno.com

Washed by the emerald waters of the River Verzasca, this is an exceptionally scenic valley lying north of Locarno. A gigantic dam, the Contra Dam, near the mouth of the valley has created the Lago di Vogorno, a large artificial lake.

The valley is lined with villages, whose stone houses cling to the mountainsides. Vogorno has a small church decorated with Byzantine frescoes. Near Lavertezzo, the river is spanned by the

💬 INSIDER TIP
Bungee Jump

James Bond did it, so they call the 220 m- (722 ft-) bungee jump from the Contra Dam "the 007". The tallest bungee in the world, you can jump at night, or even go backwards.

←
The handsome Italian-style buildings and cobbled streets of Ascona's Old Town

The Ponte dei Salti, a medieval double-arched bridge in Valle Verzasca

Ponte dei Salti, a medieval double-arched bridge. A modern art trail, running for 4 km (2.5 miles) between Brione and Lavertezzo, is lined with works by 34 Italian, Swiss and German sculptors.

At Brione-Verzasca is a church with origins that go back to the 13th century. Its façade is decorated with a painting of St Christopher, and the interior features 15th-century frescoes.

 19

Valle Maggia

🅰 E5 🔯 Ticino 🚉
ℹ️ www.vallemaggia.ch

This deep valley runs for about 50 km (30 miles) northwest of Ascona up to Cevio. At its lower levels, the valley is wide, though as it ascends it becomes increasingly rugged, with forests of pine and larch. The valley is also dotted with historical buildings and churches, and rugged stone houses. At Maggia, the largest village in the valley, you'll find the 15th-century Chiesa Santa Maria delle Grazie. The exterior is unremarkable but the interior is decorated with dazzling 16th- and 17th-century frescoes.

Past Giumaglio, where there are dramatic waterfalls, the road leads further up the valley to Cevio. A notable feature of this village is the 17th-century Palazzo Pretorio, its façade featuring the coats of arms of the bailiffs who successively occupied the building. Nearby stands the Palazzo Franzoni (1630), which houses a museum of regional history.

The hamlet of Mogno contains the serenely beautiful Chiesa di San Giovanni Battista. Designed by the Ticinese architect Mario Botta and completed in 1996, this extraordinary church is built of local stone. The interior is lined with white marble and grey granite arranged in stripes and chequer patterns. The light pouring in through the translucent ceiling only enhances the effect.

EAT

Grottos are shady, secluded outdoor restaurants with stone tables, typical of Ticino.

Grotto San Michele
A wide choice, handy for the castle.

🅰 E5 🏠 Salita al Castell, Bellinzona
🅦 castelgrande.ch

 ⓈⒻ ⓈⒻ ⓈⒻ

Grotto Canvett
The epitome of tradition.

🅰 E5 🏠 Cà d'Varénzin 6, Semione
📞 078 625 48 77

 ⓈⒻ ⓈⒻ ⓈⒻ

Grotto del Cavicc
Beloved of writer Hermann Hesse.

🅰 E5 🏠 Via Canvetti, Montagnola
🅦 grottocavicc.ch

 ⓈⒻ ⓈⒻ ⓈⒻ

↑ The village of Foroglio, Val Bavona, a popular base for hiking

Val Bavona

🅰 E5 🏔 Ticino 🚌 ℹ️ Centro Commerciale, Maggia; 91 753 18 85; www.ascona-locarno.com

Said to be the steepest and rockiest valley anywhere in the Alps, the beautiful Val Bavona is very wild – almost a world apart from the lush meadows and hills found elsewhere in the country. It is deserted in winter and still not connected to the Swiss electricity grid, despite being under a hydroelectric

plant. All the houses are made of grey stone, and massive boulders have been adapted into shelters for animals and humans alike. These structures, which are sometimes built into the rock, are called *sprügh*. In such precipitous terrain, waterfalls abound. The most impressive in all Ticino is the Cascata di Foroglio which falls 111 m (365 ft). The waterfall is an easy walk from the hamlet of Foroglio, which is on the Swiss postal bus route.

Valle di Blenio

🅰 E5 🏔 Ticino 🚌 ℹ️ Via Lavorceno, Olivone; 91 872 14 87; www.blenio.com

This scenic valley, washed by the River Brenno, leads up to the Lucomagno Pass (1,916 m/6,286 ft). The road up the valley and over the pass leads into the canton of Graubünden. Val di Blenio lies in the heart of rural Ticino. One of the sunniest spots in the country, it has great scenery and is dotted with picturesque villages.

Biasca, at the foot of the valley, has a Romanesque church with Gothic frescoes. Just north of Biasca lies

Malvaglia. The 16th- to 17th-century church here has a Romanesque tower and its façade features a large painting of St Christopher.

Negrentino is notable for its early Romanesque church of St Ambrose, whose tall belfry tower can be seen from afar. The interior of the church is decorated with frescoes dating from the 11th to the 16th centuries. Lottigna has an interesting museum of regional history (the Museo Storico del Valle di Blenio). The villages higher up the valley, such as Olivone, are good bases for mountain excursions and hikes.

Airolo

🅰 E5 🏔 Ticino 🚉🚌 From Airolo station ℹ️ Casella Postale 145, Airolo; 091 869 15 33; www.airolo.ch

Located just below the St Gotthard Pass, Airolo lies at the point where the motorway and railway line through the St Gotthard Tunnel emerge. As it is bypassed by these major routes, Airolo is a quiet town. With several hotels, it is a convenient base for exploring the valley that stretches out

Negrentino's church with its beautiful Romanesque and late-Gothic frescoes ↑

Did You Know?

The old road up to the St Gottard Pass has 37 bends, each with its own name.

below. A plaque in the town commemorates the 177 people who died during the tunnel's construction in the 1880s.

Valle Leventina, below Airolo, carries the motorway and main railway line that run from Zürich to Bellinzona and Lugano. The valley is dotted with small towns and villages, worth exploring for their interesting historic churches. Chiggiogna has a church with 15th-century frescoes, while Chironico has a 10th-century church with 14th-century frescoes. The 12th-century church in Giornico is one of the finest in Ticino. The interior is decorated with frescoes dating from 1478.

 23

St Gotthard Pass

AE5 **W**passosan gottardo.ch

With the Reuss valley in the canton of Uri to the north, and the Ticino valley to the south, the St Gotthard Pass lies at an altitude of 2,108 m (6,916 ft). It is on the principal route from northern Europe to Italy and has been used as a major alpine pass for over 700 years.

The pass is crossed by three tunnels. In 1882 the Gotthard Rail Tunnel opened, but it was not until almost a century later that a road tunnel followed, in 1980. In 2016, Switzerland inaugurated the world's longest rail tunnel here, the 57-km- (35-mile-) long Gotthard Base Tunnel, allowing for speeds of up to 200 km/h (124 mph) and reducing the journey time from Zürich to Milan to two hours and 40 minutes.

↑ The old cobblestoned Tremola road, leading up to the St Gotthard pass

The 19th-century hospice on the St Gotthard pass houses the **Museo Nazionale del San Gottardo**. The museum documents the history of the pass and describes the flora and fauna of this high alpine region.

Marked trails lead up to the summit of many of the surrounding peaks, including Pizzo Lucendro, and to mountain terraces from which there are splendid views.

Museo Nazionale del San Gottardo

⊘ **C** 091 869 15 25 **O** Jun-Oct: 9am-6pm daily

24

Museo Sasso San Gottardo

AE4 **O**Passo del S Gottardo, Airolo ▤ **O**May-Aug: 10:30am-3pm Mon & Wed-Fri (from 10am Sat & Sun); Sep-Oct: 10:30am-3pm Wed-Fri (from 10am Sat & Sun) **W**sasso-sangottardo.ch

Located on the historic mountain pass of the same name, the Museo Sasso San Gottardo is set in a

former secret military bunker buried deep in the mountains. Two museums in one, it is in part a natural history museum and in part a military museum. Visitors delve hundreds of metres into the mountains before taking the "Metro del Sasso", an underground cable car to the fortress. Inside, it is as if the 420 soldiers that once occupied it have only just left: dining hall, cannons, hospital, communications and map rooms are all as they were. The bunker was fully operational from 1943 to 1998, as dozens of Swiss mountain redoubts still are. In the natural history part of the museum is an exhibition on climate, ecology and the minerals that make up the Alps. Displays include enormous crystals – weighing over 1.5 tons – found near the St Gotthard Pass. Together, these two museums provide fascinating insight into the Swiss military mentality.

> 💬 INSIDER TIP
> **Wrap Up at the Museum**
>
> Visiting the Museo Sasso San Gottardo? Then dress warmly. Even during summer, the underground tunnels and caverns are cold and damp.

A DRIVING TOUR
LAKE MAGGIORE

CENTRAL
SWITZERLAND
AND TICINO

Lake
Maggiore

Locator Map
For more detail see p200

Length 40 km (25 miles) **Stopping-off points** Ascona and Locarno for a wide choice of restaurants

Only the northern tip of this long, slender pre-alpine lake lies in Switzerland, with the remaining portion curving southwards into Italian territory. Some 60 km (40 miles) long and 6 km (4 miles) wide, Lake Maggiore is hemmed in by mountains to the north, south and west. Follow this route through beachy resort towns, mountainside vineyards and terraced villages that boast jaw-dropping views. Boats and hydrofoils cross the lake from Ascona, Locarno and Brissago, carrying passengers down to the resorts in its Italian section.

Did You Know?

According to legend, Napoleon Bonaparte declared the lake a "wellspring of happiness".

With its balmy climate and beautiful setting, palm-fringed **Ascona** (p230) is a Swiss slice of la dolce vita.

Towering over Locarno, **Santuario della Madonna del Sasso** (p223) can be climbed on foot or by funicular.

The mountainside town of **Ronco** has stunning views of the lake below.

Cimetta
1,672 m (5,485 ft)

Lago di Vogorno

Monti di Motti

Tegna

407

Gordola

Riazzino

Intragna

560

Losone

Minusio

Tenero

406

Cugnasco

13

Verdasio

Arcegno

Locarno

Cadenazzo

Ascona

FINISH

13

Lake
Maggiore

San
Nazzaro

Vira

Magadino

Quartino

Ronco

Isole di
Brissago

Piazzogna

405

Rivera

A2

Brissago

Gerra

Piodina

START

Caviano

Monte Tamaro
1,960 m (6,430 ft)

Indemini

Mezzovico

Brissago is renowned for its botanical gardens. Pagliacci composer Ruggero Leoncavallo (1857–1919) was buried here.

Subtropical gardens flourish on the **Isole di Brissago**, once a bohemian haven.

A labyrinth of narrow alleys, the picturesque village of **Vira** is one of the ports of call for boats cruising around the lake.

Tenero, at the northern tip of the lake, has good camping grounds and a positively Caribbean beach.

↑ The lofty Santuario della Madonna del Sasso rising from the town of Locarno

The town of Hospental ↑
dwarfed by snowcapped
peaks in the distance

A DRIVING TOUR
THREE PASSES

Length 120 km (75 miles) **Stopping-off points** Andermatt and Göschenen for small hotels and restaurants

The circular route over the Uri Alps traverses some of the most spectacular alpine scenery in Switzerland. On the route are three mountain passes – the Susten Pass, Grimsel Pass and Furka Pass – each of which marks cantonal borders. A feat of 19th-century engineering, the road twists and turns, makes tightly winding ascents and descents, crosses bridges over dramatically plunging valleys, and passes through tunnels cut into the rock. All along the route are spectacular views of snow-capped mountains, majestic glaciers and beautiful mountain lakes.

CENTRAL SWITZERLAND AND TICINO

Three Passes

Locator Map
For more detail see p200

*A skiing resort in winter and hiking centre in summer, **Andermatt** lies in the heart of the St Gotthard massif.*

*The **Susten Pass** lies on the border between the cantons of Bern and Uri.*

*A bridge on the **Meienreuss Pass** spans a deep gorge in the Meien valley.*

BERN

Geissholz

Innertkirchen

Gadmen

Fuhren

Hopflauenen

Susten Pass

Schneestock 3,503 m (11,493 ft)

Tierberg 3,445 m (11,302 ft)

Steingletscher

Guttannen

Triftgletscher

Schneestock 3,608 m (11,837 ft)

Göscheneralpsee

Rhone-gletscher

Hühnertal-gletscher

Handeggfall

Grimsel Pass

Grimselsee

Furka Pass

Oberwald

VALAIS

Amsteg

Gurtnellen

Meien

Meienreuss Pass

Wassen

Göschenen

URI

START ▷ Andermatt

FINISH ▢ Hospental

Gotthard Tunnel

Realp

Innertkirchen runs routes down from the passes with the road heading north.

At an altitude of 2,165 m (7,103 ft), **Grimsel Pass** marks the border between the cantons of Bern and Valais.

Furka Pass lies between the Bernese and Pennine Alps.

*Built in the 1860s, the hairpin turns of **Furkastrasse** offer spectacular views round each corner.*

Hospental *lies at the convergence of roads from the north, south and west.*

Did You Know?

At Hospental stand the ruins of the 13th-century castle that once guarded the crossroads.

0 kilometres   6

0 miles   6

N ↑

EASTERN SWITZERLAND AND GRAUBÜNDEN

Traversed by the Rhine, which flows through Bodensee, eastern Switzerland is a relatively low-lying region of lush pastures and rural outposts, rising up into the high Alps at its most southerly extent. Known as Rhaetia in medieval times, much of the eastern part of Switzerland evolved strong German connections, in both trade and culture, while to the south, the rugged terrain increasingly cut communities off from would-be invaders.

As the Swiss Confederation spread its reach, most of the cantons to the east were partial members or subject territories, but following the defeat of Napoleon in 1815, two cantons were given full status: St Gallen and Graubünden. A university town, St Gallen has been a seat of learning since 747 when a Benedictine monastery was founded, requiring the contemplative study of books and the presence of a library. That library is now a UNESCO World Heritage Site, housing some 170,000 documents. Graubünden joined the Swiss Confederate in 1803, but it was in 1864 that it really came into its own – a hotelier in St Moritz lured summer residents back to stay for free that winter, and with this gesture, Swiss Alpine tourism was born. Home to some of the country's best ski slopes and greatest resorts, Graubünden is now a major centre for winter sports, and half of its population is involved in the tourist industry.

EASTERN SWITZERLAND AND GRAUBÜNDEN

Must Sees

① Schaffhausen
② St Gallen
③ Chur
④ Swiss National Park

Experience More

⑤ Rheinfall
⑥ Frauenfeld
⑦ Bodensee
⑧ Stein am Rhein
⑨ Appenzell
⑩ Toggenburg
⑪ Rapperswil
⑫ Walensee
⑬ Bad Ragaz
⑭ Maienfeld
⑮ Davos
⑯ Arosa
⑰ Engadine Valley
⑱ Müstair
⑲ Pontresina
⑳ Bernina Pass
㉑ Val Bregaglia
㉒ St Moritz
㉓ Sils
㉔ Zillis
㉕ San Bernardino Pass
㉖ Glarus
㉗ Klosters
㉘ Poschiavo
㉙ Mesocco

❶

SCHAFFHAUSEN

🗺E2 **🏛Schaffhausen** **🚆🚌** **ℹHerrenacker 15; schaffhauserland.ch**

Capital of the canton of the same name, the picturesque medieval town of Schaffhausen is set on the north bank of the Rhine, upriver from the spectacular cataracts known as the Rheinfall.

Thanks to its location at the point where the falls forced ships to unload their cargoes, the town was an important centre of trade from the early Middle Ages. The streets of its Altstadt (Old Town) are lined with Gothic, Renaissance, Baroque and Rococo buildings, such as the Haus zum Ritter, boasting frescoed façades and oriel windows. At the centre of its historic core lies Fronwagplatz, a square with two 16th-century fountains, the Metzgerbrunnen, topped by a statue of a mercenary, and the Mohrenbrunnen, with a statue of a Moorish king. A short walk to the southeast stands the austere Romanesque Münster, part of an 11th-century Benedictine abbey. The adjoining monastery is now home to a museum with prehistoric finds and Swiss art The abbey cloisters hold the Schillerglocke, whose sound inspired German poet Friedric Schiller to write the "Song of the Bell". Above the town to the east lies the Munot, whose keep offers fine views of the town, the river and the countryside.

↑ The circular keep of the 16th-century Munot, now the symbol of Schaffhausen

↑ The Haus zum Ritter, with a façade covered in Renaissance frescoes dating from 1568–70

← Statue depicting a soldier at the Platz

Did You Know?

Schaffhausen has 171 oriel windows - more than any other Swiss town - built as status symbols.

The town and the 11th-century Kirche St Johann, seen from the Munot fortress

↑ The beautiful Rococco reading hall of St Gallen Abbey's Stiftsbibliothek

②

ST GALLEN

F3 **St Gallen** **** Bankgasse 9; www.stgallen-bodensee.ch

The origins of St Gallen, eastern Switzerland's largest town, go back to 612, when Gallus, an Irish monk, chose the spot for his hermitage. A Benedictine abbey was founded here in 747 and soon became a centre of learning and culture; today, the abbey is a UNESCO World Heritage Site. By the 19th century, St Gallen was renowned for its textile industry. While the city's focal point is its magnificent cathedral, built in 1847, it also has a beautiful medieval centre.

①

Textilmuseum

 Vadianstrasse 2
 10am–5pm daily
 textilmuseum.ch

Reflecting St Gallen's role as a centre of the European textiles industry, this museum is filled with a comprehensive array of pieces from Switzerland and abroad, including antique fabrics from Coptic graves in Egypt. The well-presented displays examine social questions through design and fashion, connecting Swiss history with the art of weaving, as well as intricate embroidery and exquisite handmade lace. Local patterns and products, and the implements that were devised to produce them, are also shown.

②

Stiftsbibliothek

 Klosterhof 6d 10am–5pm daily stibi.ch

Although most of the abbey was destroyed during the Reformation, its important library, the Stiftsbibliothek, was spared. The main room, designed by Peter Thumb in 1758–67, is a stunning Baroque masterpiece, with elaborate Rococo touches. The wooden floor was intricately inlaid by Gabriel Loser, and the ceiling is decorated with stuccowork by Johann Georg and Mathias Gigl and trompe l'oeil paintings by Josef Wannenmacher.

The library contains more than 170,000 books and documents, including an important collection of Irish manuscripts dating from the 8th to the 11th centuries, and rare works dating from the 8th century.

 HIDDEN GEM
Bierflaschen Museum

A must-visit for any beer lover, Switzerland's first beer bottle museum *(www.schuetzen garten.ch)* features more than 2,000 bottles from over 260 Swiss breweries – all empty. The well-curated exhibits are arranged by region forming an impressive display of Swiss beer history.

Books printed after 1900 may be borrowed, but anything older can only be read onsite in the reading rooms

---

Marktplatz

Once the town's main market square, Marktplatz lies on the northern side of the old town. The square is surrounded by fine 17th- and 18th-century houses with intricately painted façades or decorated with delicate relief carving. Many also have attractive oriel windows, a feature typical of St Gallen's architecture.

On Marktgasse, the street leading off the southern side of Marktplatz, Labhart is a

---

Did You Know?

St Gallen's university was decorated by some of the most innovative artists of the 20th century.

---

long-standing watchmaker's shop with a fascinating collection of musical boxes.

St Laurenzenkirche

🏛 Marktgasse ⏰ 9:30-11:30am & 2-4pm Mon, 9:30am-4pm Tue-Sat (to 6pm Tue-Fri in summer) 🌐 ref-sgc.ch

This church was originally part of the abbey complex. During the 16th century it became a centre of the Reformation in St Gallen. The building's present Neo-Gothic façade is the result of remodelling carried out in the mid-19th century.

---

⑤ Historisches und Völkerkundemuseum

🏛 Museumstrasse 50 ⏰ 10am-5pm Tue-Sun 🌐 hvmsg.ch

The museum of history and ethnology focuses on the people and past of the town

and region of St Gallen. As well as archaeological pieces, there are documents, mementos and reconstructions of domestic life from various periods, going back as far as prehistory. Highlights include a scale reconstruction of St Gallen's abbey and a model of the city as it was in the 17th century. The ethnographic collection also has Asian, African and South American artifacts.

---

⑥ Kunst Halle Sankt Gallen

🏛 Davidstrasse 40 ⏰ Noon-6pm Tue-Fri, 11am-5pm Sat & Sun 🌐 kunsthallesankt gallen.ch

This contemporary art hall sees itself as "a large small exhibitor", and an experimental space for artists to express themselves freely. The exhibits change regularly, keeping pace with developments in the world of contemporary art.

⑦ 🖉 🖉

ST GALLEN ABBEY

170,000
The number of documents in the Abbey Library.

🏠 Klosterhof 6a ⏰ Cathedral: 6am-6:30pm Mon-Wed, 7am-6:30pm Thu-Sat, 7:30am-8:30pm Sun; Stiftsbibliothek: 10am-5pm daily 🌐 stiftsbezirk.ch

Nestled in the centre of the historic town, this abbey is one of the most spectacular examples of Baroque architecture in Switzerland. As well as containing the elegant cathedral, there is a fascinating lapidarium with archaeological displays, as well as the magnificently decorated Stiftsbibliothek (abbey library), the oldest library in Switzerland.

The Benedictine abbey was established in 747 and was at the height of its importance from the 9th to the 11th centuries. The Romanesque church and monastery, built during that period, have not survived, their only remains being the crypt containing the tombs of the abbots. The present Baroque cathedral and monastery, designed by master architect Johann Michael Beer von Bildstein, were completed in 1767. The interior decoration was executed by the foremost artists of the day. Such is the importance of this sight, with its works of art and its renowned library (p244), that it was made a World Heritage Site in 1983.

→
St Gallen Cathedral, with its Baroque architecture

The twin Baroque bell towers

High altar

←
Frescoes by Josef Wannenmacher adorning the cathedral ceiling

The twin bell towers ↑
of St Gallen Cathedral
on a sunny day

Josef Wannenmacher
ceiling frescoes

The 16 Baroque
confessionals are
crowned with
medallions.

The late Baroque
pulpit is decorated
with figures of
the Evangelists
and angels.

Main entrance
to the stunning
Stiftsbibliothek

The Baroque
stalls, made of
walnut, are by
Joseph Anton
Feuchtmayer.

Two thrones,
decorated by
the Dirr brothers,
stand among
the choir stalls.

💬 INSIDER TIP
Look Up

Ornate stuccowork is
everywhere you look
in the cathedral, but
don't neglect to cast
your gaze upwards:
the ceiling is decorated
with dramatic and
colourful frescoes by
Josef Wannenmacher.

3

CHUR

F4 **Grisons** **Bahnhofplatz 3; www. churtourismus.ch**

Located at the head of the Rhine valley, Chur lies at the crossroads of ancient trade routes that linked the alpine passes to the south and Bodensee to the north. Settled for over 5,000 years, today Chur calls itself "the oldest Swiss city". The city prospered under the rule of prince-bishops from the 12th to the 16th centuries. Following the Reformation, Chur passed into secular rule, becoming the capital of the canton of Graubünden in 1803. The narrow streets and squares of the Old Town are quiet and pleasant to explore.

① Rätisches Museum

Haus Buol, Hofstrasse 1
10am–5pm Tue–Sun
raetischesmuseum.gr.ch

Built in 1675 by patrician Baron von Buol Strassberg und Rieyberg, this Baroque patrician house in a quiet courtyard behind Kirche St Martin is now home to this comprehensive local history museum. Although the information available in English is sometimes lacking, the displays at this museum neatly illustrate the history of Chur and its environs, with artifacts from prehistoric times to the 19th century. Among the exhibits are archaeological finds from the time of the Rhaetians – alpine tribes who colonized the region in around 3000 BC –and items from Graubünden's Roman period. Precious pieces from the cathedral treasury, including medieval reliquaries, are also showcased. Other exhibits include rooms of 17th-century furnishings and other domestic objects. The culture and folk arts of the Graubünden region from the 19th century through to the present day are also attractively documented.

② Bischöflicher Hof

Hofplatz

The complex of buildings set on the terrace that rises to the east of the Old Town make up the oldest seated bishopric north of the Alps. Standing next to the cathedral, the bishop's palace was founded in the 6th century on the site of a Roman fort. The palace was extended on several occasions, and its thick walls reflect the ruling bishops' need for defence. The palace's present appearance is mainly the result of remodelling in the 18th and 19th centuries. Since it is still the residence of the bishops of Chur, it is not open to visitors.

Sunlight bathing the vineyards on the hills outside the city of Chur

UNDERGROUND CHUR

Subterranean remains of the city's 5th-century Kirche St Stephen were first discovered during the construction of a school in 1850. Once the cemetery church for the bishops of Chur, it lies next to Kirche St Luzi, which has a ring crypt. Both can be visited on a guided tour.

③
Kirche St Martin

St Martinsplatz ☎081 52 22 92 ⏰8:30–11:30am 2–5pm Mon–Fri

Since at least AD 769 there has been a church dedicated to St Martin on this spot. The late Gothic church that stands here today was completed in 1491, replacing the earlier church that was destroyed by fire in 1464. The steepled tower, which dominates the city's landscape, was completed in 1534, and remained unaltered until 1917 when it was replaced by the tower seen today. According to local tradition, Protestant reformer Martin Luther himself delivered a sermon in the mid-1520s, which prompted the congregation's conversion.

Among the most notable features of its interior are the carved stalls and the stained-glass windows, on the right of the main doors, created by Augusto Giacometti in 1917–9, which depict the Nativity story. In the north and south façades is some of the original Carolingian masonry.

④
Kirche St Luzi

Alte Schanfiggerstrasse 9

This massive church, which is dedicated to the missionary who is said to have brought Christianity to the region, sits atop a vineyard-covered hill on the east side of the old

town. Built in the 12th century as the church of a monastery, the building overlies the crypt of an 8th-century structure, including a ring crypt, where the relics of Saint Lucius were once displayed. Amid the church's soaring Carolingian arches and grand capitals, Romanesque carvings are visible. A seminary is on site.

Alien Barscape

On the unassuming Comercialstrasse, lurks the Giger Bar (www.hrgiger.com). The bar is themed on the most famous (and Oscar-winning) work of Swiss artist H R Giger - the surrealistic creatures and nightmare landscapes of Hollywood blockbuster Alien. The entire bar, from the fittings to the roofs, are all designed in his iconic biomechanical style.

⑤

Bündner Kunstmuseum

🏛 Postplatz 📞 081 257 28 70 🕙 10am-5pm Tue-Sun (to 8pm Thu) 🌐 buendner-kunstmuseum.ch

Chur's museum of fine arts is spread across two buildings. One is a large, handsome Neo-Renaissance villa dating from 1874–5, built for Jacques Ambrosius von Planta, a merchant who traded in Egypt. This heritage accounts for the Middle Eastern character of the building's interior decoration. The exterior also reflects an affinity for Middle Eastern culture, with two sphinxes that greet visitors, flanking both sides of the front steps, and a golden dome designed in the Byzantine style. The pinnacle of this style takes the shape of the crescent moon that crowns the top of the dome. Next to the villa stands the award-winning annexe, designed by the Barcelona-based architect Barozzi Veiga. On the upper floors are airy public spaces, while the exhibitions are laid out on the lower floors underground. A pedestrian zone links the two buildings.

Most of the paintings and sculptures that fill the rooms of the two spaces are by artists who either were born or lived and worked in Graubünden between the 18th and 20th centuries. The impressive roster includes Angelica Kauffmann, Giovanni Segantini, Ferdinand Hodler, Giovanni and Alberto Giacometti, and Ernst Ludwig Kirchner, as well as members of the Basel group of artists Rot-Blau (Red-Blue).

Did You Know?

Chur-born painter Angelica Kauffmann was a well-known portraitist by the age of 12.

⑥
Rathaus

🏛 Poststrasse 🕙 By prior arrangement 📞 081 254 41 13

Built in 1465, the Gothic town hall stands on the site of an earlier building that was destroyed by fire. At ground level is a handsome arcaded area that was once used as a marketplace. The upper floors of the town hall contain two finely decorated council chambers, one with a wooden ceiling and the other with Renaissance panelling. Both chambers have 17th-century tiled stoves.

The house that stands at Reichsgasse 57, nearby, is the birthplace of the Swiss painter Angelica Kauffmann. Born in 1741, she later moved to London, where she became a well-known portraitist and painter of mythological themes, such as Cupid.

⑦
Regierungsplatz

Lining this square, on the north side of the Old Town, are several historic buildings, which now serve as the seat of the cantonal authorities. One of the finest is Graues Haus (Grey House), a stately three-storey residence dating from 1752. It is also known as the New Building, to distinguish

←

The gridded cube-shaped annexe of the Bündner Kunstmuseum

One of the ornately decorated houses lining Obere Gasse

EAT

Bündner Stube

Candlelit meals of fresh, seasonal fare, much grown in the on-site kitchen garden.

🏠 Reichsgasse 11
🌐 stern-chur.ch

Calanda

A trendy spot with a popular lunch menu and new specials every day.

🏠 Postplatz
🌐 calanda-chur.ch

Zum Alten Zollhaus

Light meals in a *Stübli* (alpine restaurant) opposite the Obertor.

🏠 Malixerstrasse 1
🌐 zollhaus-chur.ch

---

from the Altes Gebäu (Old Building), which stands on Fontanapark. In the centre of the square is the Vazerol-Denkmal, an obelisk installed to commemorate the free association formed by the communes of Graubünden in the 14th century, when the local population began to organize itself in an effort to ward off foreign domination.

Bündner Naturmuseum

🏠 Masanserstrasse 31
📞 081 257 28 41 ⏰ 10am–pm Tue–Sun 🌐 natur museum.gr.ch

The displays of this modern museum showcases the beautiful natural environment of the canton of Graubünden. The well-presented displays include a large collection of minerals from the region's mountains, including gold, gemstones and micro-minerals which can be seen through a microscope, as well as plants and stuffed animals.

Obere Gasse

Chur's smartest shopping street, Obere Gasse runs from St Martinsplatz to Obertor, the Gothic city gate on the banks of the Plessur. All along this narrow, flag-hung street, the

historic houses have been converted into boutiques, restaurants and cafés.

On Saturday mornings during the summer, a market is held in Obere Gasse and Untere Gasse.

→
A stonework ibex, which flanks one side of the city's coat of arms

CHUR CATHEDRAL

📍 Hofplatz 🕐 6am-7pm Mon-Sat (from 8am Tue & 7am Sun)
🌐 bistum-chur.ch

Officially known as the Cathedral of St Mary of the Assumption, Chur's Catholic church is a historic place of worship. During the Swiss Reformation, the town's Catholic community were confined to the cathedral and the surrounding bishop's court.

Begun in 1151 and completed in the mid-13th century, Chur Cathedral represents a mixture of the Romanesque and Gothic architectural styles. The earliest part of the basilica is its eastern section. The nave, with Romanesque columns and Gothic vaulting, and the bell tower, topped by a lantern, are later elements. The exterior was remodelled in the early 19th century, after the building was damaged by a fire that destroyed the original towers and roof. Peculiarly, the cathedral is built to an irregular plan, with the axis of the sanctuary and that of the nave being out of alignment. The sanctuary is home to one of the finest features of the cathedral – the renovated 15th-century golden altar triptych, which gleams in the light slanting through the small side windows.

The 15th century stall exemplify late Gothic wood carving

The main altar has an ornate, golden triptych.

Side door to the choir of the cathedral

The crypt is supported by columns with capitals in the form of animal figures.

The Gothic sanctuary is decorated with delicate figures of saints.

← A capital in the shape of a man riding a lion in the cathedral's crypt

① Chur Cathedral is easily recognized by its single bell tower, peeking through the town's trees.

② The cathedral has an elaborate high altar, built in 1492 by Jacob Russ.

③ The stained-glass window in the west wall features scenes from the life of the Virgin Mary.

The capitals of the columns in the nave are outstanding examples of Swiss Romanesque stone carving.

Carvings of biblical scenes adorn the Baroque pulpit.

The west wall's magnificent stained-glass window

Did You Know?

The cathedral claims to house the relics of St Lucius, who brought Christianity to Britain.

The cathedral is attached to other buildings in the bishop's court.

Main entrance

↑ Chur's magnificent Cathedral of St Mary of the Assumption

④

SWISS NATIONAL PARK

🅰 G4 **🚩 Graubünden** **🚌 🕐 Zernez** **🕐 Jun-Oct: 8:30am-6pm daily; Nov-May: 9am-5pm daily** **🌐 nationalpark.ch**

Established in 1914, the Swiss National Park, or Parc Naziunal Svizzer in Romansch, was the first national park to be created in the Alps. This pristine nature reserve covers an area of 170 sq km (66 sq miles) and its topography ranges from sheltered valleys and dense forests to flower-covered meadows and rocky, snow-covered peaks.

The best way to appreciate the park is to follow its 80 km (50 miles) of well-marked hiking trails. Many of these start from parking areas off Ofenpassstrasse, the only highway through the park. A free app has detailed maps and park information, including where to find overnight accommodation in the park. Walkers are also reminded that they are forbidden to stray from these trails for conservation reasons. On the park's western border, Ova Spin overlooks rugged mountain terrain. To the east are magnificent snowy views of Piz Nair and Munt la Schera, while in the north the vista is of mountains blanketed in pine forests.

TOP 5 TOP FIVE ALPINE ANIMALS

Ibex
The Alps' iconic goats are instantly recognizable by their long horns.

Chamois
These skittish alpine antelopes dart easily up and down cliffsides.

Golden Eagles
These regal birds spiral, disappear and swoop on the mountain wind.

Northern Viper
The park's only snake, vipers are often found motionless in the grass.

Marmots
These adorable rodents thrive in the park's meadowlands.

→
A pair of hikers negotiating the terrain, which is dotted with mountain huts *(inset)*

① The *Aussichtplattform* (viewing platform) at Piz Nair offers incredible views over Silvaplanersee.

② Throughout the park there are well-marked hiking trails, open from June to October.

③ A statue of an ibex, one of the park's most iconic animals, overlooks snow-capped Munt la Schera.

EXPERIENCE MORE

❺

Rheinfall

 E2 🚉 Schaffhausen 🚌
ℹ Neuhausen, Rheinfallquai 3; www.rheinfall.ch

Creating a spectacle of rainbow-tinted spray, the waters of the Rhine tumble off a cataract at Neuhausen, 4 km (2.5 miles) downriver from Schaffhausen. The waterfall, Rheinfall, is the largest in Europe. Although it is only 23 m (75 ft) high, it is known for its width (about 150 m/ 492 ft) and its setting between tree-covered banks. Schloss Laufen, a turreted Renaissance castle overlooking the river from the south, has the best view of the falls. From the castle, steps lead down to viewing platforms. A fireworks display is staged at the Rheinfall during the evening of 31 July, the eve of National Day (1 August), each year.

> 📷 PICTURE PERFECT
> **Behind the Falls**
>
> Capture the full majesty of the Rheinfall on a boat trip. Leaving from nearby Schaffhausen (p242), tours stop at a mighty rock standing virtually in the middle of the falls, where platforms let you feel the vibration of the water as you snap the torrents up close.

❻

Frauenfeld

 E2 🚉 Thurgau 🚌
ℹ Bahnhofplatz 75; www.frauenfeld.ch

Located on the River Murg, west of Bodensee, Frauenfeld is the capital of Thurgau canton. The town has burgher houses in its historic centre, the Baliere in Kreuzplatz that is now an art gallery, and the Luzemhaus, a Baroque building that houses a natural history museum. The origins of Frauenfeld's castle go back to the 13th century. Its restored rooms house the Thurgau History Museum, a museum of local history.

At Ittingen, located 4 km (2.5 miles) north of Frauenfeld, is the Kartause Ittingen, a Carthusian monastery founded in the 15th century. No longer inhabited by monks, the monastery is open to visitors. As well as a hotel, a restaurant and a farm shop, the monastery also has a museum illustrating monastic life and a gallery of 20th-century Swiss painting.

❼

Bodensee

 F2 🚉 St Gallen, Thurgau and Schaffhausen 🚌
ℹ Hauptstrasse 39, Kreuzlingen; www.kreuzlingen-bodensee.ch

Bodensee, also known as Lake Constance, has become a summer playground for visitors attracted by the sailing, swimming and development of resort hotels along the shores. There is a wealth of watersports, including sailing and paddle-boarding. There are 337 km (209 miles) of protected bike trails touching four borders: Switzerland, Austria, Germany, and Liechtenstein.

The lake, which is both fed and drained by the Rhine, is 64 km (40 miles) long and 12 km (7 miles) wide. Its western and southern shores, which belong

→ Europe's largest waterfall, the Rheinfall, overlooked by pretty Schloss Laufen

The cobbled Rathausplatz, with its fine medieval buildings, in Stein am Rhein

o Switzerland, are lined with mall resorts that have fishing nd watersports facilities. reuzlingen is the principal wiss town here, with the aroque Kirche St Ulrich s finest building. Schloss renenberg and the medieval astle of Gottlieben are both n the Swiss shoreline, as is ne 14th-century Turmhof ortification in Steckborn.

tein am Rhein

E2 ⌂ Schaffhausen
🚋🚌🚢 ℹ Oberstadt 3;
ww.steinamrhein.ch

/ith its medieval half-timbered uildings and 16th-century ouses with frescoed façades, tein am Rhein is one of the puntry's most beautiful sights. punded in Roman times, nis small town began to pros-er and expand in the late 1th century, when German mperor Heinrich II established Benedictine monastery here. ne outline of the town walls

can be made out, and two of the town gates, Obertor and Untertor, still stand. The main square, Rathausplatz, is lined with handsome wood-framed houses painted with motifs reflecting their names, such as House of the Sun or House of the Red Ox. The **Lindwurm Museum** re-creates 19th-century middle-class life over four floors of a beau-tifully restored house in the historic Old Town.

Overlooking the Rhine stands Kloster St Georgen, a Benedictine monastery, and its 12th-century church. The well-preserved monastery rooms, decorated in the early 16th century, now house the **Klostermuseum St Georgen**, devoted to local history.

Lindwurm Museum
⊛ ⌂ Understadt 18
🕐 Mar–Oct: 10am–5pm
Tue–Sun 🚫 Nov–Apr
🌐 museum-lindwurm.ch

Klostermuseum
St Georgen
⊛ ⌂ Fischmarkt 3
🕐 Apr–Nov: 11am–5pm
Tue–Sun; Jun–Aug:
11am–6pm Tue–Sun
🚫 Dec–Mar 🌐 kloster
sanktgeorgen.ch

THE RHAETIAN RAILWAY

Riding a mountain train when in Switzerland is almost an inevitability. The most scenic line is the private Rhaetian Railway, running across 383 rail bridges and through 84 tunnels. Its Albula/Bernina Line, climbing up the Albula Valley past the drama-tic Landwasser viaduct, is now a UNESCO World Heritage Site and one of Europe's truly great rail journeys.

⑨ Appenzell

🄰F3 🄰 Appenzell 🄰🄰
🄸 Appenzell, Hauptgasse 4;
www.appenzell.ch

Surrounded on all sides by the canton of St Gallen, the region known as Appenzell consists of two half-cantons, Appenzell-Ausserrhoden in the north and west, and Appenzell-Innerrhoden in the south. From the 10th to the 15th centuries, Appenzell formed part of the territory owned by the abbey at St Gallen (p246). Having gained its independence, Appenzell joined the Swiss Confederation in 1513.

While the bigger Appenzell-Ausserrhoden is Protestant and largely industrialized, Appenzell-Innerrhoden is Catholic and markedly more bucolic, with a farming economy and a developed tourist industry. It is renowned for its cattle-breeding and its dairy products, most especially its cheeses. Along with its rural character, Appenzell-Innerrhoden has strong folk traditions and a pristine natural environment.

Like many other towns in the region, Appenzell, capital of Innerrhoden, has a Landsgemeindeplatz, a square on which regular voting sessions are held. The well-preserved historic centre of this small town is filled with

←
A beautifully decorated bed on display in the Museum Appenzell

colourfully painted wooden houses. Also of interest are the 16th-century town hall and the parish church, Kirche St Mauritius, which was built in the 16th century in the Baroque style and remodelled in the 19th century.

The history and culture of Appenzell is amply documented by the varied and extensive collections of the **Museum Appenzell**. These range from costumes and headdresses to embroidery and cowbells.

To the south of Appenzell lies the Alpstein massif. The highest peak here, the Säntis, rises to 2,504 m (8,215 ft). Popular with hikers and mountaineers, the Säntis can be reached by road or by cable car from Schwägalp.

The picturesque village of Urnäsch, in Ausserrhoden, also has the **Appenzeller Brauchtumsmuseum**, a folk museum. Its collection includes reconstructed farmhouse interiors, as well as costumes and craft items.

North of Urnäsch lies Herisau, capital of the canton of Appenzell-Ausserrhoden. The town boasts attractive wooden houses and a church with Rococo furnishings dating from 1520.

The impressive cascade of Thurwasserfälle at Unterwasser, Toggenburg

Stein, a quiet village east of Herisau, has an interesting folk museum and show dairy. While the displays at the **Appenzell Folklore Museum** illustrate the lives, culture and crafts of the local people, at the **Appenzeller Showcase Dairy (Schaukäserei)**, visitors can watch cheese being made using local methods.

The market town of Gais, at the centre of Appenzell, is of interest for its colourfully painted wooden houses, many of which have ornate gables. It is also an excellent base for exploring the region.

Museum Appenzell

🄰 Appenzell, Hauptgasse 4 🄰 Apr-Oct: 10am-noon & 1:30-5pm Mon-Fri, 11am-5pm Sat & Sun; Nov-Mar: 2-5pm Tue-Sun 🅆 museum.ai.ch

Appenzeller Brauchtumsmuseum

🄰 Urnäsch 🄰 Apr-Oct: 9-11:30am & 1:30-5pm Mon-Sat, 1:30-5pm Sun; Nov-Mar: 9-11:30am Mon-Fri, 9-11:30am & 1:30-5pm Sat, 1:30pm-5pm Sun 🅆 museum-urnaesch.c

Appenzell Folklore Museum

🄰 Stein 🄰 10am-5pm Tue-Sun 🅆 appenzeller-museum.ch

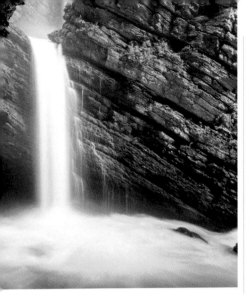

ppenzeller Showcase airy (Schaukäserei)

🏠 Stein ⏰ 9am–5pm (heese-making until 3pm) schaukaeserei.ch

10
oggenburg

🗺 E3 🏠 St Galle 🚌🚆 Wildhaus, Hauptstrasse; ww.toggenburg.org

ashed by the River Thur, e Toggenburg is a long valley at lies on a north-south is between Wil and Wattwil, en veers eastwards just ove Alt St Johann, where it comes Oberes Toggenburg, hich then opens out onto e Rhine valley.

The Toggenburg has over 0 km (185 miles) of marked king and cycling trails, and gentle slopes provide easy iing pistes. The valley is otted with attractive small wns and villages, among em are Wil and Lichtensteig, hich has historic houses. Wildhaus, a pleasant resort the eastern extremity of beres Toggenburg, is the rthplace of Ulrich Zwingli, e leader of the Reformation Switzerland. The farmhouse

where he was born in 1484 is open to visitors. Unterwasser is worth a visit too, for its impressive waterfall, the Thurwasserfälle.

11
Rapperswil

🗺 E3 🏠 St Galle 🚗🚌🚆 ℹ Fischmarktplatz 1; www.rapperswil.ch

This small town, in the canton of St Gallen, sits on a promontory on the north side of Zürichsee. Although the modern part of Rapperswil has nothing of great interest,

the traffic-free medieval centre is a pleasant place to stroll. Behind the lakeside promenade lie narrow streets lined with houses fronted by arcades, and small squares with cafés and restaurants serving fresh locally caught fish. From May to October the air is filled with the delicate perfume of more than 15,000 roses. Known as the City of Roses, Rapperswil has more than 16,000 roses flowering in walled gardens, including one within a Capuchin monastery and a particularly serene one specially designed for the visually impaired and those with mobility issues.

Besides the 15th-century town hall and the parish church, Rapperswil's main feature is its looming Gothic castle, whose three forbidding towers rise above the town. From the castle there are views of Zürich to the north and of the Glarus Alps to the southwest. The village makes a good base for hiking in summer and skiing in winter.

↑ An attractive rose garden in a courtyard of Rapperswil's medieval castle

Walensee

E3-F3 **St Gallen and Glarus** 🚂🚌
ℹ️ Walenseestrasse 18; www.heidiland.com

This slender lake marks the border between the cantons of St Gallen and Glarus. About 15 km (9 miles) long and just 2 km (1 mile) across at its widest point, it lies in a steep-sided valley, with the rugged Churfirsten massif on its northern side and the Glarner Alps to the southeast. This lovely region is also known as Heidiland after Johanna Spyri's famous children's novel.

The railway line and the motorway linking Zürich and Chur run along the south side of the lake. Most of the towns and villages on the steep north shore are accessible only by boat or on foot. Cruises on the lake take in the charming town of Weesen.

A short distance south is Näfels, which boasts a late-Renaissance palace, the Freulerpalast. The building houses a museum of local history. The neighbouring town of Mollis contains well-preserved burgher houses and fine 18th-century man-

sions, while Walenstadt, on the lake's eastern shore, is a convenient base for exploring the mountains, including Walenstadtberg and Berschis.

Bad Ragaz

F4 **St Gallen** 🚂🚌 ℹ️ Am Platz 1; www.heidiland.com

Bad Ragaz, set on the River Tamina, is one of Switzerland's foremost spa resorts, with grand old palace-style hotels and an outstanding golf course. Its natural thermal springs have been used to cure ailments since the 13th century. The resort has several indoor and outdoor pools – Tamina-Therme, in the centre of the resort, is the best known.

Bad Ragaz also has an early 18th-century parish church with Baroque wall paintings. The town hall contains a display of paintings and other works of art of Bad Ragaz and its environs.

1535

The year Swiss doctor Paracelsus recognized the healing powers of Bad Pfäfers' hot springs.

As well as skiing on the slope of Pizol, Bad Ragaz offers go tennis and other sporting activities. It is also an excelle base for hiking in the surrounding hills.

About 5 km (3 miles) sout of Bad Ragaz is Bad Pfäfers, a spa town with a beautiful Baroque church and a forme Benedictine monastery that houses a local history museu

Southwest of Bad Ragaz is the Taminaschlucht, a deep gorge carved out by the rushing waters of the Tamina. Also of interest is Sargans, which has beautiful Neo-Classical buildings and a Gothic castle.

> Davos has some famous "off-piste" powder snow runs, but beginners are catered for, too: there are several ski and snowboarding schools.

aienfeld

F3 🏠 **Graubünden** 🚉🚌
**Bahnhofstrasse 1; www.
idiland.com**

e village of Maienfeld, across
e Rhine from Bad Ragaz,
lso part of the Heidiland
urism area. It was this part
the Swiss Alps that Johanna
yri chose as the setting
Heidi (1881), the story of an
ohaned girl that has become
lassic of children's litera-
e. A very easy walking trail
ds from Maienfeld up to
e hamlet of Oberrofels. Here
itors can see Heidi's House,
vooden chalet in which the
tional surroundings of Heidi's
with her grandfather are
idly re-created.

vos

F4 🏠 **Graubünden** 🚉🚌
**Promenade 67; www.
vos.ch**

iginally a remote village,
vos developed into a health
sort for tuberculosis suf-
ers in the 1860s, and was
insformed into a winter
orts resort in the 1930s.

Today it is one of the largest
of Swiss resorts and hosts
world leaders at the Davos
World Economic Forum.

Davos has close associations
with German writer and Nobel
laureate Thomas Mann, who
visited in 1911 and was
inspired to write *The Magic
Mountain*. The town is also
associated with the German
Expressionist painter Ernst
Ludwig Kirchner, who settled
here in 1917. The largest collection of his work in the
world, including many of
the alpine landscapes that
he painted during his years
in Davos, are displayed in
the **Kirchner Museum** here.

Davos has some famous
"off-piste" powder snow runs,
but beginners are catered
for, too: there are several ski
and snowboarding schools,
as well as some less demanding slopes. There are also
toboggan runs and a large
natural ice rink, where ice
hockey is played.

In summer visitors can
enjoy golf and tennis, hiking
along trails, rock climbing
and trekking on horseback.

Kirchner Museum
 🏠 **Promenade 82**
⏰ 11am–6pm Tue–Sun
🌐 kirchnermuseum.ch

←
The small port of Weesen
in an idyllic lakeside
setting on Walensee

↑ The slopes of the Hörnli
near Arosa, ideal for
intermediate skiers

16

Arosa

F4 🏠 **Graubünden** 🚉🚌
**Poststrasse; www.arosa.
ch**

Set in a bowl in the narrow
Schanfigg valley, Arosa is
one of Switzerland's most
beautiful resorts. Although it
lies at an altitude of 1,800 m
(5,900 ft), it enjoys a gentle
climate, with lots of sunshine.

The town is divided into two
areas. Ausserarosa is the main
resort and Innerarosa the
original village. The crafts
and folk art on display in the
Schanfigg Heimatmuseum
reflect mountain life in the
days before the town became
a popular winter holiday spot.

In winter the neighbouring
slopes of Weisshorn, Hörnli
and Prätschli provide superb
downhill pistes. There are also
cross-country trails, a sleigh
run and an ice rink. In summer
visitors can enjoy over 200 km
(125 miles) of hiking trails and
mountain biking routes, and
the resort's two lakes offer a
variety of watersports.

Schanfigg Heimatmuseum
 🏠 **Poststrasse, Innerarosa**
⏰ Jun–Oct: 2:30–4:30pm Mon,
Wed & Fri; Dec–Apr: 2:30–
4:30pm Tue & Fri 🌐 arosa-
museum.ch

Hikers in the village of Ardez, notable for its houses painted with beautiful murals

(Schuls in German), with a spa and a regional museum. On the opposite bank of the Inn lie the villages of Vulpera, which has picturesque houses and an 11th-century castle, and Tarasp, with a spa. Chas Tarasp, a castle, perches on a rocky spur above the village. At S-charl, nearby, is a lead and silver mine, which is open to visitors.

Most of the towns and villages in the Lower Engadine make good bases for exploring the Silvretta mountain range to the north and the Swiss National Park (p254) to the south.

Müstair

🅰G4 🅰Graubünden 🚆
🚹 Chasa Cumünala, Tschierv; www.val-muestair.ch

Tucked away at the bottom of Val Müstair (Münstertal in German), and almost on the border with Italy, Romansh-speaking Müstair (Münster in German) takes its name from

---

⑰

Engadine Valley

🅰G4 🅰Graubünden 🚆🚌
🚹 Via San Gian 30, St Moritz; www.engadin.stmoritz.ch

The Engadine Valley is generally acknowledged as one of Switzerland's most scenic. It begins at the foot of the Rhaetian Alps, near St Moritz, and extends northeastwards as far as the border of Austria. It is named after the River Inn (En in Romansh), which runs along the valley and on into Austria, where it joins the Danube.

This deep valley between high cliffs is divided into an upper, southwestern section and a lower, northeastern section. The Upper Engadine (Oberengadin in German, Engiadin' Ota in Romansh) lies between the Maloja Pass and Zernez. With glaciers and snowy peaks on either side, the valley floor of the Upper

Engadine lies at an altitude averaging 1,800 m (5,900 ft) and is dotted with several popular winter sports resorts, including Pontresina and St Moritz (p264).

The Lower Engadine (Unterengadin in German, Engiadina Bassa in Romansh) lies between Zernez and Martina. Remote, unspoiled and very picturesque, this region is dotted with attractive villages set on either side of the River Inn. Many of these villages have houses with painted façades or sgraffito decoration, in which the upper layer of plaster is cut away to create a design. Particularly fine sgraffito decoration can be seen in Guarda, a village overlooking the River Inn. The village of Ardez is also notable for its painted houses, one of which has an exterior covered with a beautiful depiction of Adam and Eve in the Garden of Eden.

The principal town of the Lower Engadine is Scuol

CROSS-COUNTRY SKIING IN THE ENGADINE

Even more popular with Swiss families than downhill skiing is shuffling along the flats, through the woods and over the frozen lakes, on more than 230 km (142 miles) of trails in the Engadin Valley. The Engadin Skimarathon takes place every March, with many cross-country skiers racing over a 42-km (26-mile) course.

he Carolingian monastery
ounded here in about AD 780.
he working convent is one
f the oldest buildings in
e country.

The convent church, known
Romansh as the **Baselgia
an Jon** and in German as
losterkirche St Johann, is a
orking convent decorated
ith exceptionally well-
eserved 12th- and 13th-
entury Romanesque fres-
es. Because of these, the
hurch has been declared a
NESCO World Heritage Site.
hile the frescoes on the side
alls depict scenes from the
fe of Christ, those in the
resbytery show scenes from
e life of St John. A depiction
f the Last Judgement covers
e west wall. Some of the
escoes have now been
oved to the Schweizerisches
ationalmuseum in Zürich
164). The church also has a
2th-century statue of Charle-
agne and an 11th-century
elief of the baptism of Christ.
e small museum near the
hurch contains Carolingian
atuary and Baroque figures.

aselgia San Jon

⦿ ⊛ ⊙ May–Oct: 9am–5pm
on–Sat, 1:30–5pm Sun; Nov–
pr: 10am–noon & 1:30–
30pm Mon–Sat, 1:30–
30pm Sun ⊠ muestair.ch

Pontresina

⛰G4 ⬡ Graubünden 🚆🚌
🛈 Via Maistra 133; 081 838
83 00 ⊠ pontresina.ch

A mountaineering resort since
the 19th century, Pontresina,
in the Upper Engadine, lies at
the foot of Val Bernina at an
altitude of 1,800 m (5,900 ft).

Among Pontresina's historic
buildings are the Spaniola
Turm, a Romanesque tower,
and the chapel of Santa Maria,
containing Romanesque frescoes, some of which depict
scenes from the life of Mary
Magdalene. Exhibits in the
Museum Alpin illustrate the
history of the town.

Pontresina is a year-round
resort. In winter the slopes
of Diavolezza and Lagalb
are linked into the 350-km
(217-mile) network of the
Engadine ski region. In summer, Pontresina offers gentle
walking along wooded paths,
as well as more demanding
hiking and mountaineering
up to the summits of Alp Ota
and Munt della Bescha. The
hiking trail up Val Roseg leads
to a glacier at the foot of Piz
Roseg. Experienced climbers
can tackle Piz Bernina, at
4,049 m (13,284 ft) the highest
peak in the Rhaetian Alps.

Did You Know?

Legend has it a red-
haired siren lured
mountineers to their
doom on Diavolezza.

Museum Alpin

⊛ ⬡ Via Maistra 199 ☎ 081
842 72 73 ⊙ Mid-Jun–mid-
Oct & end Dec–mid-Apr: 3:30–
6pm Mon–Sat

Bernina Pass

⛰G5 ⬡ Graubünden 🚆🚌

At an altitude of 2,328 m
(7,638 ft), the Bernina Pass
is the highest point on the
ancient route from St Moritz
to Tirano, in Italy.

A road climbs up Val
Bernina on the north side
of the pass and descends Val
di Poschiavo on its southern
side. The pass is also served
by ordinary trains and by the
Bernina Express (p274). The
breathtaking view from the
pass takes in the peaks of the
Rhaetian Alps to the north and
Lago Bianco, an artificial lake.

↑ The Bernina Express train
making its dramatic ascent
up to the Bernina Pass

㉗
Val Bregaglia

F5 Grisons Strada Principale 101, Stampa; www.bregaglia.ch

The western continuation of the Inn valley culminates at the Maloja Pass (1,815 m/ 5,955 ft), which marks the western boundary of the Engadine. On the western side of the pass a road winds down the canton's predominantely Italian-speaking valleys.

Dotted with ruined castles and small churches, Val Bregaglia is popular with mountaineers for its many scenic hiking trails and extraordinary rock formations.

The main village in the valley is Vicosoprano, which has mansions and historic law courts. Further south lies Stampa, birthplace of the artists Augusto Giacometti and his son, Alberto. Their works can be seen in Stampa at the 16th-century Casa Granda, where there is also a museum of local history.

The charming hamlet of Soglio sits on the north side of the valley and is the starting point for numerous scenic hiking trails.

FOOD IN ST MORITZ

Known as a foodie place in the snow, St Moritz has a buzzing culinary scene, with its share of celebrity chefs and Michelin stars. Central to its epicurean reputation is the town's Gourmet Festival. Held every January, it entices gourmands with the chance to sample elaborate and inventive dishes cooked by master chefs, taste local delicacies from around the world and quaff award-winning wines.

㉒
St Moritz

F5 Graubünden Via Maistra 12; www. stmoritz.ch

The birthplace of winter tourism, still celebrated for its "champagne atmosphere" at 1,800 m (5,900 ft), St Moritz (San Murezzan in Romansh) lies on a sunny terrace on the north shore of Moritzersee. Surrounded by mountains, it offers superb skiing and snowboarding, and is a base for hiking and mountaineering in summer. Visitors will also find the world's oldest and only natural-ice bobsled run

75

The number of seconds it takes to zoom down the St Moritz bobsled run.

here. It is also known for its curative springs, exploited at least since the Middle Ages.

The town has two districts: St Moritz-Bad, the spa area on the southwestern side of the lake, and St Moritz-Dorf, on the northern side, with hotels, restaurants and boutiques.

Although little remains of the original village, St Moritz is an interesting place with two diverting museums. The **Giovanni-Segantini Museum** on Via Somplaz, is devoted to the Symbolist painter, who spent the final years of his life in the Upper Engadine. On Via dal Bagn, just below Via Somplaz, is the **Museum Engiadinais**, which looks at life in the Engadine and the history of the spa.

Giovanni-Segantini Museum

Via Somplaz 30
Mid-May–Oct & Dec–mid-May: 11am–5pm Tue–Sun Nov
segantini-museum.ch

The traditional Engadine village of Sils on the north shore of Silsersee

useum Engiadinais

⏺ 🅐 Via dal Bagn 39 ⏺ Mid-ay-Oct: 10am-5pm Wed-Mon; ec-Apr: 2-6pm Wed-Mon �🌐museum-engiadinais.ch

---

ils

🅵5 🅐 Grisons 🚌 ℹ sils.ch

e village of Sils (Segl in mansh) is set on the north ore of Silsersee. The village nsists of two parts: Sils selgia, on the lakeshore, and s Maria, to the south. Many iters, painters and musicians ve been drawn to Sils. From 31 to 1889, Sils Maria was e summer residence of the rman philosopher Friedrich etzsche. The house where he ed, and where he wrote *Also* *Sprach Zarathustra,* has been converted into a small museum, the **Nietzsche Haus**.

Nietzsche Haus

⊛⊛ 🅐 Via da Marias 67 ⏺ Mid-Jun-Oct & mid-Dec-Apr: 3-6pm Tue-Sun ⏺ May-mid-Jun & Nov �🌐nietzsche haus.ch

---

28
Zillis

🅵4 🅐 Graubünden 🚆 Thusis 🚌 ℹ Poststelle Hauptstrasse; www. zillis-reischen.ch

In the village of Zillis (Ziràn in Romansh), a remarkable cycle of Romanesque frescoes adorn a small church, on the east bank of the Hinterrhein.

The wooden ceiling of **Kirche St Martin** is covered with 153 square panels, painted between 1109 and 1114. The exterior panels depict an ocean filled with sea monsters; those in the interior show scenes from the life of Christ and of St Martin.

Kirche St Martin

🅐 Am Postplatz ⏺ 10am-5:30pm daily �🌐zillis-st-martin.ch

←

Paintings displayed at the Giovanni-Segantini Museum, St Moritz

29
San Bernardino Pass

🅴4 🅐 Graubünden 🚌 ℹ Strada Cantonale; www. sanbernardino.ch

On the great transalpine route running from Bodensee, in the far northeast of the country, down to Lake Como, in Italy, San Bernardino is one of Europe's most important mountain passes, lying at an altitude of 2,066 m (6,778 ft). Although snow usually blocks the pass from November to May, the 7-km (4-mile) tunnel beneath it is permanently open. The village resort of San Bernardino, located on the south side of the pass, makes an excellent base for hiking and exploring the surrounding mountains.

STAY

Suvretta House St Moritz

Impeccable service and Alpine luxury perched high above the Engadine Valley.

🅵5 🅐 Via Chasellas 1, St Moritz �🌐suvretta house.ch

🅢🅕 🅢🅕 🅢🅕

A spectacular waterfall near the Klausen Pass in the canton of Glarus ↑

26

Glarus

 E3 ◙ Glarus 🚌🚃
**🛈 Glarnerland Rätstätte
A3, Niederurnen; www.
glarnerland.ch**

Capital of the canton of Glarus, this small town is also the urban centre of Glarnerland, a rather isolated and mountainous but beautiful region that lies between Walensee and the Klausen Pass. Largely rebuilt after it was destroyed by fire in 1861, the town is laid out on a grid pattern and as such is a classic example of 19th-century urban planning. Notable buildings here include the town hall, the Kunsthaus Glarus – an art gallery with a collection of 19th- and 20th-century Swiss paintings – and the Neo-Romanesque parish

> **With beautiful lakes and valleys, the mountains around Glarus, particularly those of the Glärnisch massif, are popular with hikers.**

church with a treasury that contains a collection of liturgical vessels.

With beautiful lakes and valleys, the mountains around Glarus, particularly those of the Glärnisch massif, are popular with hikers. Many of the slopes have excellent pistes. South of Glarus, the main road goes on to Linthal, from where a funicular climbs to Braunwald. This tranquil car-free resort is set on a plateau that offers superb hiking. Beyond Linthal the road leads through some spectacular scenery over the Klausen Pass (1,948 m/6,391 ft) and down to Altdorf *(p229)* and Lake Lucerne.

27

Klosters

F4/F5 ◙ Graubünden
🚉🚌 **🛈 Alte Bahnhof
strasse 6; www.klosters.ch**

Quieter and smaller than Davos *(p261)*, its neighbour

to the south, the discreetly chic ski resort of Klosters has an intimate atmosphere. The only remaining trace of the medieval monastery from which it takes its name is Kirche St Jacob, which has beautiful stained-glass windows by Augusto Giacometti. The history of the village and its development into a resort are documented by displays in the **Nutli-Hüschi**, a 16th-century chalet.

Klosters shares a ski-pass region with Davos, encompassing 320 km (199 miles) of ski terrain. It is suitable for all levels of experience, from beginner to master skier.

Nutli-Hüschi

⊘ 🏠 Talstrasse ⏰ 3–5pm Wed & Fri 🌐 museum-klosters.ch

Did You Know?

Klosters is known as "Hollywood on the Rocks" because it attracts so many celebrities.

Poschiavo's cent
square with
Italianate buildin

28

Poschiavo

G5 Grisons
Stazione; www.081 844
05 71 valposchiavo.ch

The descent down Val di
Poschiavo, the valley on the
south side of the Bernina Pass,
reveals a very different side of
Switzerland. Here the climate
and vegetation, as well as the
language and the culture, are
Mediterranean. Buildings show
an Italian influence, the cuisine
turns to pastas and antipasti,
and cypress trees and palms
grow in sheltered gardens.

Poschiavo (Puschlav in
German) is the main town in
the valley. At its heart is the
Piazza Communale, a square
lined with Italianate *palazzi*
and two churches, a late 15th-
century Catholic church and
a 17th-century Protestant
church. Other notable buildings include the Casa Torre, a
Romanesque tower, and the
Palazzo Albricci. The so-called
Spaniolenviertel (Spanish
Quarter) boasts imposing
houses painted in a colourful
Moorish style.

At nearby Cavaglia are
remarkable geological features known as cauldrons.
These are natural wells, up
to 3 m (10 ft) in diameter, that
were carved into the rock by
the circular action of stones
and water released by
a melting glacier.

29

Mesocco

F5 Graubünden
mesocco.ch

The picturesque stone houses
of Mesocco cluster on the
banks of the River Moesa,
which runs along the Valle
Mesolcina. This valley stretches
from the San Bernardino Pass
southwards to Bellinzona and,
although it is located in the
canton of Graubünden, it has
strong cultural links with Ticino.

The Castello di Misox, a
ruined fortress set on a rocky
outcrop above the town,
commands a stunning view
of the valley and the villages
in it. Built for the counts of
Sax von Misox during the
12th century, the castle was
significantly extended in the
15th century and in 1480 it
passed into the ownership
of the Trivulizio family, from
Milan. The slender campanile
is a remnant of the castle
complex, which was almost
completely destroyed in 1526.

At the foot of the castle
stands the Romanesque
church of Santa Maria del
Castello. Built in the 12th
century, the church was partly
remodelled in the 17th century. The nave has a coffered
ceiling, and the walls are decorated with well-preserved
15th-century murals, which
depict St George and the
Dragon, St Bernard of Siena,
patron saint of Valle Mesolcina,
and scenes symbolizing the
months of the year.

About 4 km (2.5 miles)
south of Mesocco is Soazza,
a village with an attractive
17th-century church. About
15 km (9 miles) south of
Soazza is the sleepy village
of San Vittore, where there
is an 8th-century chapel. The
Val Calanca, which runs into
Valle Mesolcina, is
also well worth
exploring for
its beautiful
scenery.

EAT

Chesa Grischuna
Award-winning French
cuisine in a grand chalet.

F4/F5
Bahnhofstrasse 12,
Klosters
chesagrischuna.ch

(SF)(SF)(SF)

White Marmot
Fine wines and haute
cuisine at high altitude.

F5 Corviglia,
St Moritz 81 833 76 76

(SF)(SF)(SF)

NEED TO KNOW

A classic cypress-line road in Val d'Orcia

BEFORE YOU GO

Things change, so plan ahead to make the most of your trip. Be prepared fo all eventualities by considering the following points before you travel.

AT A GLANCE

CURRENCY
Swiss Franc
(SF)

AVERAGE DAILY SPEND

SAVE	SPEND	SPLURGE
SF 200	SF 350	SF 600

BOTTLED WATER	COFFEE	BEER	DINNER FOR TWO
SF 3.30	SF 4	SF 7	SF 100

ESSENTIAL PHRASES

Hello	Guten tag/bonjour/ buongiorno
Goodbye	Auf wiedersehen/ au revoir/arrivederci
Please	Bitte/s'il vous plaît/ per favore
Thank you	Danke/merci/ grazie
Do you speak English?	Sprechen Sie Englisch?/ Parlez-vous anglais?/ Lei parla inglese?

ELECTRICITY SUPPLY

Power sockets are type J, fitting type J (3-pin) plugs and type C (2-pin) plugs. Standard voltage is 230V.

Passports and Visas

For entry requirements, including visas, consul your nearest Swiss embassy or check Switzerland **Online Visa System**. EU nationals and citizens the UK, US, Canada, Australia and New Zealand need a valid passport but do not need visas fo stays of up to three months.
Online Visa System
W swiss-visa.ch

Government Advice

Now more than ever, it is important to consult both your and the Swiss government's advice before travelling. The **US Department of State** the **UK Foreign and Commonwealth Office**, t **Australian Department of Foreign Affairs an Trade** and the **Swiss Federal Council** offer the latest information on security, health and local regulations.
Australian Department of Foreign Affairs and Trade
W smartraveller.gov.au
Swiss Federal Council
W admin.ch
UK Foreign and Commonwealth Office
W gov.uk/foreign-travel-advice
US Department of State
W travel.state.gov

Customs Information

You can find information on the laws relating to goods and currency taken in or out of Switzerland on the **Federal Customs Administration** website.
Federal Customs Administration
W ezv.admin.ch

Insurance

We recommend taking out a comprehensive insurance policy covering theft, loss of belongings, medical care, cancellation and delays, and read the small print carefully.

UK and EU citizens are eligible for free emergency medical care in Switzerland provid

...ey have a valid European Health Insurance ...rd (**EHIC**). Note the UK Global Health Insurance ...rd (GHIC) is not valid in Switzerland.
EHIC
ec.europa.eu

Vaccinations

...r information regarding COVID-19 vaccination ...quirements, consult government advice *(p270)*.

Booking Accommodation

...witzerland offers accommodation to suit all ...stes and budgets. The **Swiss Hotel Association** ...fers a comprehensive list of accommodation. ...dvanced booking is essential in the mountain ...gions during the ski season (December to April).
Swiss Hotel Association
swisshotels.com

Money

...ost establishments accept major credit, debit ...nd prepaid currency cards. Contactless pay-...ents are becoming more widely accepted, but ...s always a good idea to carry cash for smaller ...ems and tips. Cash machines are found at ...anks and at various points in town and city ...ntres. Taxi drivers, hotel porters and concierges ...ill expect to be tipped SF 5–10, housekeeping ...ould be given SF 2–5 per day and you should ...und up restaurant bills to the nearest SF 5 or ...F 10 for wait staff.

Travellers with Specific Requirements

...witzerland offers a high standard of facilities ...r travellers with specific requirements, but it is ...ways worth calling ahead to check that your ...quirements will be met.

...For assistance at train stations, phone the ...BB Call Centre Handicap one hour before ...eparture (or three working days beforehand ...r international travel). **Mietauto** has details ...n adapted hire vehicles.

...Switzerland Tourism can provide full details ...f suitable hotel facilities for guests with specific ...quirements. The website of the **Swiss ...ational Association of and for the Blind** ...dvises travellers with visual impairments.

Mietauto
mietauto.ch
SBB Call Centre Handicap
0800 007 102 (within Switzerland, toll-free), +41 51 225 78 44 (from abroad, subject to charge)
Swiss National Association of and for the Blind
snab.ch
Switzerland Tourism
myswitzerland.com

Language

Switzerland has four national languages – French, German, Italian and Romansh. Although English is not an official language, it is often used to bridge the language divides (especially in cities), and much official documentation is available in English. German is spoken mostly in the east, French mostly in the west, and Italian mostly in the southern canton of Ticino and the southern parts of neighbouring Graubünden. Romansh is spoken only in the canton of Graubünden.

Opening Hours

> **COVID-19** Increased rates of infection may result in temporary opening hours and/or closures. Always check ahead before visiting museums, attractions and hospitality venues.

Monday Some places are closed on Monday mornings or for the entire day.
Thursday Cities, including Geneva and Zürich, have late-night shopping until 8pm.
Saturday Post offices and shops close at noon.
Sunday Most businesses are closed for the day.
Public holidays Shops, churches, museums and restaurants either close early or all day.

PUBLIC HOLIDAYS

1 Jan	New Year's Day
19 Apr	Good Friday
30 May	Ascension Day
1 Aug	National Day
25 Dec	Christmas Day

GETTING AROUND

Whether you are visiting for a short city break, a ski weekend or a rural retreat, discover how best to reach your destination and travel like a pro.

AT A GLANCE

PUBLIC TRANSPORT COSTS

BERN

SF 2.80

One-way
tram, bus, trolley bus

GENEVA

SF 3.00

One-way
tram, bus, ferry, local train

ZÜRICH

SF 2.70

One-way
bus, tram, local train

TOP TIP
Major cities offer travel passes, better value if you plan to use public transport often.

SPEED LIMIT

MOTORWAY

120 km/h
(75mph)

DUAL CARRIAGEWAYS

100 km/h
(62mph)

SECONDARY ROAD

80 km/h
(50mph)

URBAN AREAS

50 km/h
(31mph)

Arriving by Air

Zürich and Geneva airports are the main hubs for long-haul flights into Switzerland. Transatlantic flights are provided by SWISS, the national airline, as well as American Airlines, United Airlines, Delta and Air Canada. Both airports also offer flights to all major European cities with SWISS and a large number of carriers including several budget airlines, such as easyJet, which has a hub at Geneva.

A number of smaller airports at Bern, Basel and Lugano also serve destinations within Europe. The airports of Sion, St Gallen and Engadin are used more for private business jets and internal flights than for scheduled international departures.

For information on distances and journey times between airports and cities, see the table opposite.

Train Travel

International Train Travel

Situated at the crossroads of major European routes, Switzerland has excellent international rail links. Regular high-speed trains connect the country to all major cities in the neighbouring countries of France, Germany, Austria and Italy, and beyond. Train journeys into the country can often compete with flights on price, and, for some short-haul routes, are not very much longer than flights door to door. Additionally, the opening of the 57-km- (36-mile-) long Gotthard Base Tunnel – the world's longest railway tunnel – in 2016 has significantly reduced rail journey times for passengers transiting the Alps.

Making reservations early is strongly recommended, especially on overnight sleeper trains, as tickets get booked up quickly. **Eurail** and **Interrail** sell tickets for multiple international journeys and international rail passes for trips lasting from five days up to three months.
Eurail
w eurail.com
Interrail
w interrail.eu

GETTING TO AND FROM THE AIRPORT

Airport	Distance to City	Taxi Fare	Public Transport	Journey time
Euro Airport Basel-Mulhouse-Freiburg (MLH)	6 km (4 miles)	SF 50	Bus	18 mins
Bern Airport (BRN)	6 km (4 miles)	SF 50	Bus	35 mins
Geneva International Airport (GVA)	4 km (2 miles)	SF 35	Train	6 mins
Lugano -Agno Airport (LUG)	6 km (4 miles)	SF 35	Bus	15 mins
Engadin Airport St Moritz-Samedan (SMV)	7 km (4 miles)	SF 100	Bus	17 mins
Sion Airport/Aéroport de Sion (SIR)	2.5 km (2 miles)	SF 46	Bus	4 mins
St Gallen-Altenrhein Airport (ACH)	20 km (12 miles)	SF 82	Bus	45 mins
Zürich Airport (ZRH)	10 km (6 miles)	SF 70	Train	10 mins

RAIL JOURNEY PLANNER

This map is a handy reference for intercity rail travel between Switzerland's main towns and cities.

••• Direct train routes

Bern to Basel	1 hr	**Geneva to Lausanne**	1 hr
Bern to Geneva	2 hrs	**Geneva to Lugano**	5 hrs
Bern to Zürich	1 hr	**Lugano to Basel**	3.5 hrs
Bern to Lucerne	1.5 hrs	**Zürich to Basel**	1 hr
Bern to Lugano	3.5 hrs	**Zürich to Lucerne**	1 hr
Bern to St Gallen	2 hrs	**Zürich to Lugano**	2.5 hrs
Geneva to Basel	3 hrs	**Zürich to St Gallen**	1 hr
Geneva to Zürich	3 hrs		

Domestic Train Travel

Travelling by train is one of the best ways to see the country. The comprehensive Swiss rail network is operated by Swiss Federal Railways or **SBB/CFF/FFS** (Schweizerische Bundesbahnen/ Chemins de Fer Fédéraux Suisses/Ferrovie Federali Svizzere). Safety and hygiene measures, timetables, ticket information, transport maps, and more can be obtained from the SBB/CFF/ FFS website.

Tickets must be validated in machines set at platform entrances. There are heavy on-the-spot fines for travellers caught with an unstamped ticket. **Swiss Travel System** (part of Switzerland Tourism) offers a range of discounted travel passes for use on all modes of transport. One of the most popular is the Swiss Travel Pass, which allows unlimited travel on most train, bus, tram and boat services, discounts on some funiculars and cable cars and entry to over 500 museums. There is also a Junior Travelcard for children aged 6 to 16 years. Most travel passes can be purchased in advance from travel agencies and Swiss tourist offices in your country.

Switzerland is known for its scenic railways, where visitors can enjoy the spectacular scenery in special trains with glass-roofed carriages. Among the most popular are the **Bernina Express** (Chur or Davos to Tirano, Italy), **Golden Pass Line** (Montreux to Lucerne), **Gotthard Panorama Express** (Lucerne to Lugano) and **Glacier Express** (St Moritz to Zermatt). It is essential to book in advance for these.

Bernina Express
W rhb.ch
Glacier Express
W glacierexpress.ch
Golden Pass Line
W mob.ch
Gotthard Panorama Express
W sbb.ch
SBB/CFF/FFS
W sbb.ch
Swiss Travel System
W swisstravelsystem.com

Long-Distance Bus Travel

Eurolines offers several coach routes between Swiss destinations and other European cities. Switzerland has an extensive network of routes covered by local buses and **Swiss Post**'s distinctive yellow postbuses. The latter vary in size depending on the remoteness of the destination and are useful for reaching alpine locations inaccessible by rail. They also carry unaccompanied luggage, which is handy for hikers.

Eurolines
W eurolines.de
Swiss Post
W swisspost.ch

Boats and Ferries

In some cities, boats form an integral part of the transport system. Yellow *mouettes* (bus-boats) operated by **Mouettes Genevoises Navigation** shuttle foot passengers across Lake Geneva, while quirky *fähri* (cable-ferries) run by **Fähri-Verein Basel** have been ferrying people across the Rhine in Basel since the mid-19th century.

A cruise on one of Switzerland's lakes and rivers is a relaxing way to explore the country. Plying the waters of many of the major lakes are old-fashioned paddle steamers and other vessels, including those run by **SBS** across Bodensee, **CGN** on Lake Geneva, **SGV** on Lake Lucerne and **ZSG** across Zürichsee.

CGN
W cgn.ch
Fähri-Verein Basel
W faehri.ch
Mouettes Genevoises Navigation
W mouettesgenevoises.ch
SBS
W sbsag.ch
SGV
W lakelucerne.ch
ZSG
W zsg.ch

Public Transport

S-Bahn and RER

Some cities, including Basel, Bern, Geneva and Zürich, have comprehensive urban rail networks (called S-Bahn in German and RER in French) which radiate out from the city centres to the suburbs and neighbouring towns. Some towns built on steep cliffs or hillsides, such as Lausanne and Fribourg, also have funicular railways.

Metro

Lausanne is the only Swiss city to have a metro. It has two lines and 30 stops, and operates from 5:30am to midnight, with trains every five to seven minutes.

Lausanne Metro
W t-l.ch

Buses and Trams

The quickest and easiest way of getting around towns and cities is by hopping on a bus or tram. These run at frequent intervals from around 5am to midnight. Larger cities also operate a reduced night-bus service at weekends.

Tickets are available from machines at every bus and tram stop, and are usually valid on all modes of transport. In most towns, the transport network is divided into zones; the more zones you traverse the higher the fare. Tickets valid for limited periods, from 30 minutes to a full day or more, are also available. These includ

...VV's ZürichCard and **TPG**'s GenevaPass; both
...f these also offer free entry to some city attrac-
...ons. Tickets must be validated in the machine
...n the vehicle as you board.
PG
W tpg.ch
VV
W zvv.ch

Taxis

...large cities, buses and trams are ubiquitous
...nd inexpensive, and few people use taxis. They
...e expensive compared with public transport,
...nd metred by distance; charges are higher at
...ght and at weekends. If you do choose to
...avel by taxi, note that they cannot be hailed –
...ey must be booked in advance or engaged at
...taxi rank.

Driving

...ne of the best ways to explore Switzerland is
...y car. Driving here is pleasurable – the Swiss
...ave a high regard for rules of the road and
...ke pride in having the safest roads in Europe.
...U driving licences are valid. If visiting from
...utside the EU, or if your licence is not in English,
...erman, French or Italian, you may need to
...pply for an International Driving Permit (IDP).

Driving to Switzerland

...you bring your own foreign-registered car into
...e country, you must carry the vehicle's regis-
...ation and insurance documents and a valid
...river's licence.

...Fuel is generally less expensive than in
...eighbouring countries. Bigger petrol stations
...e usually open from 7am to 8pm; smaller ones
...ntil 6pm. Outside these hours, petrol is widely
...vailable from automatic pumps. Some motor-
...ay service stations are open 24 hours.

...To use Swiss motorways, which are indicated
...y green signs, drivers require a sticker called a
...gnette, which costs SF 40. It is sold at border
...ossings, petrol stations, tourist offices and
...ost offices. Driving on a motorway without
...valid vignette incurs a fine.

Driving in Switzerland

...ell-maintained motorways and major roads
...nk the major towns, and there are some spec-
...cularly scenic routes over mountain passes
...d down alpine valleys to more remote towns
...d villages. Most of the high alpine passes are
...pen between June and October; alternative
...ays of crossing the Alps is to take advantage of
...e Gotthard and San Bernardino road tunnels,
...hich are open year-round (some have tolls),
... to drive your car onto a train to transit via
...e Lötschberg, Furka, Albula or Vereina tunnels.

Car Rental

To rent a car, you must be over 20 years of age
and have held a valid driver's licence for at least
a year. Drivers under 25 may incur a surcharge.

All major international car-hire companies
have offices in the main cities and airports, and
Swiss Railways also offers a **Mobility Click &
Drive** online rental service with pick up from
400 railway stations.
Mobility Click & Drive
W mobility.ch

Rules of the Road

The legal car driving age in Switzerland is 18
(20 or 25 in a hire car). The Swiss drive on the
right, and seatbelts are compulsory. It is illegal
to use mobile phones while driving, or to drive
under the influence of alcohol (the blood-
alcohol content limit is 0.05 per cent). Children
under 12 must travel in the back seat, and
under-sevens must use a child seat. All vehicles
must carry a warning triangle, a first aid kit and
a reflective jacket, and full headlights should
be on at all times. In winter, drivers are required
by law to use snow tyres and/or chains on
mountain roads when indicated by special
warning signs.

Cycling

Environmentally conscious Switzerland
encourages pedal power and, with the growing
use of e-bikes, cycling has taken on a new popu-
larity. Bike routes crisscross the entire country
(marked by red signs with a white bicycle symbol) and include many long-distance paths.

Public bike-sharing schemes are available in
most major cities, such as **Zürirollt** in Zürich and
Genèveroule in Geneva. **PubliBike** is a popular
nationwide bike-sharing programmes. Contact
local tourist offices for details of schemes in
their town. Bicycles can also be hired at main
train stations (these need not be returned to
the same station), and can be carried on most
postbuses and trains for a fee.
Genèveroule
W geneveroule.ch
PubliBike
W publibike.ch
Zürirollt
W zuerirollt.ch

Walking

Laced with paths and trails, Switzerland is
a hiker's paradise (*p43*). Find your nearest walk
on the **Switzerland Mobility** website. As well as
detailed maps, guides and safety tips, it advises
on the accessibility of each route.
Switzerland Mobility
W schweizmobil.ch

PRACTICAL
INFORMATION

A little local know-how goes a long way in Switzerland. Here you will find all the essential advice and information you will need during your stay.

AT A GLANCE

EMERGENCY NUMBERS

EMERGENCY	POLICE
112	**117**

AMBULANCE	FIRE SERVICE
144	**118**

TIME ZONE
CET/CEST: Central European Summer Time runs from the last Sunday in March to the last Sunday in October.

TAP WATER
Unless otherwise stated, tap water in Switzerland and water from fountains in towns and villages is safe to drink.

WEBSITES AND APPS
Switzerland Tourism
Produces excellent free apps, including Family Trips, SwitzerlandMobility, Swiss Events and Snow Report *(www.my switzerland.com)*.
Swiss Museums
Discover the latest exhibitions on this app.
Via Michelin
App providing live speed restriction and traffic alerts, navigation and other tools.
Meteo Suisse
The country's official weather app.

Personal Security

Switzerland is a safe country to visit but, like anywhere, petty crime does take place. Pickpockets work known tourist areas, public transport and busy streets. Use your common sense and be alert to your surroundings, and you should enjoy a stress-free trip.

If you do have anything stolen, report the crime within 24 hours to the nearest police station. Obtaining a police report will enable you to make an insurance claim. Contact your embassy if you have your passport stolen, or in the event of a serious crime or accident.

As a rule, the Swiss are accepting of all people, regardless of their race, gender or sexuality. Homosexuality was legalized in 1942 and Zürich has held a huge annual Pride event since 1994. That being said, some forms of homophobic discrimination have only been criminalized since 2020 and same-sex marriage is not yet legal. Conservative attitudes prevail, especially outside of urban areas, and overt displays of affection may receive a negative response from locals. If you do feel unsafe, head for the nearest police station or contact **Diologai**, an LGBTQ+ association in Geneva.
Diologai
w dialogai.org

Health

Switzerland has a world-class healthcare system but the country does not have a government health program, so medical treatment of any kind must be paid for. A reciprocal agreement exists with all EU nations, so if you have an EHIC *(p271)*, present this as soon as possible. You may have to pay the fee and claim it back later. Private health insurance is essential, especially if you are planning a skiing, mountaineering or hiking holiday, or any extreme sports.

For minor ailments, seek medical supplies and advice from pharmacies. Search the website of the **SOS-Pharmacy** organization for open emergency pharmacies in your area.
SOS-Pharmacy
w sos-pharmacie.ch

Smoking, Alcohol and Drugs

Smoking is banned on public transport and in enclosed public places, and it is illegal to drive under the influence of alcohol (the blood alcohol content limit is 0.05 per cent). Drug possession is taken very seriously and there are heavy penalties, jail sentences and fines depending on the type of narcotic (possession of very small amounts of cannabis will incur no penalties). Taking drugs across an international border automatically constitutes drug trafficking and has a heavy penalty.

ID

By law you must carry valid identification at all times. A photocopy of your passport photo page (and visa if applicable) should suffice.

Local Customs

Be respectful of the religious beliefs and political opinions of the local people and try to adhere to local customs, both at national and cantonal level.
National customs include a commitment to the environment (the Swiss take their recycling seriously and expect tourists to do the same) and punctuality. It'll come as no surprise that a country famed for its timepieces has little tolerance for tardiness, whether you're attending a business meeting or a dinner reservation.

Visiting Churches and Cathedrals

Most churches and cathedrals will not permit visitors during Sunday Mass. Generally, entrance to churches is free, however a fee may apply to enter special areas, like cloisters. When visiting places of worship, ensure that you are dressed respectfully, with your torso, shoulders and knees covered.

Mobile Phones and Wi-Fi

Wi-Fi is widely available throughout Switzerland, and cafés and restaurants will usually give customers their Wi-Fi password. Visitors with EU tariffs are able to use their devices abroad without being affected by roaming charges. Check with your service provider for details.

Post

You can purchase stamps *(Briefmarken/timbres/francobolli)* in post offices and some news-agents. Allow from a couple of days to one or two weeks for delivery of international mail, depending on the service you select.

Taxes and Refunds

Switzerland's standard VAT rate is 7.7 per cent, although there is a reduced rate of 2.5 per cent on certain everyday consumer goods such as food, non-alcoholic beverages, newspapers, magazines, books and medicines. Hotel stays (including breakfast) are taxed at a special rate of 3.7 per cent. Due to the four official languages, VAT may be called Mwst (Mehrwertsteuer), TVA (Taxe sur la valeur ajoutée), IVA (Imposta sul valore aggiunto) or TPV (Taglia sin la Plivalur). Non-EU residents get a tax refund on purchases over SF 300, subject to conditions. Ask for a tax receipt and relevant documentation at the time of purchase, and show these at customs (with ID) when leaving the country for your refund.

Discount Cards

Switzerland Tourism *(p273)* offer a range of passes and tickets exclusively for visitors. Its Swiss Museum Pass allows free entrance into 490 museums and galleries and is available from tourist offices, railway stations, post offices and larger museums. It also offers travel passes for three regions – Bernese Oberland, Central Switzerland and Lake Geneva-Alps.
Some cities (Bern, Lucerne, Neuchâtel and Winterthur) offer their own visitor's pass or discount card. Others also cover the cost of public transport, for instance, the **Zürich Card**, the **BaselCard** and the **GenevaPass**. Certain regions (including the Engadin, Davos-Klosters, Arosa, Saas Fee, Villars and Adelboden) offer schemes whereby guests staying more than one night in a participating hotel receive free transportation during the summer.

BaselCard
w basel.com/en/BaselCard
GenevaPass
w geneve.com/en/see-do/geneva-pass/
Zürich Card
w zuerich.com/en/zurichcard

INDEX

Index

Page numbers in **bold** refer to main entries

PHRASE BOOK

German is the most widely spoken language in Switzerland, followed by French and Italian. Swiss German, which is used in everyday speech, differs from standard German, so some of the most commonly used expressions in Swiss German are marked by an asterisk.

IN EMERGENCY	German	French	Italian
Help!	Hilfe!	Au secours!	Aiuto!
Stop!	Halt!	Arrêtez!	Alt!
Call a doctor!	Holen Sie einen Artz!	Appelez un médecin!	Chiami un medico!
Call an ambulance!	... einen Krankenwagen!	... une ambulance!	... una ambulanza!
Call the police!	... die Polizei!	... la police!	... la polizia!
Where is the hospital?	Wo finde ich das Krankenhaus?	Où est l'hôpital?	Dov'è l'ospedale?

COMMUNICATION ESSENTIALS

Yes	Ja	Oui	Si
No	Nein	Non	No
Please	Bitte	S'il vous plaît	Per favore
Thank you	Danke vielmals	Merci	Grazie
Excuse me	Entschuldigen Sie *Äxgüsi	Excusez-moi	Mi scusi
Hello	Guten Tag *Grüezi	Salut	Salve/Ciao
Goodbye	Auf Widersehen *Ufwiederluege	Au revoir	Arrivederci
Bye!	Tschüss!	Salut!	Ciao!
Here	hier	ici	qui
There	dort	là	la
What?	Was?	Quel/Quelle?	Quale?
When?	Wann?	Quand?	Quando?
Where?	Wo/Wohin?	Oé?	Dove?

USEFUL PHRASES AND WORDS

Where is ...?	Wo befindet sich...?	Où est ...?	Dov'è...?
Where are ...?	Wo befinden sich...?	Oùsont...?	Dove sono...?
Do you speak English?	Sprechen Sie Englisch?	Parlez-vous anglais?	Parla inglese?
I understand	Ich verstehe	Je comprends	Capisco
I don't understand	Ich verstehe nicht	Je ne comprends pas	Non capisco
I'm sorry	Es tut mir leid	Je suis désolé	Mi dispiace
big	gross	grand	grande
small	klein	petit	piccolo
open	auf/offen	ouvert	aperto
closed	zu/geschlossen	fermé	chiuso
left	links	à gauche	a sinistra
right	rechts	à droite	a destra
near	in der Nähe	près	vicino
far	weit	loin	lontano
early	früh	de bonne heure	presto
late	spät	en retard	tardi
entrance	Eingang/Einfahrt	l'entrée	l'entrata
exit	Ausgang/Ausfahrt	la sortie	l'uscita
toilet	WC/Toilette	les toilettes/les WCs	il gabinetto
this	diese	ce	questo
that	das	cette	quello

MAKING A TELEPHONE CALL

I'd like to make a long-distance call.	Ich möchte ein Fernsgespräch machen.	Je voudrais faire un interurbain.	Vorrei fare una interurbana.
I'll try again later.	Ich versuche es später noch einmal.	Je rapellerai plus tard.	Ritelefono pié tardi.
Can I leave a message?	Kann ich etwas ausrichten?	Est ce que je peux laisser un message?	Posso lasciare un messaggio?

STAYING IN A HOTEL

Do you have a vacant room?	Haben Sie ein Zimmer frei?	Est-ce que vous avez une chambre libre?	Avete camere libere?
double room	ein Doppelzimmer	une chambre à deux	una camera doppia
twin room	ein Doppelzimmer mit zwei Betten	une chambre à deux lits	una camera con due letti
single room	ein Einzelzimmer	une chambre à une personne	una camera singola
with a bath/shower	mit Bad/Dusche	avec salle de bains/douche	con bagno/doccia
How much is the room?	Wievel kostet das Zimmer?	Combien coûte la chambre?	Quanto costa la camera?
Where is the bathroom?	Wo ist das Bad?	Où est la salle de bains?	Dov'è il bagno?
with breakfast	mit Frühstück	avec petit-déjeuner	con prima colazione
with half-board	mit Halbpension	en demi-pension	mezza pensione
dormitory	Schlafsaal	le dortoir	il dormitorio
key	Schlüssel	la clef	la chiave
I have a reservation	Ich habe ein Zimmer reserviert	J'ai fait une réservation	Ho fatto una prenotazione

SIGHTSEEING

English	German	French	Italian
bus	der Bus	l'autobus	el autobus
tram	die Strassenbahn	le tramway	el tram
train	der Zug	le train	il treno
bus station	der Busbahnhof	la gare routière	l'autostazione
train station	der Bahnhof	la gare	la stazione
boat	das Boot	le bateau	la barca
parking	der Parkplatz	la place de stationnement	il parcheggio
car park	das Parkhaus	le parking	l'autosilo
(hire) bicycle	das Fahrrad/das Mietvelo	le vélo (de location)	la bicicletta (a noleggio)
airport	der Flughafen	l'aéroport	l'aeroporto
church	die Kirche	l'église	la chiesa
cathedral	der Dom	la cathédrale	il duomo/la cattedrale
main square	der Hauptplatz	la place centrale	la piazza principale
post office	das Postamt	le bureau de poste	la posta
tourist office	das Verkehrsamt	l'office du tourisme	l'ente turistico

TIME

English	German	French	Italian
morning	der Morgen	le matin	la mattina
afternoon	der Nachmittag	l'après-midi	il pomeriggio
evening	das Abend	le soir	la sera
yesterday	gestern	hier	ieri
today	heute	aujourd'hui	oggi
tomorrow	morgen	demain	domani
Monday	Montag	lundi	lunedì
Tuesday	Dienstag	mardi	martedì
Wednesday	Mittwoch	mercredi	mercoledì
Thursday	Donnerstag	jeudi	giovedì
Friday	Freitag	vendredi	venerdì
Saturday	Samstag/*Sonnabend	samedi	sabato
Sunday	Sonntag	dimanche	domenica

SHOPPING

How much does this cost?	Wieviel kostet das?	C'est combien, s'il vous plaît?	Quant'è, per favore?
I would like...	Ich hätte gern...	Je voudrais...	Vorrei...
Do you have...?	Haben Sie...?	Est-ce que vous avez...	Avere...?
bank	Bank	la banque	la banca
chemist/pharmacy	Apotheke	la pharmacie	la farmacia
market	Markt	le marché	il mercato
travel agent	Reisebüro	l'agence de voyages	l'agenzia di viaggi

EATING OUT

Have you got a table for...?	Haben sie einen Tisch für ...?	Avez-vous une table pour...?	Avete una tavola per ...?
The bill/check, please	Zahlen, bitte	L'addition, s'il vous plaît	Il conto, per favore
I am a vegetarian	Ich bin Vegetarier(in)	Je suis végétarien(ne)	Sono vegetariano(a)
waitress/waiter	Fräulein/Herr Ober	Mademoiselle/Monsieur	Cameriera/Camariere
menu	die Spiesekarte	le menu/la carte	il mené
wine list	die Weinkarte	la carte des vins	la lista dei vini
breakfast	das Frühstück	le petit déjeuner	la prima colazione
lunch	das Mittagessen	le déjeuner	il pranzo
dinner	das Abendessen	le dîner	la cena

MENU DECODER

English	German	French	Italian
baked	gebacken	cuit au four	al forno
beans	Bohnen	des haricots	fagioli
beef	Rindfleisch	boeuf	manzo
boiled	gekocht	bouilli	bollito
cheese	Käse	fromage	formaggio
chicken	Hendle/Hahn/Huhn	poulet	pollo
chocolate	Schokolade	chocolat	cioccolato
cream	Schlag	cream	crema
egg	ei	oeuf	uovo
fish	Fisch	poisson	pesce
garlic	Knoblauch	ail	aglio
grilled	vom Grill	grillé	alla griglia
ham	Schinken/Speck	jambon	prosciutto
ice cream	Eis	glace	gelato
lamb	Lamm	agneau	agnello
meat	Fleisch	viande	carne
milk	milch	lait	latte
pepper	Pfeffer	poivre	pepe
poached	pochiert	poché	in camicia
pork	Schwein	porc	carne di miale
potato	Kartoffel/Erdäpfel	pommes de terre	patate
red/white wine	Rot-/Weisswein	vin rouge/blanc	vino rosso/blanco
roasted	gebraten	rôti	arrosto
salad	Salat	salade	insalata
salt	Salz	sal	sale
sausage	Wurst	saucisse	salsiccia
seafood	Meeresfrüchte	fruits de mer	frutti di mare
vegetables	Gemüse	légumes	contorni
water	Wasser	l'eau	acqua

ACKNOWLEDGMENTS

K would like to thank the following for
eircontribution to the previous edition: Caroline
shop, Mike MacEacheran, Anthony Lambert.

ie publisher would like to thank the following for their
nd permission to reproduce their photographs:

y: a-above; b-below/bottom; c-centre; f-far; l-left;
right; t-top

23RF.com: Roman Babakin 29tr, 122-23b; Stefan
mber 218cl; Janos Gaspar 22crb; jakobradlgruber
.8cr; Chon Kit Leong 242bl; Narongsak Nagadhana
lcra; photogearch 242clb; rudi1976 248-9t;
slankphoto 46tr; Fedor Selivanov 246bl; theyok
.2bl; Eleonora Travostino 222t.

orners: Andreas Gerth 30bl; Gianni Krattli 19, 174;
ca Da Ros 76-7b.

g-images: 166cl; Cameraphoto 69tl; André Held 191br.

amy Stock Photo: age fotostock 67br, 126cra, 157tr;
gencja Fotograficzna Caro / Bastian 255ca; AGF Srl
3tr; Stephen Allen 56bc; Leonid Andronov 67t; Anvalo
1tl; AR Photo 150tr; Architecture2000 186clb; Arco / J.
eiffer 255t; ART Collection 57cra; Arterra Picture
orary 228tr; Udo Bernhart 36-7t; Eva Bocek 45br,
4-15b, 266t; Tibor Bognar 18bl, 158; byvalet 75b;
nnaro Caninchello 45bl; Josse Christophel 58tl; Aiden
arke 263b; Sorin Colac 72b; Chris Craggs 112tl; Peter
ghton 251br; Ian Dagnall 22bl; dpa picture alliance
2-13b; Pavel Dudek 145tl; Ros Drinkwater 194-95t;
iner Elsen 168bl; Stefan Ember 232b; EThamPhoto
br; Archie Fisher 230bl; Francesco Gavazzeni 264-5b;
°C Collection 24t, 40-1t, 55tl; Godong 121bc; Tim
aham 262tl; Granger Historical Picture Archive 58bc;
mis.fr 118bl, 154bl, 173tr, / Giuglio Gil 24crb, / Ludovic
aisant 123ca, / Bertrand Rieger 187; The History
llection 181bc; imageBROKER 17t, 31b, 197b, 198clb,
8b, 232tl, / Werner Dieterich 220bl, / Marina Horvat
bl, / Iris Kürschner 254-5b, / Meinrad Riedo 210t, /
rald Wenzel – Orf 250bl; Image Professionals GmbH /
rnard van Dierendonck 44bl, / Ingrid Firmhofer 53cla;
TERFOTO / Fine Arts 167cra; JBTravel 118crb, 147bl;
chael Jenner 267b; Christian Kober 259br; Christian
ber 1 96cr; Jitraporn Leeniva 227b; Arnaud Lesueur
8t; LOOK Die Bildagentur der Fotografen GmbH
clb; MARKA / giulio andreini/ exhibition of work by
gmar Ploke at art museum,Kunsthaus,Zurich © The
tate of Sigmar Polke, Cologne / DACS 2018 167tr, /
ovanni mereghetti 214ca; Hilke Maunder 28cla;
auritius images GmbH 13cr, 53br, 107br, 127br, 199tl,
1cr, 258-9t, 265t, / Walter Bibikow 35b, / enricocaccia-
ografie 221; McPhoto / Protze 49c; mediacolor's
2crb; Melba Photo Agency 24cr; Hercules Milas 16, 62;
berto Moiola 42-43b; Peter Moulton 112cb; National
ographic Image Collection / Robbie Shone 94cra;
rgio Nogueira 147br; Alexander Novikov 256-7b;
orge Oze 162t; Panther Media GmbH 99t, 150b, 228tr,
lena Klippert 150b; vichai phububphapan 104b,
2cr; PjrTravel 182b, 184cb; Prisma Archivo 56crb;
ısma by Dukas Presseagentur GmbH 10clb, 11cr, 98bl,
3br, 108b, 110t, 110bl, 154-55t, 156t, 156-57b, 207tl,
8-29b, Olaf Protze 46tl, / Sonderegger Christof 52bl;
mon Reddy 74tr; Paolo Romiti 117bl; RossHelen
itorial 226tl; Alistair Scott 54clb, 55bl, 152-53b,
2-53b; Kumar Sriskandan 261tr; Dominic Steinmann
clb; Geoffrey Taunton 100bl; Erik Tham / template /
riant / friend / stranger by Tony Oursler at the modern
t show "Art Basel 2016" 54cr; The Protected Art
hive 56t; Glyn Thomas 170cra; Rosengart Museum,
cerne / TravelCollection / Inga Wandinger works by
casso © Succession Picasso/DACS, London 2018
8tr; travelstock44 8clb, 169t, 171br, 178cr;
velstock44.de / Juergen Held 161cl; Jorge Tutor
7ca; Universal Images Group North America LLC
3cra, 186bl; Sebastian Wasek 100-01t; Westend61
bH 8cl, 121t, / Werner Dieterich 130bl; Peter Wey 95;
ott Wilson 172b; World History Archive 57br; Juriaan

Wossink 120bl; Patrizia Wyss 188bl, 258bl;
YesPhotographers 260-1b.

AWL Images: Jon Arnold 129tl; Jean-Francois
Hagenmuller 60-1; Christian Kober 210cr, 211;
Doug Pearson 218cb.

Bern Welcome: 70cra.

Cabaret Voltaire: Thus I Spoke-«Dying on Stage»,
Performance by Christodoulos Panayiotou & Jean
Capeille 39br.

Chur Tourismus: Andrea Bradrutt 249tr.

Crans-Montana Tourisme & Congrès: 111bl.

Depositphotos Inc: pandionhiatus3 170t.

Dorling Kindersley: Katarzyna Medrzakowie /
Wojciech Medrzakowie 121fbl, 252bl, 253tr.

Dreamstime.com: Akulamatiau 54cla; Alexirina27000
138tr; Andreykr 124tl; Leonid Andronov 43tr, 80-81, 148,
184bl; Astra490 217tr; Baselxg 181tr; Eva Bocek 97bc,
206-07b; Burben 44-5t; Roberto Cerruti 93br; Elena
Duvernay 17bl, 114; Stefano Ember 48-49t, 215ca, 79br;
Janos Gaspar 255cla; Gayane 138-39b; Diego Grandi 70c;
Jojjik 90-91t; Thomas Jurkowski 121cra; Rachapol
Kitjanukit 20, 200; Makasanaphoto 93cla; Mihai-bogdan
Lazar 136-37t; Minnystock 42tl; Emanuele Leoni 109ca;
Lianem 218b; Milosk50 192-93b; Moniphoto 142bc;
Monner 54cra; Morseicinque 224-25t; Dmytro Nikitin
231t; Nuvisage 46-7b; Vichai Phububphapan 94clb; Ivano
Piacenza 91tr; Ppy2010ha 36bl; Beatrice Preve 33cb;
Prasit Rodphan 59tr; Rosshelen 70bl, 128b, 192tr;
Sculpies 96-97t; Sforzza1 166-67b; Sophyphotos 37tc;
Michal Stipek 41ca, 109t; Susazoom 253tl; Swisshippo
47cl, 55cr, 242br, 243; Tnuangthong 59crb; Verryfe 97br;
Victorflowerfly 213tr; Vogelsp 30-1t; Bram De Vrind 43cb;
Xantana 26cla, 86b, 178t, 204-05t.

The Fondation Beyeler: Mark Niedermann 149tl.

Getty Images: AFP / Fabrice Coffrini 24cl, 51cb, 68-9b, /
Valeriano Di Domenico 33cla; AGF / Hermes Images 247t;
Ascent Xmedia / Milo Zanecchia 2-3; Bettmann 58cla,
59clb; cdbrphotography 50-1b; Corbis / VCG / Francis G.
Mayer 68clb; Harold Cunningham 32-3t, 69tr, 69cla;
EyeEm / Marcus Tischer 26t; Fine Art Images / Heritage
Images 123t; Sean Gallup 31cl; Gamma-Rapho / Marc
Deville 28tl; Historical 58clb; Hulton Deutsch 58-9t;
Lightcapturing by Björn Abt 190-91t; Frank Lukasseck
8-9; March Of Time 57tl; Francesco Meroni 21, 238;
Martin Moos 189tr; Neumann 228-9; Mathieu Polak 59bc;
robertharding / Julian Elliott 4; Michele Tantussi /
Accumulation: Searching for Destination (2014-2016) by
Chiharu Shiota, Art Basel 2016 © DACS 2018 12-3b; Jean
Bernard Vernier 57bl; VCG Wilson 38b; Suphanat
Wongsanuphat 8cla; xenotar 18tl, 130; Lingxiao Xie 36br.

Heididorf: Gaudenz Danuser 50tl.

iStockphoto.com: AleksandarGeorgiev 213br; alxpin
216bl; Leonid Andronov 178br; anouchka 78tr, 144-45b;
antares71 141tr; AsianDream 217cra; assalve 55tr;
bhidethescene 22t, 121br; cdbrphotography 12clb,
28-9t; Dmitry Chulov 215cr; dblight 121tr; E+ / Bim
142-43t, / mbbirdy 52-53t; Elenarts 40b; elettro24
134-35t, 151br; fotoember 214clb, 233tr; fotoVoyager
22cr; Gatsi 180b; genekrebs 32b; Aleksandar Georgiev
6-7; Andreas Haas 257tr; Yuliia Hrozian 26-7t; Janoka82
10-11b; Alexander Jung 102-03t; JurgaR 11t; LianeM 27tr;
lucentius 105tl, 210cl; MatteoCozzi 141cr; merc67 11br;
Mor65 236, 253ca; OGphoto 51tr, 141crb; olli0815
186crb; PixHound 208-09b; RomanBabakin 24bl, 73t;
Rostislavv 66bl; Juergen Sack 55br; Oleh Slobodeniuk
268-9; Somatuscani 88-89t; Michal Stipek 215ca;
swisshippo 13br; syolacan 219; TheShihan 28-9ca;
taranchic 84-85t; TomasSereda 254cra; Flavio Vallenari
57tr; Rafael_Wiedenmeier 93c; Xantana 26cra; yanisapae
210br; zorazhuang 106t.

Kunsthaus Zurich: 167cla.

This book was made with Forest Stewardship Council ™ certified paper – one small step in DK's commitment to a sustainable future. For more information go to www.dk.com/our-green-pledge

MIX
Paper from responsible sources
FSC
www.fsc.org **FSC™ C018179**

A NOTE FROM DK EYEWITNESS
The rapid rate at which the world is changing is constantly keeping the DK Eyewitness team on our toes. While we've worked hard to ensure that this edition of Switzerland is accurate and up-to-date, we know that opening hours alter, standards shift, prices fluctuate, places close and new ones pop up in their stead. So, if you notice we've got something wrong or left something out, we want to hear about it. Please get in touch at travelguides@dk.com

---

Penguin Random House

This edition updated by
Contributor Craig Turp
Senior Editor Alison McGill
Senior Designers Stuti Tiwari Bhatia, Laura O'Brien, Ben Hinks
Project Editors Dipika Dasgupta, Rebecca Flynr
Project Art Editor Ankita Sharma
Editors Nayan Keshan, Arushi Mathur, Anuroop Sanwalia, Manjari Thakur
Picture Research Manager Taiyaba Khatoon
Assistant Picture Research Administrator Vagisha Pushp
Jacket Coordinator Bella Talbot
Jacket Designer Jordan Lambley
Cartographer Ashif
Cartography Manager Suresh Kumar
Senior Cartographer Subhashree Bharati
Senior DTP Designer Tanveer Zaidi
Senior Production Editor Jason Little
Production Controller Kariss Ainsworth
Deputy Managing Editor Beverly Smart
Managing Editors Shikha Kulkarni, Hollie Teague
Managing Art Editor Bess Daly
Senior Managing Art Editor Priyanka Thaku
Art Director Maxine Pedliham
Publishing Director Georgina Dee

First edition 2005
Published in Great Britain by Dorling Kindersley Limited, DK, One Embassy Gardens, 8 Viaduct Gardens, London SW11 7BW

The authorised representative in the EEA is Dorling Kindersley Verlag GmbH. Arnulfstr. 124, 80636 Munich, Germany

Published in the United States by DK Publishing, 1450 Broadway, 8th Floor, New York, NY 10018

Copyright © 2005, 2022 Dorling Kindersley Limited
A Penguin Random House Company
21 22 23 24 10 9 8 7 6 5 4 3 2 1

A CIP catalogue record for this book is available from the British Library.

A catalogue record for this book is available from the Library of Congress.

ISSN: 1542 1554
ISBN: 978 0 2414 6279 9

Printed and bound in China.

www.dk.com